15.20

THE WADSWORTH MUSIC SERIES

MUSIC LITERATURE

English Folk Song, Fourth Edition by Cecil J. Sharp
Five Centuries of Keyboard Music by John Gillespie
The Musical Experience by John Gillespie
The Musical Experience Record Album by John Gillespie
Scored for the Understanding of Music—Supplemented Edition by Charles R. Hoffer
  and Marjorie Latham Hoffer
Scored for the Understanding of Music Record Album by Charles R. Hoffer
Talking about Symphonies by Antony Hopkins
The Search for Musical Understanding by Robert W. Buggert and Charles B. Fowler
The Understanding of Music, Second Edition by Charles R. Hoffer
The Understanding of Music Record Album by Charles R. Hoffer
The Understanding of Music Enrichment Record Album by Charles R. Hoffer

MUSIC FOUNDATIONS

Basic Concepts in Music by Gary M. Martin
Basic Resources for Learning Music by Alice Snyder Knuth and William E. Knuth
Foundations in Music Theory, Second Edition with Programed Exercises by Leon Dallin
Introduction to Musical Understanding and Musicianship by Ethel G. Adams
Music Essentials by Robert Pace
Music Fundamentals by Howard A. Murphy with John F. Park

MUSIC SKILLS

Advanced Music Reading by William Thomson
Basic Piano for Adults by Helene Robinson
Basic Violin for Adults by Albert Lazan
Intermediate Piano for Adults, Volume I by Helene Robinson
Intermediate Piano for Adults, Volume II by Helene Robinson
Introduction to Ear Training by William Thomson and Richard P. DeLone
Introduction to Music Reading by William Thomson
Keyboard Harmony: A Comprehensive Approach to Musicianship by Isabel Lehmer
Keyboard Skills: Sight Reading, Transposition, Harmonization, Improvisation
  by Winifred K. Chastek
Music Dictation: A Stereo-Taped Series by Robert G. Olson
Music Literature for Analysis and Study by Charles W. Walton
Music Reading through Singing by Charles W. Walton and Harry Robert Wilson
Steps to Singing for Voice Classes by Royal Stanton

MUSIC THEORY

Harmony and Melody, Volume I: The Diatonic Style by Elie Siegmeister
Harmony and Melody, Volume II: Modulation; Chromatic and Modern Styles by Elie Siegmeister
A Workbook for Harmony and Melody, Volume I by Elie Siegmeister
A Workbook for Harmony and Melody, Volume II by Elie Siegmeister

MUSIC EDUCATION

Exploring Music with Children by Robert E. Nye and Vernice T. Nye
First Experiences in Music by Lyman C. Hurd, III, and Edith J. Savage
Help Yourself to Music, Second Edition by Beatrice P. Krone and Kurt R. Miller
Music in the Education of Children, Third Edition by Bessie R. Swanson
Planning for Junior High School General Music by William O. Hughes
Singing with Children, Second Edition by Robert E. Nye, Vernice T. Nye, Neva Aubin,
  and George Kyme
Teaching Music in the Secondary Schools by Charles R. Hoffer
Toward World Understanding with Song by Vernice T. Nye, Robert E. Nye,
  and H. Virginia Nye
Toward World Understanding with Song Record Album by Vernice T. Nye, Robert E. Nye,
  and H. Virginia Nye

Harmony and Melody

ELIE SIEGMEISTER

HOFSTRA UNIVERSITY

Harmony

and

Melody

VOLUME II: MODULATION; CHROMATIC
AND MODERN STYLES

WADSWORTH PUBLISHING COMPANY, INC.

BELMONT, CALIFORNIA

Music autography by Alfredo Seville

HARMONY AND MELODY, Volume II, by Elie Siegmeister

8 9 10—80 79 78 77 76 75

L. C. Cat. Card No.: 65–17537
Printed in the United States of America

A
Prefatory
Note

This volume of *Harmony and Melody* carries the approach and method of Volume I further along the path. The study of harmony leads from secondary dominants, modulation, diminished sevenths, and ninth chords to more complex areas of chromatic borrowed and altered chords and, finally, to the vigorous appearance of complex modern techniques. At the same time, the study of melody, starting with the period, double period, phrase group, and two- and three-part forms, leads to contemporary melodic practice.

In writing melodies in small form, harmony is often called for at one point or another to help plan the structure and to add roundness to the conception. By the same token, melodies sometimes arise out of existing chord patterns. Thus line and chord suggest and depend on each other; melody and harmony intertwine in contemporary music as in the past.

In this volume, as in its predecessor, general principles are derived directly from the music of the masters; and no artificial barriers are raised between various musical styles or periods. The spectrum shifts broadly from Monteverdi to Bartók and back again from Ives to Claude le Jeune, with passing salutes to Chopin or Wagner, to Gershwin or Burton Lane, along the way.

A considerable territory is traversed here. No class need necessarily cover it all. Moreover, the order of chapters can be altered and the time given to each varied according to the needs of the individual class. One instructor may choose to spend several weeks on chorale harmonization; another may wish to expand the time allotted to variation writing; a third may decide to devote two or three months to the study of contemporary techniques.

By coming into contact with music at the source, in the works of the masters, the student finds his musical horizons broadened and (it is hoped) his curiosity piqued. Sometimes the small extracts quoted may serve as an *aperitif*, leading the questing individual to examine the entire work. Through analysis of the techniques of chromatic and modern harmony and melody, and through the personal use of these techniques in original composition, the student comes to grips with music as a living force.

Elie Siegmeister

Contents

Chapter VI

Chapter VII

Chapter VIII

Harmony and Melody

I

The
Secondary
Dominant

Backgrounds of Chromatic Harmony

The study of chromatic techniques is a key not only to Romantic music but also to large areas of Renaissance, Baroque, Classical, and contemporary styles as well. Chromaticism was formerly viewed as a late phase of the development of music, an end-product of harmonic evolution. More recent study, however, has shown otherwise. The ancient Greeks had a form of chromatic melody; chromatic steps are found in the music of the Orient and Africa and in the folk blues of our own South. Chromaticism emerged in European music soon after the beginnings of the chordal style itself, well before 1600—the date usually given for the establishment of the major-minor system.

Side by side with the diatonic idiom, or intertwined with it, chromatic motion has formed a basic part of European music for more than four hundred years. Chromatic harmony was first developed by Vicentino, Monteverdi, and Gesualdo da Venosa, after 1550. During the middle Baroque, interest in chromatic experiments receded somewhat; but even in the basically diatonic late Baroque and Classical periods, chromatic passages and compositions served to express moments of high drama or intense emotion—as in "Dido's Lament" from Purcell's *Dido and Aeneas*, the *Crucifixus* from Bach's B minor Mass, and Mozart's C minor Fantasy.

The Romantic spirit gave birth to a new and more powerful wave of chromaticism, with Wagner's *Tristan and Isolde* as the high-water mark. In their enthusiasm, the Wagnerians envisaged an end to diatonic harmony;

3

from their time forward, they were certain, music would follow a consistently chromatic course.

But the evolution of music rarely follows the neat pathways laid out for it. Tristan, composed in 1859, was followed by the diatonic masterpieces of Brahms, Verdi, Bizet, Tchaikovsky, and Wagner himself (*Die Meistersinger*), and by a work revealing a revolutionary type of diatonic harmony, Moussorgsky's *Boris Godunov*.

Since 1550, all the great composers have blended diatonic and chromatic techniques, in proportions dependent on their expressive intentions and on the language of the times. Between the period of *Tristan* and the present, the two tendencies have see-sawed back and forth, sometimes engaged in bitter rivalry, at other times mingling in friendly embrace. The German school, by and large, has carried chromaticism to its ultimate stage— the complete abandonment of tonality. The French, Russian, and American schools explored, until about 1950, the new modal and polytonal possibilities of the diatonic language. In the early '20s Schönberg codified pure chromaticism into a formal system (the twelve-tone method); but as late as the '40s, composers such as Bartók, Prokofiev, and Revueltas produced masterpieces in a fresh and modern transformation of the diatonic concept. The interrelation of diatonic and chromatic practices forms an age-old and perhaps still unfinished line of musical evolution.

Chromatic Alterations

Chroma means color, *chromatic*, colorful. The first development of chromatic harmony arose out of a search for color variation. Chromatic alterations, which raise or lower a note by one half step, are signalled by sharps, flats, or naturals appearing in the course of a phrase (not all passing accidentals result from chromatic changes; some are inherent in the diatonic minor scales). An expressive example of such alteration appears in Monteverdi's opera *Orfeo*.

Ex. 1   Monteverdi: *Orfeo*, Act III (1607)

The slowly rising melody of *Orfeo* acquires special poignancy through the raising of two notes (*a* and *b*), which adds expressive color to an otherwise diatonic line. Such half-step motion—more intense than motion by whole step—became an integral part of the melodic language from the late Renaissance onward.

Chromatic melody tones are of two kinds: (1) embellishing tones that do not change the structure of the underlying chords, and (2) those that do change the chord structure, as in *Orfeo*, bringing about a new type of harmonic function, as we shall see.*

Structure of the Secondary Dominant

Even more important than its effect on melody is the power of chromaticism to intensify harmonic motion. The falling fifth, as we have seen, forms the most dynamic root movement; and of all falling fifths, V—I is the strongest. The latter acquires its special force from the half-step drive of leading tone to tonic. Sixteenth-century composers discovered that the third of a minor triad, when raised chromatically, becomes a *secondary leading tone*, and the triad, a *secondary dominant*. Any triad containing this alteration† can act as a secondary dominant of the chord a fifth below. Changing a diatonic chord into a secondary dominant increases its active quality; and adding secondary dominants to a phrase sharpens its harmonic

---

* In Ex. 36 (page 22), C sharp and D sharp in bars 2 and 3 are chromatic embellishing tones; they do not change the structure or function of the I and V chords. G sharp at (*a*) and C sharp at (*b*) do change the structure and function of the chords.

† Or in some cases without alteration—see pages 9, 10, and 11.

drive. A basic chromatic formation, the secondary dominant has played a vital role in harmony since Monteverdi's time.

V of V

Most important of secondary dominants is the *V of V*. Formed by raising the third of the minor triad on II, it adds energy to the movement from II to V, giving it the sharpness of a V—I progression.

Ex. 2   V of V

Note the greater harmonic drive of "All Through the Night" when II (Ex. 3, *a*) is changed by chromatic alteration into V of V (*b*).

Ex. 3   Welsh hymn: All Through the Night

The V of V often serves a special function in the half cadence, strengthening the progression to V. The half cadence V of V—V is found in both serious and popular music (Exs. 4 and 5).

Ex. 4   Schumann: A Little Piece, from *Album for the Young*, Op. 68

Ex. 5   Dacre: Daisy Bell

It is apparent from Ex. 5 (*a*) that V⁷ plays the role of secondary dominant just as effectively as V—in certain cases, even more so.

V's of II and VI

Two other secondary dominants are formed by altering minor triads in major—*V of II* by raising the third of VI, and *V of VI* by raising the third of III.

Ex. 6   V's of II and VI

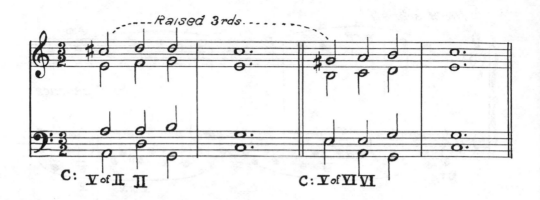

Brahms introduces the V^7 of II in a particularly lyrical phrase; Beethoven uses the V of VI in a crisp scherzo.

Ex. 7   Brahms: Sonata No. 2 for Violin and Piano, Op. 100

Ex. 8   Beethoven: Sonata, Op. 106 (*Hammerklavier*), second movement

V of IV

The tonic triad in major possesses a major third and thus needs no alteration to serve as a *V of IV*. But to distinguish this function from that of the tonic triad itself, a minor seventh is frequently added, making the chord a *V⁷ of IV*.

Ex. 9   V and V⁷ of IV

For a V⁷ of IV in Beethoven, see Ex. 20, page 15; for one in Bach, see Ex. 17, page 67.

V of III

While VII, as we have seen, has but limited use as an independent chord, the *major* triad on 7 makes an excellent secondary dominant—*V of III*. It is formed by adding two sharps to the diminished triad on VII.

Ex. 10   V of III

The V⁷ of III occurs in Schubert's *Unfinished* Symphony.

Ex. 11   Schubert: Symphony No. 8 (*Unfinished*), second movement

Secondary Dominants in Minor

Because of the structure of the minor mode, secondary dominants are formed differently than in major. To create a V of V, both the third and fifth of II—a diminished triad—must be raised (see Ex. 16, *c*). To form a V of IV, it is necessary to raise the third of the tonic triad, as in Monteverdi's *Orfeo* (Ex. 1, *c*). The V of III appears without alteration on lowered VII (the *subtonic**)—a diatonic triad in falling melodic minor.

Ex. 12   V of III in minor

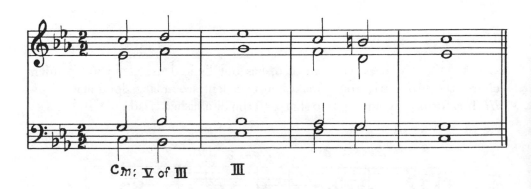

* Lowered 7 is called the subtonic to distinguish it from the leading tone. The two steps differ in harmonic structure and function, the former tending downward, the latter up.

Ex. 13   Beethoven: Piano Concerto No. 4, Op. 58, second movement

Similarly, the V of VI is formed by the diatonic lowered III (as in Ex. 16, *a*.)

Functions of the Secondary Dominant

Secondary dominants play a variety of roles in music, among them:

1. To enhance harmonic activity within a phrase or at the cadence.
2. To add color or a special accent to a chord or a phrase.
3. To widen the harmonic boundaries of a key.
4. To create a special form of deceptive cadence.

Enhancing Harmonic Activity

In Ex. 14, a series of secondary dominants appears in close order—V of II, V of IV, and V of VI—each followed by the triad a fifth below. Starting at (*b*), these active chords produce a harmonic progression of great energy. The linear bass adds to the feeling of strongly directed motion.*

---

* This illustrates once more the point made in Volume I—that melodic motion of the bass enhances harmonic activity (see Volume I, page 236).

Ex. 14   Schubert: Ecossaise, Op. 18a, No. 1

Secondary dominants are particularly useful in adding drive to the cadence. We have already noted the role of V of V in the half cadence; it serves with equal effectiveness in the perfect cadence.

Ex. 15   Schumann: Harvest Song, from *Album for the Young*, Op. 68

Adding Harmonic Color

Secondary dominants enrich the harmonic color of a phrase. The chords in Ex. 16, beautifully scored to take advantage of the dark middle and low registers of the piano, include the V^7's of VI (*a*); IV (*b*); and V (*c*). The latter appears twice, lending special emphasis to the half cadence (*d*).

Ex. 16   Chopin: Prelude, Op. 28, No. 20

Often a composer adds an expressive accent by substituting a secondary dominant for the diatonic chord on the same degree. In Ex. 17 (*a*), V of V, the sole chromatic chord in a diatonic context, reinforces the melodic climax with harmonic emphasis.*

Ex. 17   Verdi: *Falstaff*, Act II†

Widening Tonal Boundaries

The addition of secondary dominants serves to widen the boundaries of a key. Appearing at times to move outside the limits of a given tonality, these chromatic chords expand its harmonic content while remaining within its borders. Sometimes a composition even begins with a secondary dominant —as, for example, Beethoven's Symphony No. 1 in C major.

Ex. 18   Beethoven: Symphony No. 1, Op. 21

* For another example of secondary-dominant accent, see Ex. 31 (*b*), page 241.
† Quoted in Murphy and Melcher: *Music for Study* (Englewood Cliffs, N.J., 1960).

Upon hearing this opening, critics of Beethoven's time attacked the composer for starting a C major symphony in another key. *If taken alone*, it is true, the first chords might well be V⁷ and I of F major.

Ex. 19   Beethoven: Symphony No. 1, first bar analyzed in F

But Beethoven was well aware that the key of a work is not necessarily determined by its first bar; the phrase continues:

Ex. 20   Beethoven: Symphony No. 1

Accidentals forming secondary dominants are purely temporary, and are usually cancelled very quickly. Thus the B flat at (*a*) is replaced by a B natural at (*b*). In view of this change, the opening chord is recognized as V of IV in C major, rather than V of F. Similarly, the F sharp at (*c*) has only temporary significance, forming part of the V of V and being cancelled at (*d*).

By starting the phrase with secondary dominants and delaying the appearance of the tonic chord until bar 6 (*e*), Beethoven creates a feeling of uncertainty and suspense. Taking a broad view, there can be no doubt that the entire passage is in C major—but a C major with chromatic chords that widen its tonal boundaries.*

Forming a Deceptive Cadence

In the last of its functions, the secondary dominant serves as a "surprise" chord in the deceptive cadence. Wagner often introduced secondary dominants in this way; but almost a century earlier, Mozart anticipated the practice (Ex. 21, *a*).

Ex. 21   Mozart: Sonata, K. 533

V⁷ and VII as Secondary Dominants

As we have seen, a secondary dominant can take the form of a V^7 rather than a triad. Ex. 22 presents a lovely V^7 of V followed by V^7. (Note the temporary nature of the chromatic alteration F double sharp, followed in bar 3 by the single sharp.)

---

* Beethoven's critics—hardly great scholars—were unaware of a similar example in Bach, some sixty or seventy years earlier (see Ex. 17, page 67).

Ex. 22   Chopin: Waltz, Op. 64, No. 2

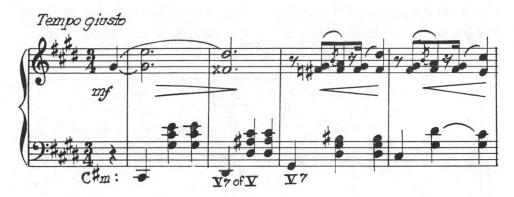

The secondary-dominant V^7 appears in inversion as well as in root position. Thus we find $V\frac{6}{5}$ of VI (Ex. 23), $V\frac{4}{3}$ of V (Ex. 24), and $V\frac{4}{2}$ of II (Ex. 25).

Ex. 23   Schumann: *Frühlingsgesang*, from *Album for the Young*, Op. 68

Ex. 24   Schumann: *Botschaft*, from *Albumblätter*, Op. 124

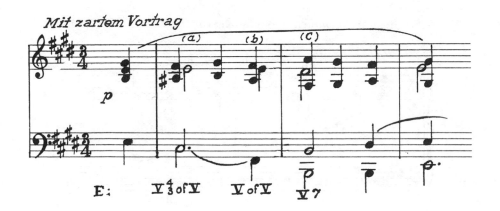

Ex. 25   Schumann: *Schneeglöckchen*, Op. 79, No. 27

The VII can also serve as a secondary dominant, usually in first inversion (Ex. 26, *a*), but sometimes in root position as a passing chord (Ex. 27).

Ex. 26   Schumann: *Fröhlicher Landmann*, from *Album for the Young*, Op. 68

Ex. 27   Schumann: *Abendlied*, from *Sonata for the Young*, No. 2, Op. 118b

A comparison of the major triad, the dominant seventh chord, and the diminished triad used as secondary dominants is revealing (Ex. 28). Of the three, V⁷ has the most drive and VII probably the least, since it generally functions in a passing or embellishing role rather than as an independent chord.*

Ex. 28   Various forms of secondary dominant compared

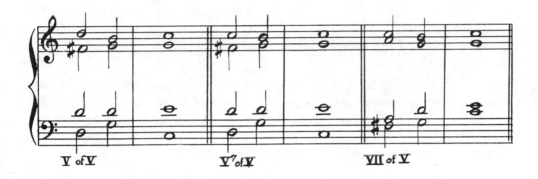

Preparation and Resolution of the Secondary Dominant

A secondary dominant can be preceded by any chord of the key that leads to it smoothly. When a tone is altered to form a secondary leading tone, *both tones should remain in the same voice* for the best voice leading (*a*); introduction of the altered step in another voice produces a cross-relation (*b*).

Ex. 29   Chromatic alteration retained in same voice

*For the use of the diminished seventh chord as a secondary dominant, see pages 164–165; for the ninth chord, pages 225–226.

If the tone to be altered is doubled in the preparatory chord, one voice moves chromatically to the altered tone and the other to a different tone of the second chord.

Ex. 30   Preparatory tone doubled

In resolving by falling fifth, a secondary dominant follows the same voice-leading principles as those that govern the resolution of V to I. The secondary leading tone progresses upward; like 7, it is not doubled.

Ex. 31   Regular resolution of secondary dominant

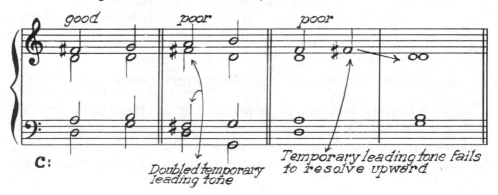

A secondary dominant, like V, can resolve irregularly to a chord other than the triad a fifth below. In Ex. 32, the V⁷ of VI (*a*) progresses to IV instead of VI.

Ex. 32   Beethoven: Sonata, Op. 101

Another irregular resolution, often encountered at the cadence, finds V of V moving to I$_4^6$ and *then* to V (Ex. 33).

Ex. 33   Beethoven: Sonata, Op. 7, second movement

In still another type of resolution, a secondary dominant resolves down a fifth to a V^7 instead of to the usual triad. Thus, in Ex. 34, V^7 of V leads to V^7, which, in turn, moves to V^7 of IV. Such substitution of V^7 for the triad creates added harmonic momentum.

Ex. 34   Beethoven: Sonata, Op. 2, No. 2, third movement

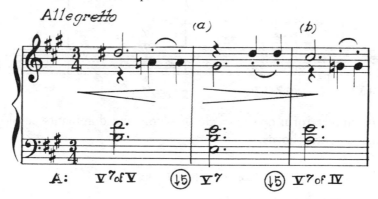

The Cycle of Secondary Dominants

The motion from V^7 to V^7 can continue in a sequence of falling fifths; this sequence is called the *cycle of secondary dominants*.

Ex. 35   Cycle of secondary dominants

One of the most dynamic forms of the cycle of fifths, this progression is illustrated in Ex. 36 (*a–d*).

Ex. 36   Chopin: Mazurka, Op. 33, No. 3

A simpler form of the cycle of secondary dominants employs triads rather than seventh chords.

Ex. 37   Beethoven: Piano Concerto No. 4, Op. 58

A most imaginative concentration of secondary dominants in irregular resolution is found in Ex. 38.*

* For another example of irregular resolution in Bach (V^6 of II—V^6_5 of III) see page 2, Volume I.

Ex. 38   Bach: Sarabande, from English Suite No. 6

Between (*a*) and (*b*) the falling chromatic bass supports a succession of secondary dominants, whose movements are irregular—and beautiful. Although the progression contains quite a few accidentals, there is no change of key. This example vividly illustrates the expansion of tonality by means of chromatic harmonies.

To turn from Bach to a song of the Gay '90s may be a startling jump; but it illustrates the versatility of the chords in question. Secondary dominants ("barbershop" chords) can be found in almost any old-time sentimental song: "Sweet Adeline," "Down by the Old Mill Stream," "Strolling through the Park," "Sidewalks of New York," or "Aura Lee" (Ex. 39).

Ex. 39   College song: Aura Lee

Sun-shine came a-long with thee, and swal-lows in the air.

V of V

To become more keenly aware of the value of secondary dominants, play the examples in this chapter first without and then with the written accidentals.

Centering and Traveling Motion

The addition of secondary dominants to our harmonic palette sheds new light on broad harmonic motion. Examined briefly in Volume I, this motion appears in new perspective with the widening of our harmonic resources. Schubert's *Ecossaise* (page 12), for example, shows a sharp contrast in the broad harmonic progression of its two phrases. The first phrase (*a*) contains only I and V chords. Since its entire effect is to emphasize the tonal center, we call this *centering motion*. The second phrase (*b*) develops a different kind of harmonic action. Moving rapidly through a series of secondary dominants, and progressing from point to point without emphasizing the tonic, the harmony creates a strong directional drive—*traveling motion*.

These two types of progression serve different musical functions. Centering motion, often found in folk songs, popular dances, and the opening themes of many Baroque and Classical compositions, circles around the tonic, establishing the key firmly. Traveling motion, often found in the second part of short pieces and in the development section of longer ones, moves continuously away from the tonic, producing a greater harmonic momentum. The contrast between the two types of broad harmonic motion is an important aspect of musical structure, as we shall see in later chapters.*

Summary

1. Chromatic alterations, which raise or lower a diatonic note one half step, can be used to enhance the dynamic or expressive quality of a melody or chord.

* For further examples of centering motion, see the first four bars of Exs. 15 and 36. For traveling motion, see Exs. 16, 36 (*a*), and 37. More radical types of harmonic traveling involve modulation (Chapters II–IV and XI), and the use of complex chromatic chords (Chapters X, XII, and XIII). See especially pages 105–106, 118–120, and Exs. 58–60, pages 282–283.

2. Secondary dominants are chords that act as temporary dominants of degrees other than I.
   a. They are formed by raising the third of a minor triad one half step, making it a secondary leading tone and making the chord a major triad.
   b. As major triads, the V of IV in major and the V's of III and VI in minor can act as secondary dominants without alteration.

3. The most important secondary dominant is V of V, which often adds drive to the cadence.

4. Next in importance are the V's of II, VI, III, and IV.

5. Secondary dominants serve:
   a. To heighten harmonic activity.
   b. To add color or accent to a chord or phrase.
   c. To widen the harmonic boundaries of a key.
   d. To create a special type of deceptive cadence.

6. Chords other than major triads can serve as secondary dominants:
   a. V^7, with greater drive.
   b. VII, with less drive.
   c. Inversions of the triad, V^7, and VII, with gentler effect.

7. The secondary dominant resolves:
   a. Regularly, down a fifth.
   b. Irregularly, to other degrees.

8. The secondary dominant can be preceded by almost any chord of the key.

9. The secondary leading tone is handled similarly to the diatonic 7:
   a. It is not doubled.
   b. It resolves one step upward.
   c. When it follows the diatonic tone on the same degree, both remain in the same voice.

10. Secondary dominants can appear consecutively in a cycle of fifths, called the "cycle of secondary dominants." Most active is the cycle of dominant sevenths.

11. Broad harmonic motion can take two forms:
    a. Centering motion—gravitating around the tonic.
    b. Traveling motion—moving actively from point to point without stressing the tonic.

The Parallel Period

Symmetry, one of the shaping principles in music, often arises, as we have seen, from patterns based on dance movement—the repeated motive, the repeated phrase.* A higher type of structure appears in the *parallel period:* two phrases similar in length and content, contrasted in their cadences. The combination of symmetrical shape and opposing cadences adds dynamic tension to the period form, which has been basic and universal for many centuries—from the dance tunes of primitive peoples and the songs of medieval troubadours, through Renaissance madrigals and the works of Bach, Beethoven, Schubert, and Brahms, to the music of Prokofiev, Bartók, and the popular songs of our time.†

Varieties of Parallel Periods

The parallel period allows for the immediate restatement of a phrase, avoiding the monotony of literal repetition by a change in the second cadence. Whether in miniature periods or those of large dimension, the joining of symmetry and contrast produces a balanced, clearly articulated form.

The shortest period usually spans four measures.

---

* See Volume I, pages 280–283.

† For parallel periods already quoted, see Volume I, pages 113–114.

Ex. 40   Haydn: Symphony No. 103 (*The Drumroll*)

One of the longest periods—36 measures—occurs in Porter's song "Begin the Beguine."*

Both periods just mentioned form parts of larger compositions and are therefore called *dependent* periods. We shall work for the present with *independent* periods—those that are complete compositions in themselves (such as folk songs and short dance pieces).

Cadences in the Parallel Period

Most independent periods consist of either eight or sixteen bars. The principle of *cadential suspense* is illustrated by the first cadence, an "open" one. In order to keep the movement flowing and avoid a full stop, this cadence must clearly be of a temporary nature: a half or imperfect cadence. Only at the second pause is the suspense resolved—hence a perfect cadence. Thus a period contains two broad lines of melodic and harmonic motion, leading (1) to a tentative goal and (2) to a final one. †

Ex. 41   Pattern of period

The first phrase of a parallel period generally ends on a half or imperfect cadence. Occasionally it closes on V of V (Ex. 42) or on another chord.‡

---

* For the first phrase of this song, see Ex. 31, page 282 of Volume I.
† The contrast in the goals toward which various phrases of a composition move is a basic element in musical form, from the smallest period to the largest sonata or symphony.
‡ For a first cadence on V of VI, see Ex. 39.

Ex. 42   Beethoven: Sonata, Op. 2, No. 3, last movement

Sometimes a parallel period whose outer structure is perfectly symmetrical contains an irregular inner pattern. Example 43 consists of two three-bar phrases; Ex. 44, two phrases of five bars each.

Ex. 43   Beethoven: String Quartet, Op. 18, No. 2, second movement

Ex. 44   Brahms: *Variations on a Theme of Haydn*, Op. 56A

Melodic Variation in the Second Phrase

In a parallel period, as we have seen, both phrases generally begin alike. Sometimes, however, the opening of the second phrase is varied; but the variation does not go so far as to conceal the similarity of the two phrases. Among the most common methods of variation are (1) sequence, (2) ornamentation, and (3) inversion.

1. Sequence appears in Exs. 45 and 46. In the former, the second phrase starts a tone below the first; in the latter, a tone above.

Ex. 45   American folk song: Polly Wolly Doodle

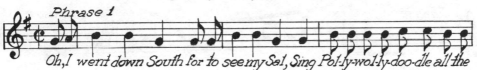

Ex. 46   Mozart: Sonata, K. 576

2. Ornamentation and octave displacement are used to vary the second phrase in Ex. 47 (b).

Ex. 47   Mozart: Symphony No. 41 (Jupiter), K. 551, second movement

Often only the beginnings of the two phrases are parallel; thus the second phrase of Ex. 47, after its first bar, turns in a direction different from that of the first phrase.

3. Inversion serves to vary the second phrase in Ex. 48. The reversal of direction is delightful: where the first phrase descends, the second mounts in a rising line.

Ex. 48   Haydn: Symphony No. 100 (*Military*), third movement

Many other techniques of variation studied in connection with the motive are also applied to the phrase, producing changes in the second half of a parallel period. For interval change, see Ex. 2, page 38; for extension, Ex. 25, pages 75–76; and for expansion, Ex. 26, pages 76–77.

Bridging the Cadence

In the writing of parallel periods, too sharp a division of the phrases can lead to a mechanical construction (Exs. 49 and 50).

Ex. 49   Mozart: *A Musical Joke*, K. 522, fourth movement

Ex. 50   Student work

Both examples have the same fault: a rigid compartmentalization of the rhythmic structure, producing a "box-like" feeling. Each phrase seems to be in its own pigeonhole; the line does not flow. To avoid such a sharp break within the period, composers invented two ways of bridging the half cadence:

1. Continuous melodic flow through the cadence bar (Ex. 51).
2. A melodic rest, with the rhythmic flow continuing in another voice or voices (Ex. 52).*

Ex. 51   Bach: Minuet, from French Suite No. 3

* See also Ex. 2 (*a*), page 38.

Ex. 52   Mozart: *Là ci darem*, from *Don Giovanni*

Summary

1. A parallel period consists of two phrases with similar openings and differing cadences. It combines symmetry and contrast.

2. Periods vary in length from 4 to 16 bars. Exceptionally, they run to 32 bars.

3. Following the principle of cadential suspense, the first cadence of a period is "open" or suspended, and the second "closed," resolving the suspense.

4. An independent period is a complete entity in itself. A dependent period is incomplete, forming part of a larger composition.

5. In an independent period, the first cadence generally rests on V or on an imperfect cadence; occasionally it rests on IV or V of V. The second cadence is a perfect one.

6. The second phrase of a parallel period starts:
   a. Similarly to the first.
   b. With a variation—a sequence, ornamentation, or inversion of the first.

7. To avoid too sharp a break between the two phrases of a period, the first cadence is bridged, by:
   a. Continuous melodic flow through the cadence bar.
   b. A melodic pause, with the rhythmic flow continuing in another voice or voices.

II

Modulation
to the
Dominant

When chromatic alterations began to be common in music, producing new dominants on degrees other than V, it was inevitable that new tonics would also be produced on degrees other than I. The emergence of new tonics was a more significant event, for it entails a *change of key center*. Change of key, or *modulation*, shifts the axis on which music rotates. The discovery of this technique had untold consequences for the evolution of musical expression and form.

When, in Monteverdi's *Orfeo*, the hero learns of the death of his wife, Euridice, his shock is emphasized by an abrupt modulation.

Ex. 1   Monteverdi: *Orfeo*, Act II

The Messenger's music (*a*) is in E major. When Orfeo hears the words "Your lovely Euridice," he has a premonition of catastrophe; his music modulates suddenly to the dark key of G minor (*b*), interrupting the Messenger's phrase. When the latter continues (*c*), the phrase leaps back to the original key, E major.

Such key changes, characteristic of Monteverdi's dramatic style, were a striking novelty in the early Baroque; but they soon became a familiar operatic technique and later (in a more restrained way) part of the musical language.

How do chromatic changes in a modulation differ from those that produce secondary dominants? The difference, basically, is a matter of degree and duration. Accidentals introducing secondary dominants, as we have seen, are only momentary—they tend to be cancelled as soon as possible. Those producing a modulation are more persistent, remaining long enough at least to *establish* the new key, often much longer.*

---

* Yet even they, too, are temporary, eventually being cancelled in the return to the home key. See pages 47–48.

Modulation involves traveling motion away from the home key; in setting up a new tonal center, it creates an *area of contrast* pitted against the *area of the home key*. Such an area of contrast becomes important, as we shall see, in the design of such basic musical patterns as two- and three-part forms.

Comparing diatonic motion within a key and modulating motion among various keys, we find a gentle contrast in the former:

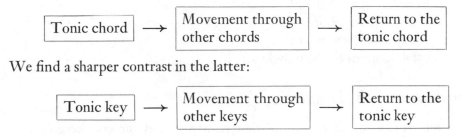

We find a sharper contrast in the latter:

Functions of Modulation

Once absorbed into the general language of music, modulation became an important expressive and structural device. Among its functions are:

1. To intensify harmonic motion.
2. To underscore dramatic changes.
3. To produce contrasts of mood and color.
4. To emphasize structural divisions.

The evolution of modulatory techniques was very important in the development of Western music. From the sixteenth through the twentieth centuries, change of key provided a means of unparalleled power for the achievement of emotional, psychological, and dramatic contrasts. It also provided the architectural basis for the evolution of the great musical forms, especially those of the opera, the fugue, the sonata, and the symphony.

I—V, the Basic Modulation

The relation of 1 and 5 has been fundamental in our study—in melodic motion, chord structure, and the movement of harmonies. It comes, then, as no surprise that the basic modulation from a major key also leads to V. Because it launches the harmonic motion of a work on an active note and adds brightness and color to the music, it was the opening modulation in most Baroque and Classical compositions in major keys; Romantic composers continued its use well into the twentieth century. Having left the home key and become established in the dominant, the music holds a favored position, "dominating" the tonic: one step and it reaches home again, rounding out the modulatory circle. Modulation to the dominant is still a familiar procedure in dance and popular music today.

The Four Stages in Modulation

A modulation usually takes place in four stages:

1. Establishment of the home key.
2. Use of a pivot chord.
3. Entry into the new key.
4. Establishment of the new key.

Establishment of the Home Key

One cannot speak of modulation to a new key unless there is an original or *home* key to leave. The home key, therefore, must be firmly established at the outset. This is accomplished by some form of centering motion—by a progression including a cadence, or by sufficient dwelling on the primary chords to identify the key. Usually, as in Ex. 2 (*a*), the cadence is imperfect, with no rhythmic stop (a *perfect* cadence would tend to halt the musical flow at the beginning of a composition).

Ex. 2   Mozart: Minuet from *Don Giovanni*

The four opening bars establish G major through an insistence on the tonic chord and an imperfect cadence (*a*). Bridging the cadence, the rhythm flows gracefully into the next phrase (*b*).

Pivot Chord

A *pivot chord* is one which, belonging to both keys of a modulation, serves as a link between them (Ex. 2, *a*). The music approaches the pivot chord from one key and leaves it to enter the other. Often several chords can serve as pivots. Here are the pivot chords shared by a key and its dominant, with the function of each chord in both keys:

Ex. 3   Pivot chords between I and V

The best pivot chord is one that leads strongly to V of the new key: usually a chord with subdominant function (IV or II) in that key. Thus in Ex. 2, at (*a*) the I of G major serves also as IV of D leading to the new V.

Entry into the New Key

Stage three of a modulation is signalled by the appearance of a *modulating tone*, bearing an accidental characteristic of the new key, and marking the entry into that key. In shifting from a major key to its dominant, the modulating tone is the new (raised) 7.

Ex. 4   Modulating tone in modulation from I to V

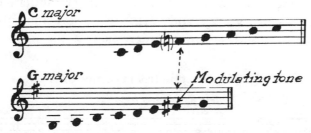

Comparing C and G major, we see that the sole difference between them is the modulating tone F sharp. This new 7 marks the point of entry into G in all modulations from C major—the "leading" function of the leading tone being apparent in such cases. In Exs. 5 and 6, it occurs in the lower voice, at (*a*). In Ex. 6, the reiteration of the new 7 in the right hand at (*b*) confirms the modulatory change. *

* For the direct appearance of the new 7 in the melody, see Ex. 15 (*a*), page 45.

Ex. 5   Bach: Fugue No. 1, from *The Well-Tempered Clavier*, Book I

(a)

Ex. 6   Clementi: Sonatina in C major

Allegro

f

p   (a)   f

(b)

Just as a modulating tone signals the entry into the new key melodically, a chord containing that tone—a *modulating chord*—marks it harmonically. The more active the chord, the stronger the harmonic drive into the new key. Thus V, V⁷, and VII⁶ are most commonly used as modulating chords to ensure a strong progression at the moment of key change.

Ex. 7   Modulating chords, in modulation from C major to G

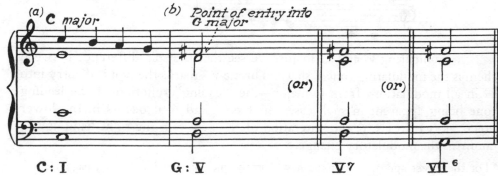

(a) C major   (b) *Point of entry into G major*

(or)   (or)

C : I   G : V   V⁷   VII⁶

In the Minuet from Don Giovanni (page 38), V^7 of the new key acts as the modulating chord (*b*). In Ex. 8 (*c*), it is $V\frac{4}{2}$; in Ex. 12 (*a*), VII; and in Ex. 14 (*a*), $VII\frac{6}{4}$.

From one altered chord alone, however, can we be sure that a change of key has taken place? Not quite. For as we have seen, a chromatically altered chord might prove to be a secondary dominant; if followed by chords of the home key, there would be no modulation. In order to produce a modulation, stage four becomes necessary: a *cadence establishing the new key.*

Cadence in the New Key

A cadence establishing the new key marks the difference between a true modulation and those momentary chromatic changes introduced by secondary dominants. Note the difference between secondary dominant and modulating chord in "Jeanie with the Light Brown Hair."

Ex. 8   Foster: Jeanie with the Light Brown Hair

At (*a*) the V^7 on G serves as a secondary dominant, leading to a half cadence (*b*). At (*c*) the same V^7 (in another inversion) appears as a modulating chord leading to I of the new key. At (*d*) it is repeated in root position as part of the perfect cadence confirming the modulation. Thus a chromatically altered chord may be either a secondary dominant or a modulating chord, *depending on what follows it.*

The confirmatory cadence is further illustrated in Exs. 2 (*c*); 16 (4); and 17 (*b*). Note that the cadence establishing a new key is generally a perfect one.

To recapitulate, the smoothest, most fully prepared modulations are produced by the establishment of a key, the use of a pivot chord, the entry into a new key by a modulating tone and chord, and, finally, a cadence establishing the new key.

Voice Leading in Modulation

When a diatonic tone changes chromatically into a modulating tone, both remain in the same voice and resolve in the direction of the alteration. Since every modulating tone has an obligatory resolution, it acts as a temporary leading tone and is not doubled.

Ex. 9   Retention of a chromatically altered tone in same voice

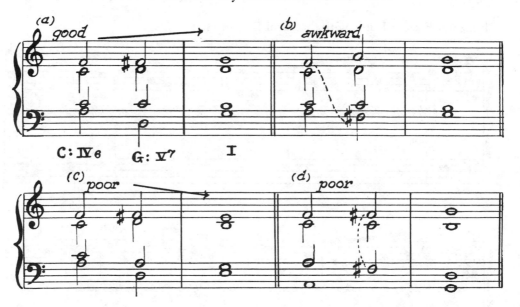

In Ex. 9 (*a*) the melodic progression F—F sharp—G is smooth and logical. At (*b*) the shift from F in the soprano to F sharp in the bass causes a cross-relation. At (*c*) the failure of the chromatic movement F—F sharp to reach its goal, G, is awkward and frustrating. At (*d*) the doubling of the modulating tone (7 of the new key) results in a crude imbalance.

Inversions as Modulating Chords

Modulating chords in root position produce sturdy motion into the new key. Used in inverted form, they lend a gentler, more flowing quality to the modulation. Thus, in Exs. 10 and 11 (*a*), V⁷ appears as a modulating chord in two different inversions.

Ex. 10   Schumann: A Chorale, from *Album for the Young*, Op. 68

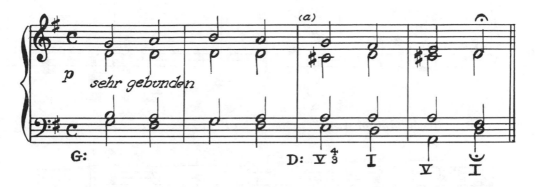

Ex. 11   Schumann: Melody, from *Album for the Young*, Op. 68

The VII and both of its inversions act as modulating chords in Exs. 12–14 (*a*).

Ex. 12   Schumann: Soldier's March, from *Album for the Young*, Op. 68

D : VII   I

Ex. 13   Bach: *Gottlob, es geht nunmehr zu Ende*

Praised be our God, the end is near-ing,
Gott-lob, es geht nun mehr zum En - de,

F: V⁶₅ I VII⁶   I

Ex. 14   Beethoven: Sonatina in F

Abrupt, Fast, and Gradual Modulations

Modulations can be abrupt, fast, or gradual. When a modulatory change occurs abruptly, it may simply involve a leap from one key to another, as in the scene from *Orfeo* (page 36). Such *abrupt* modulations serve mainly for sharp, dramatic changes.

In *fast* modulations, stage 2 (the pivot chord) is often omitted;* sometimes stages (3) and (4) are telescoped into one. Thus, in Ex. 15 the chord (*a*) that leads into the new key forms part of the cadence establishing that key.†

Ex. 15   Haydn: Symphony No. 94 (*Surprise*), second movement

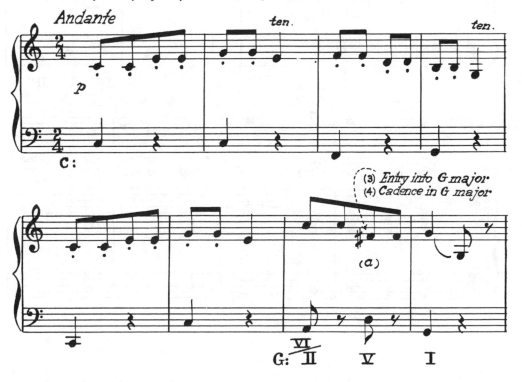

* See Ex. 10, page 63.
† See also Exs. 11, page 43, and 7, page 61.

Gradual modulations are more or less prolonged, leading more smoothly into the new key as part of the general flow of the music. Often a considerable broadening occurs in stage (4), between the point of entry and the last chord of the cadence confirming the new key. In Ex. 16, the modulation develops gradually through its four stages: (1) eight bars are used to establish the original key; (2) the pivot chord occupies a full bar; (3) the modulating V^7 fills more than two bars; and (4) the confirmatory cadence reaches its final tonic (4b) ten bars after the entry into the new key.*

Ex. 16   Mozart: O Isis and Osiris, from *The Magic Flute*

* For another example of gradual modulation, see Ex. 19, page 69.

Return to the Home Key

A return to the home key is not, strictly speaking, part of a modulation; but since it almost invariably occurs at some point after a modulation, it merits study. The process—return from V to I—involves reversing the original move from I to V, except that the change often occurs more quickly. The main elements of the return are:

1. Cancellation of the accidentals identifying the new key.
2. The reappearance of chords characteristic of the home key.
3. A perfect cadence re-establishing that key.

In Ex. 17, the modulation is initiated by the modulating tone C sharp (*a*); and consummated by the perfect cadence in the new key, D major (*b*). The *point of re-entry* into the original key is signalled by the appearance of C natural (*c*), cancelling the C sharp, and of the IV⁶ of G—a chord characteristic of the home key, G major, and not of D. A perfect cadence confirms the return.

Ex. 17   Schumann: A Chorale, from *Album for the Young*, Op. 68

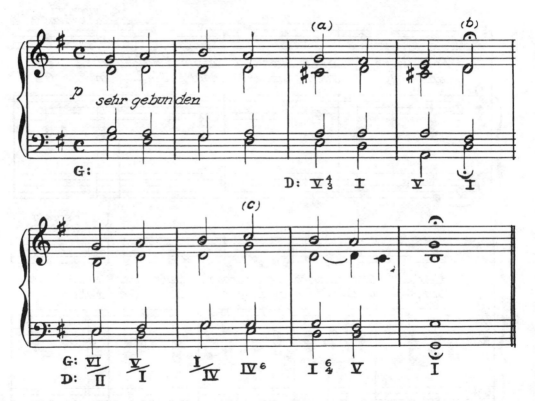

Summary

1. A modulation, or change of key, involves shifting the tonal center from I to another degree.

2. Modulations differ from secondary dominants in that the accidental changes involved are not immediately cancelled; they are retained long enough to make a cadence in the new key, sometimes much longer.

3. The functions of modulation are:
   a. To intensify harmonic motion.
   b. To underscore dramatic changes.
   c. To produce contrasts of mood and color.
   d. To emphasize structural divisions.

4. The most basic modulation, from a major key to its dominant, adds brightness and a sense of forward motion to the music.

5. The four stages of modulation are:
   a. Establishment of the home key by centering motion, involving:
      i. A cadence (usually imperfect, with no stop), or
      ii. Sufficient emphasis on the primary chords to identify the key.
   b. Use of a pivot chord—a harmony belonging to both the home key and the new key.
   c. Entry into the new key:
      i. Melodically, by a modulating tone marked by an accidental belonging to the new key but not to the old. 7 is usually (but not invariably) the modulating tone.
      ii. Harmonically, by a modulating chord, one belonging to the new key but not to the old—usually the new V, V^7, or VII^6.
   d. Establishment of the new key by a perfect cadence.

6. When a diatonic tone changes chromatically into a modulating tone, both remain in the same voice. The new 7 resolves to its tonic.

7. Inversions of V, V^7, and VII also serve as modulating chords, producing gentler modulations than root-position chords.

8. Modulations can be abrupt, fast, or gradual. ·
   a. In abrupt modulations, the music leaps into the new key.
   b. In fast modulations, the four stages are performed quickly. Sometimes stage 2 is omitted and stages 3 and 4 are telescoped into one.
   c. In gradual modulations, each stage is prolonged, often for several measures.

9. In returning to the home key, the four stages occur in reverse.
   a. Stage 1 has already been accomplished.
   b. A returning pivot chord may or may not appear.
   c. Re-entry into the home key requires use of a returning modulating tone and chord—both characteristic of the home key, not the new one.
   d. A perfect cadence reconfirms the home key.

The Contrasting Period

In a *contrasting period*, the two phrases differ in melody but maintain a similarity in general style, equal phrase lengths, and contrasted cadences. The composer, freed of the obligation to repeat his opening idea, can develop a longer, more continuous line. A contrasting period often contains a subtly constructed, free-flowing melody (Ex. 18).

Ex. 18   Beethoven: Sonata Op. 13 (*Pathétique*), second movement

While the first cadence (*a*) contrasts harmonically with the second (*b*), the melody flows over the cadence measure, creating a continuous movement throughout the eight bars. There is no repetition of the opening melodic pattern. The steady sixteenth-note figure in the inner voice adds to the feeling of unity.

At other times, a deliberate contrast is created between the two phrases. In Ex. 19, the second phrase differs sharply from the first in melody, rhythm, and texture. But the melodic curve—an arch—unites the two: the first half of the period rises to a climax, pausing for a moment of suspense (*a*); the second half falls gently toward the resolution (*b*).

Ex. 19   Beethoven: Sonata, Op. 14, No. 1, last movement

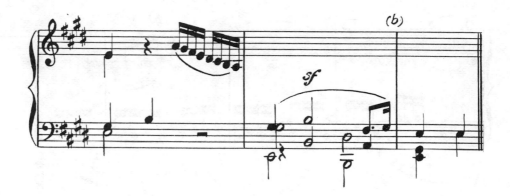

Unity in the Contrasting Period

In writing the contrasting period, a problem arises—how to maintain unity while achieving the desired contrast. Unity can be attained through one or more of the following elements:

1. A persistent rhythmic motive.
2. A continuous accompaniment figure.
3. A strong over-all melodic curve.
4. Interweaving of melodic fragments.
5. General consistency of style.

In the folk song "Barbara Allen," a rhythmic motive binds the two contrasted phrases together. A broad melodic curve (an arch) also helps to create unity, the general rise of the first phrase being balanced by the gradual fall of the second.

Ex. 20   English folk song: Barbara Allen

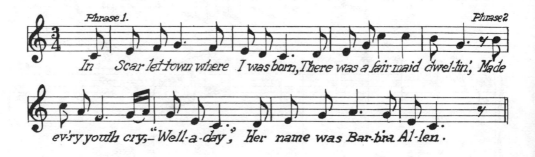

The sharp melodic and rhythmic contrast of the two phrases in Ex. 21 could easily pull them apart, were it not for the constant rhythm and texture of the accompaniment figure, as well as the strong forward drive of the chord roots. Note, incidentally, the rather unusual first cadence (*a*) on III (major region of the minor mode), which makes a fine contrast with the final perfect cadence.

Ex. 21   Chopin: Mazurka, Op. 17, No. 2

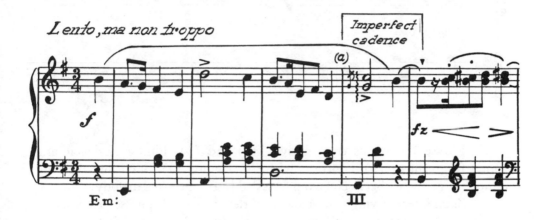

Interweaving of Motivic Fragments

A special type of contrasting period appears when the beginning of the second phrase derives from the *end* of the first (Ex. 22).

Ex. 22   Mozart: Symphony No. 35 (*Haffner*), K. 385

Phrase 1 contains two motives, (*a*) and (*b*). Phrase 2, developing from a fragment of (*b*), contrasts with the opening (*a*). Such interweaving of motive fragments between two phrases adds strength to a melody.

Such interweaving can be even subtler: in Ex. 23, phrases 1 and 2 are contrasted; but fragment (*c*) derives clearly from (*a*), and (*d*) is a varied augmentation of (*b*).

Ex. 23   Minuet, from *The Notebook of Anna Magdalena Bach*

The foregoing examples show how the phrases of a contrasting period can be related. The obvious or subtle persistence of a rhythmic or melodic fragment, or of other stylistic elements, serves to hold them together.

Summary

1. In a contrasting period, the two phrases differ in melody and in cadence but are similar in length and general style.

2. Unity between contrasted phrases may be attained through:
   a. A persistent rhythmic motive in the melody.
   b. A persistent accompaniment figure.
   c. A clear-cut over-all melodic curve.
   d. Interweaving of motivic fragments.
   e. General consistency of style.

III

Modulation
to Other Keys

In the earlier stages of evolution of the major-minor system, most modulations led to *closely related keys* (those having the same signature as the tonic, or differing by one accidental). Only later, in the Classical and Romantic periods, did more distant modulations become common practice.* Let us follow history in this respect, first studying modulations from major to the nearer keys: VI, II, III, and IV.

Modulation from I to VI

Of all the keys intimately related to a major tonic, VI, or the *relative minor*, is one of the closest. Possessing a common key signature, the two keys also share most of their chords. The comparison is somewhat complicated by the three different scale structures possible in the minor mode. Falling

---

* For exceptions and further discussion, see pages 305–306.

melodic minor, of course, has exactly the same tones and chords as the relative major. Harmonic minor differs from the relative major in its modulating tone, raised 7, and in its modulating chord, V.*

Ex. 1   Modulation I—VI: modulating tone and chord

Modulation from major to the relative minor is shown in a Bach chorale—where we observe a characteristic darkening of mood.

Ex. 2   Bach: *Was mein Gott will, das g'scheh' allzeit*

The phrase moves from the home key, C major (*a*), through two pivot chords (*b*) which belong to both C and A minor, to the modulating tone and chord (*c*) and the cadence confirming the new key (*d*).

In modulating from I to VI through the rising melodic minor scale, an additional modulating tone (R6) and two new modulating chords (RIV and RII) are often used.

* V is used here to represent all dominant-function chords, including V⁷, VII, and their inversions.

Ex. 3   Modulation I—VI: additional modulating tone and chords

Raised 6 usually appears just before raised 7, and raised IV⁶ just before raised VII (or V⁶). In Ex. 4 (*a*), R6 and R7 are the modulating tones (in the bass), and RIV⁶ and RVII the modulating chords that lead from C major to A minor.*

Ex. 4   Bach: *Was mein Gott will, das g'scheh' allzeit* (different setting)

Since a major key and its relative minor share so many chords in common, it is unnecessary to stress any particular pivot chord; a modulation can be made by introducing the new IV and V almost anywhere in the phrase (Ex. 5, *a*).

* Note that in two different harmonizations of the same chorale melody, Bach enters the new key earlier in Ex. 4 than in Ex. 2—showing that it is often possible to begin a modulation at different points in the phrase.

Ex. 5   Rimsky-Korsakoff: *Scheherazade*, Op. 35

Often the new V alone suffices to make the change of key (Ex. 6, *a*).

Ex. 6   Chopin: Mazurka, Op. 50, No. 2

In an interesting Renaissance example of a fast modulation to the relative minor, stages 3 and 4 are telescoped into one. Entry into the new key and the cadence confirming that key are one step (Ex. 7, *a*).

Ex. 7   Gervaise: *Bransles simples*, No. 6

Modulation to II

Modulation to the supertonic (II), like that to VI, involves change from a major to a minor key—from brighter to darker color. It does not however, necessarily connote a darkening of mood; there may even be a heightened intensity when the second phrase (Ex. 8, *b*) appears in sequence, one tone above the original (*a*).*

* See also Ex. 46, page 29.

Ex. 8   Schumann: *Lied der Braut*, from *Myrten*, Op. 25

Tonic and supertonic keys share very few pivot chords. The II of the home key occurs in all forms of the supertonic; the I, IV, and V only in certain forms of that key. Raised 7 of the new key is the essential modulating tone, but lowered 6 plays an important role, too.

Ex. 9   Modulation I—II: modulating tones and chords; pivot chords

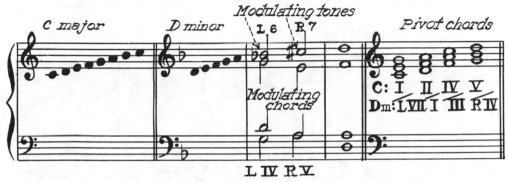

Ex. 10 shows entry into the new key (F minor) through a sudden appearance of the new V^6 (*a*). The pivot chord has been omitted, making this a fast modulation. Raised 7 of the new key (*a*) acts as modulating tone in the bass; lowered 6 (*b*) follows in the right hand. The confirmatory perfect cadence arrives at (*c*).

Sometimes lowered 6 *precedes* raised 7 as modulating tone. See, for instance, F natural in Ex. 8 (*b*), which first indicates the modulation to A minor. Note, too, in this example, that II^6 precedes V as modulating chord.

Ex. 10   Bach: Minuet, from French Suite No. 2

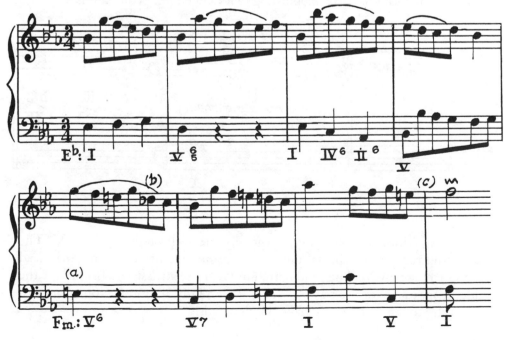

Modulation to III

Like the modulation from I to II, the shift to III brings a darkening of color. But movement to the mediant (Ex. 11) seems more emphatic than to the supertonic.

Ex. 11   Brahms: Rhapsody, Op. 119, No. 4

In modulating to III, there are two modulating tones—raised 7 and 2 of the new key. They provide a strong move in the sharp direction, especially since the new V chord contains both raised tones. There are three possible pivot chords in the modulation to III.

Ex. 12   Modulation I—III: modulating tones and chord; pivot chords

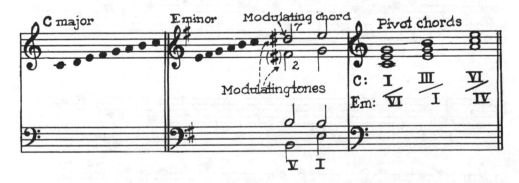

Entry into the new key is generally made through its 7 and V. The modulation requires no special pivot chord, since the original tonic may lead directly to the new V. The modulation in Ex. 13 seems rather abrupt; yet the sudden appearance of the new V⁷ (at a) is certainly pleasing. Note that both modulating tones—7 and 2—arrive simultaneously.

Ex. 13   Chopin: Mazurka, Op. 68, No. 2

Sometimes the new 2 appears (Ex. 14, *a*) before the 7 (*b*). Here, too, as in Ex. 8, II⁶ (*a*) precedes V as modulating chord.

Ex. 14   Lvov: Old Russian Anthem

Modulation to IV

Although the relation of subdominant and tonic keys is just as close as that of dominant and tonic (each being separated by one accidental), modulation from I to IV is not so common as might be supposed. It rarely occurs in the first half of a composition, appearing more frequently near the end. We can readily see why. Whereas movement to V adds brightness to the first part of a work, modulation to IV brings a darker color, considered unsuitable to the opening of a composition in major. The somberness caused by flatting the original 7—necessary for subdominant modulation—lends a gentle color to an ending.

The modulating tone leading to IV is not a new 7, as in all preceding modulations, but 4 of the new key.

Ex. 15   Modulation I—IV: modulating tone and chords; pivot chords

The modulating chords leading to the subdominant are those containing the new (lowered) 4: IV, II, and V^7 (rarely VII) of the new key. Lacking a new V,* modulation to the subdominant adds no drive to the harmony. Like the plagal cadence (also involving a I—IV relationship), it has, nonetheless, its own characteristic quality. In Ex. 16, the subdominant, D major, enters abruptly at (a) with the appearance of that key's 4 (G natural) and IV chord.

Ex. 16   Schumann: *Im Walde*, from *Liederkreis*, Op. 39

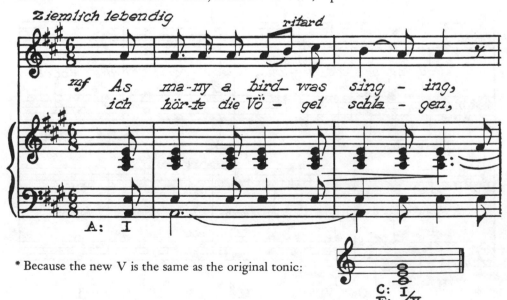

* Because the new V is the same as the original tonic:

Modulations to the subdominant before the latter part of a composition rarely appear in Bach. What seem superficially to be key changes of this
type at the beginning of a work are generally revealed as secondary
dominants—V⁷'s of IV. Their characteristic chromatic alterations are quickly
cancelled, leading to a cadence in the home key.

Ex. 17   Bach: Sarabande, from English Suite No. 4

The beautiful flatted seventh that opens Ex. 17 (*a*) lends a mellow quality to the phrase. Its downward impulse is balanced by the upward-directed V$^4_2$ at (*b*). Note that Bach was so eager to counteract the downward movement of the V of IV that he introduced the V three times in two bars.

On the other hand, modulation to IV occurs frequently in the *last* part of many Bach compositions.* A common pivot chord is the original tonic (V in the new key). In Ex. 18, I of C (*a*) serves as a pivot; at (*b*) the modulating chord V^9 leads into F major; and at (*c*) the phrase ends in a cadence.

Ex. 18   Bach: Fugue No. 2, from *Little Fugues and Preludes*

Wavering Motion in Modulation

In the modulations analyzed thus far, harmonic motion leads directly from one key to another; after entering the new key it progresses quickly to the cadence. Such examples occur by the thousands in the musical literature. But the paths of modulation are not always so neat and orderly; in the music of the great masters, it is not unusual to find passages in which the progression wavers, so to speak, moving in zigzag fashion rather than in a straight line. Sometimes the phrase enters a new key and heads for the cadence, but suddenly turns back to the home key; moving forward again, backtracking

* Modulation to the subdominant is also characteristic of the middle part, or Trio, of many Classical minuets. See, for example, the minuets in Mozart's Sonatas K. 212 and 331, and Beethoven's Op. 10, No. 3.

once more. Then, when we almost despair of finding its true direction, the music makes a perfect cadence in the new key (Ex. 19).

Ex. 19   Bach: Prelude No. 5, from *Six Preludes*

Such a "wavering" progression does not reveal indecision on the part of the composer; it shows, rather, a deliberate artistic plan. In Ex. 19, the phrase enters the dominant at (*a*), the modulating tone being reiterated at (*b*), (*c*), and (*d*). At (*e*), however, the F sharp changes back to F natural, indicating a return to the home key, C major. The sharp reappears at (*f*), repeats at (*g*), but loses out to the natural again at (*h*). Returning for the third time at (*i*), it finally reaches the perfect cadence, at (*j*). Wavering motion prolongs and adds interest to a modulation, from the point of entry to the final establishment of the new key.*

Summary

1. Keys closely related to a given key are those sharing the same signature or differing by one accidental.

2. After the modulation to V, the most common modulations from a major key are to the other closely related keys: VI, II, III, and IV.

3. Modulation to VI, the relative minor, involves a darkening of mood but a minimum of harmonic shift, due to the wide overlapping of tones and chords between the two keys.

4. Modulation to II, although to a darker key, can involve a heightening of mood, especially if the phrase in the new key is a sequence of the first phrase, a tone higher.

5. Modulation to III, in addition to a certain darkness, often connotes an emphatic quality.

6. Modulation to IV, because of its somber character, generally occurs near the end of a composition.
   a. Its modulating tone, unlike that of other closely related keys, is 4.
   b. Its modulating chords, unlike those of other closely related keys, include its II and IV in addition to V^7.

7. Wavering motion follows an indirect path to the new key, prolonging and adding interest to the modulation.

* Hindemith's discussion of wavering motion is interesting (Paul Hindemith: *The Craft of Musical Composition*, New York, 1942): "Often it is impossible to draw clear boundaries for the . . . tonal groupings; one listener hears the change as occurring at one place, another at another. But this is not a shortcoming; on the contrary, one of the greatest charms of modulation lies in the exploitation of this very uncertainty in the transitional passages."

8. Here are the pivot chords and modulating tones and chords leading to all the keys closely related to C major:

The Asymmetrical Period

Throughout the history of melody, two forces have contended for supremacy: one, the spirit of free, unmeasured, lyrical outpouring; the other, that of order, balance, and symmetry. We have seen examples of the first in old religious chants, folk songs, and the themes of certain contemporary masters, while the second has occurred in evenly balanced dance tunes, popular songs, and many eighteenth- and nineteenth-century arias and sonata themes.*

Besides competing, however, the two forces inevitably intermingle, producing a music that combines freedom with balance, spontaneity with order.

Asymmetry through Free Form

In the *asymmetrical period*, we have freedom of form—two phrases of unequal length—and yet proportion, for the two divisions complement each other. The musician who seeks an organized pattern without constricting regularity will find himself at home with this form.

* For examples of free, asymmetrical melody, see Volume I, pages 161–162 and 277–279; for symmetrical ones, pages 113–114 of that volume and 27–30 of this one.

In listening to one of Beethoven's beautiful slow movements—Ex. 20, for instance—we usually are not aware of its delicate asymmetry. The proportions are slightly uneven: five, then four measures.

Ex. 20   Beethoven: Sonata, Op. 10, No. 3, second movement

The free rhythm of Spanish folk music often produces a similar fluidity of form, in which the counting of measures seems quite irrelevant. As notated, the irregular phrases of Ex. 21 have six and five measures, respectively.

Ex. 21   Spanish folk song: *Noche clarina y serena*

From Kurt Schindler, Folkmusic and Poetry of Spain and Portugal, *Hispanic Institute, 1941. Reprinted by permission of Andrew A. W. Schindler and Veronica Moss.*

Before the commercialization of American folk music in popular recordings and TV programs, the songs of the Southern Appalachians often combined balance and asymmetry. The changing meters of the free-flowing melody in Ex. 22 reveal a freshness of invention; yet the two phrases (*a* and *b*) are bound together by period form.

Ex. 22   American folk song: Young Hunting

Asymmetry through Extension

Asymmetry arises from the basic structure of the periods in Exs. 20–22. In other periods, asymmetry results from extension or expansion of a regular phrase. When the second phrase of a parallel period fails to halt at its appointed place, but draws the melody out to greater length, the result is *asymmetry through extension*. We find a delightful example in the aria *Là ci darem*.

Ex. 23   Mozart: *Là ci darem*, from *Don Giovanni*

Don Giovanni, singing this melody to Zerlina, is completely self-contained and conscious of his purpose: the tune forms a perfect period (page 32). In Zerlina's answer (Ex. 23) the lady is carried away: the four-bar tune (*b*) does not stop at (*c*) where it should, but leaps to a climax and stretches out for an additional two bars (*d*).

Sometimes extension results from a simple repetition of the ending. "Edward," a folk song in the pentatonic scale (Ex. 24) could have stopped at (*a*). Two bars of extension, echoing the two preceding bars, add a roundness to the melody, which otherwise might have been too formal and box-like.

Ex. 24   American folk song: Edward

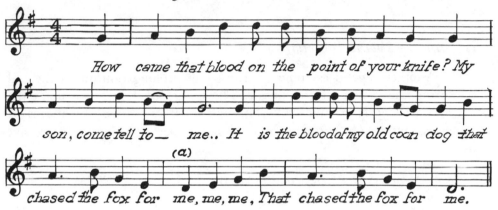

Sometimes an extension at the end of the second phrase provides the occasion for an attractive climax; avoiding a tedious squareness, the melody sweeps freely onward (Ex. 25).

Ex. 25   Mendelssohn: *Venetian Boat Song*, Op. 19, No. 6

Asymmetry through Expansion

Another type of asymmetry arises from prolongation not at the end but during the course of the phrase. Phrase (*a*) of Ex. 26 occupies the conventional length of four bars. Through *inner expansion** by means of sequences, phrase (*b*) stretches out to eleven bars, gaining in expressive power.

Ex. 26   Wagner: *Die Meistersinger*, Act III

* A technique observed in connection with the motive (see page 243, Volume I).

Summary

1. In an asymmetrical period, the two phrases are of unequal length. The imbalance often produces a feeling of irregularity and freedom.

2. Asymmetry arises from:
   a. Irregularity in the original structure of the phrases.
   b. An extension of one phrase.
   c. An expansion of one phrase.

IV

Modulation from Minor

Modulation between minor keys and from minor to major is more complex than between major keys alone. Due to the variability of the minor scales, pivot chords between minor keys and between minor and major often cannot be defined precisely. Certain triads, for example, are shared by two keys in falling melodic minor but not in the rising or harmonic forms. We shall examine this point more closely in specific modulations.

As with major, the keys most closely related to a minor key are those sharing the same signature or differing by one accidental: (1) the relative major, III; (2) V and its relative major (lowered) VII; and (3) IV and its relative major, VI.

Note that, in minor, lowered VII is closely related to a given key, but II is not.* (In major, the opposite holds true.)

The modulation from a minor key to its relative major is the simplest of all. Many compositions in minor—Baroque suites, Bach chorales, minuets and other short compositions by Classical composers—modulate first to III. Since practically all the chords in a minor key also appear in the relative major, almost any of them (except the minor's raised V) can serve as a pivot. The new V is the usual modulating chord. After establishment of the minor key, a cadence in the relative major will simultaneously make and confirm the modulation.

A fast modulation of this kind occurs in an "Ayre" by the seventeenth-century English composer Thomas Campion.

* I and II in minor are separated by two sharps.

79

Ex. 1   Campion: All Lookes Be Pale (1613)

The modulatory process, as we have seen, can be prolonged or contracted without changing its essential nature. Thus modulation accomplished by five chords in Ex. 1 spreads out over ten chords in Ex. 2.

Ex. 2   Campion: Think'st Thou to Seduce Me Then (1617)

There is something very satisfying about a modulation from minor to its relative major—as though the music, starting in a darker area, has worked into the light. Note the procedure in a stately French Renaissance dance tune.

Ex. 3   Thoinot Arbeau: Pavane (1589)

Arbeau's melody shows a modulation more fully developed than those of Campian. The home key is established by the centering motion of the four opening chords (*a*), the last of which (*b*) serves also as a pivot. At (*c*) V of B flat leads to a perfect cadence (*d*) in that key, followed at (*e*) by a second cadence confirming the modulation.

Phrase 2 modulates back from III to I. After the phrase starts in B flat (*f*), the return pivot chord IV of G minor (*g*) leads to V—the point of re-entry into the home key. A curious wavering appears at (*h*): instead of moving directly to the tonic of G minor, the music harks back momentarily to the key just relinquished, B flat—a surprising but not unpleasing progression. The wavering ceases as the phrase moves ahead into G minor (*i*), the confirmatory cadence (*j*) being doubly welcome now. A *tierce de Picardie* replaces the expected minor third in the final chord.

Two and a half centuries after the Renaissance, Schubert made the same modulation from minor to the relative major. Note the unusual use of VII^7 as a modulating chord (Ex. 4, *a*).

Ex. 4   Schubert: *Ländler*, Op. posth., No. 3

Modulation to V

To modulate from a minor key to its dominant, *two* chromatic alterations must be made. The new key can be entered through either modulating tone, 7 or 2. Both tones, however, are needed in the modulating chord, V of the new key.

Ex. 5   Modulation I—V: modulating tones

Ex. 6   Modulation I—V: modulating chord

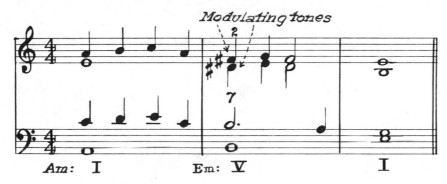

A passage from Bach illustrates this modulation. Starting in A minor, the first phrase enters E minor through its 2 (*a*), with the 7 following at (*b*) and the cadence in the new key at (*c*).

Ex. 7   Bach: Sinfonia, No. 13

Because of the variability of the minor mode, a minor key and its dominant share only three tones at all times (Ex. 8,*).

Ex. 8   Comparison of minor scales I and V

Possessing only three tones in common, I and V have only a few pivot chords.

Ex. 9   Modulation I—V: pivot chords

The triads on C, E, and G serve as pivot chords only in *melodic minor falling*. The I of the home key, however, can almost always be used as a pivot chord; in many modulations, I—considered as a new IV—leads directly to V or I of the new key (Ex. 10).

Ex. 10   Mozart: Sonata, K. 331, Rondo *alla turca*

Am: I/
Em: IV   I   V   I

In traditional music, most modulations from minor lead either to III or to V. Those leading to VII, IV, and VI are far less common.

Modulation to VII

After III and V, the most favored goal for a modulation from minor is lowered VII. Its scale differs from that of the home key by only one tone. To modulate, 6 of the home key must be raised and 7 lowered (Ex. 11); the original I acts as pivot chord. In Ex. 12, the A minor triad at (*a*) serves both as I of the first key and II of the second. The new key, G major, is entered through its 7 and V⁶ (at *b*).

Ex. 11   Modulation I—VII: modulating tones

Ex. 12   Bach: *Helft mir Gott's Güte preisen*

From now on, it will not be necessary to spell out all pivot chords; a little investigation will soon show what they are.

Modulation to IV

Because of the relatively dark nature of minor, modulations to IV—which generally reinforce this somber quality—rarely appear in short compositions. (They are also infrequent near the beginning of longer ones.) In order to make such a modulation, *two* modulating tones, R7 and L6 of the new key, are often employed (Ex. 13).

Ex. 13   Modulation I—IV: modulating tones

In the modulation to IV, the modulating chords are V and IV of the new key (Ex. 14). To form the new leading tone, the third of the original triad (*a*) is raised, changing it from a minor to a major triad (*b*).

Ex. 14   Modulation I—IV: change of tonic I to major triad

Ex. 15   Bach: *Ach wie flüchtig, ach wie nichtig*

In Ex. 15, the key of A minor, emphasized by two tonic triads at (*a*)
and (*b*), is confirmed by the cadence starting at (*c*). But Bach, mindful that
he will soon modulate to D minor, paves the way by pausing on an A *major*

triad, with *tierce de Picardie*, at (*d*). At (*e*), this triad, now the new V, leads directly into the new key. (Note that the *tierce de Picardie* appears once more, at the cadence in D minor—*f*.)

Modulation to VI

Modulations to VI in short minor compositions are even rarer than those to IV. The modulating tone is 4, and the modulating chords are II and IV of the new key (Ex. 16, *a*).

Ex. 16   Modulation I—VI: modulating tone and chord

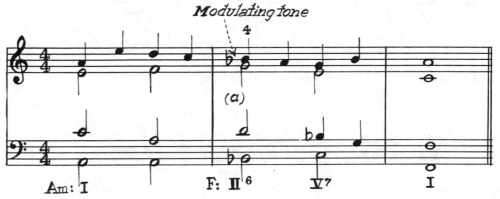

In Ex. 17, the shift to VI occurs abruptly. After the ending of the first phrase in A minor (*a*), the second phrase starts directly in F major (*b*).

Ex. 17   Schumann: The Wild Horseman, from *Album for the Young*, Op. 68

Summary

1. Modulation from a minor key is more complex than from a major one. Because the minor scale possesses such a variety of forms, the pivot chords between a minor key and its neighbors cannot be defined exactly.

2. The modulation to the relative major (III) is the most frequent and easiest of all. After the establishment of the original minor key, only a simple cadence in the relative major is needed to confirm the modulation. It often suggests a "working into the light."

3. The modulation to V is the second most common from a minor key. It brings a brightening of mood, and requires two modulating tones.

4. The modulation to lowered VII is the next most common.

5. The modulation to IV brings a darkening of mood. It often involves changing the minor I to a major I.

6. The modulation to VI is quite rare in short pieces.

7. Here are the pivot chords and the modulating tones and chords to all the keys closely related to A minor:

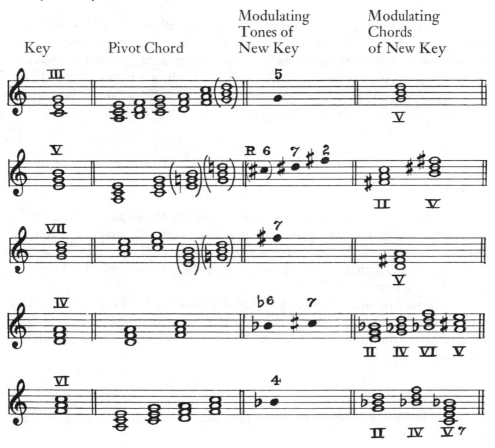

The
Three-Phrase
Group

When three phrases are joined together, with the first two ending in incomplete cadences and the third in a perfect one, the union forms a *three-phrase group*. Asymmetrical in nature, this pattern permits a certain freedom of design. It appears in three different types: (1) three parallel phrases (a-a′-a″); (2) two parallel and one contrasting phrase (a-a′-b) or (a-b-b′); and (3) three contrasting phrases (a-b-c).*

Cadences

Like the period, the phrase group embodies the principle of cadential suspense. Ending in incomplete cadences, the first two phrases create an "open" feeling and the need to push on. The last phrase, closing with a perfect cadence, brings a sense of completion: the goal toward which the first two were striving.

Sometimes one of the opening phrases modulates; it can even end in a perfect cadence in a new key. Such modulation produces a tension resolved by a return to the home key, where a perfect cadence in the tonic rounds out the form.

---

* A-b-a represents a different structural principle, the three-part form (see pages 174–175.)

Here are various cadence patterns for the three-phrase group:

	(1)	(2)	(3)
(a)	Imperfect	Half	Perfect
(b)	Half	Imperfect	Perfect
(c)	Imperfect	Perfect in new key	Perfect in home key
(d)	Perfect in new key	Half	Perfect in home key

Three Parallel Phrases

A phrase group achieves greatest unity when all phrases begin with the same motive (a-a′-a″). Starting in parallel fashion, each of the three lines goes off in a different direction, sometimes with a surprise just before one of the cadences.

In Schubert's *Heidenröslein*,* the surprise consists in extension of the second phrase to six bars, creating a pleasing asymmetry.

Harold Arlen's "Blues in the Night" (Ex. 18) makes a virtue of insistent monotony—often the essence of a good blues. All phrases share the same motive, and, in the first two, a winding figure repeats obsessively. But rhythmic contractions at (*a*) and (*b*) add pungency to the suddenly appearing "blue" notes.

Ex. 18   Arlen: Blues in the Night

* See page 450, Volume I.

The twelve-bar, three-phrase pattern shown in Ex. 18 has been standard for the blues ever since W. C. Handy's first notation of the "Memphis Blues" in 1909.

Beethoven's First Symphony provides another example of the parallel three-phrase group.

Ex. 19   Beethoven: Symphony No. 1, Op. 21

In contrast to the lazy quality of the blues, this phrase group exudes vitality; the motivic insistence, the active rhythm, and the over-all pattern of a rising wave culminating in high A (*) create a strong momentum throughout all three phrases (a, a', and a''). Note the irregular lengths: six, six, and nine measures, respectively. Such three-phrase groups, with the last phrase building to a climax, are often found in Beethoven.

Two Phrases Parallel, One Contrasting

In the second type of phrase group, the first two phrases are parallel, the third contrasting (a-a'-b); or the last two are parallel, both contrasting with the first (a-b-b'). Another famous blues (Ex. 20) illustrates the first pattern. Its second phrase forms a sequence of the opening one, and the third differs with both in intervals and rhythm.

Ex. 20   Traditional blues: Frankie and Johnny

In the a-b-b' pattern (Ex. 21), the second phrase leads to an imperfect cadence and the third (largely a repetition, except for octave displacement, a change in dynamics, and variation of the last few notes) to a perfect one.

Ex. 21   Beethoven: Symphony No. 8, Op. 93

Three Contrasting Phrases

Of all the patterns, a-b-c offers the greatest variety and freedom; each phrase starts with a different melodic and rhythmic idea. This design also makes possible the shaping of an open, asymmetrical line. Without obligation to repeat, the composer can spin out a long, freely expanding melody.

Ex. 22   Handel: Largo, from *Xerxes*

Deservedly one of Handel's best-known melodies, the Largo (Ex. 22) contains three phrases, each with a different curve, length, rhythmic structure, and cadence.

Phrase (1), a bowl 5 bars long, grows from the rhythm

and ends on a half cadence.

Phrase (2), a falling line 4 bars long, grows from the rhythm

and ends in an imperfect cadence.

Phrase (3), a falling wave 6 bars long, grows from a free rhythm of quarter and eighth notes, and ends in a perfect cadence.

The unusual variety of this melody—especially of its rhythms—raises the question: how does it achieve unity?

Apart from the steady pulse of the accompaniment and the logical march of the harmonies (not shown in Ex. 22), there are three unifying factors in the melody itself:

1. The falling melodic pattern,

appearing in different rhythmic guises, binds the three phrases together. In the second phrase, it occurs a sixth higher than in the first, and in the third, an octave higher—extended, moreover, to cover the entire octave range.

2. The motivic fragment,

which appears six times, produces an inner connection among the various phrases. *Inner unity has special importance in binding together phrases that have contrasted beginnings.**

3. Unity is further emphasized by the broad sweep of the over-all melodic curve—an arch. Its elegant proportions of rise and fall create a feeling of unbroken movement from beginning to end.

Another distinguished melody, written nearly two hundred years after Handel's *Largo*, presents three contrasting phrases that reveal a similar unity-in-diversity.

---

* This means of achieving unity is also important in two- and three-part forms (see pages 149–156 and 180–181).

Ex. 23   Prokofiev: Gavotte, from the *Classical* Symphony, Op. 25

As in Handel's *Largo* (Ex. 22), the three Prokofiev phrases (Ex. 23) all start differently. Unity results, however, from the persistent appearance of two motivic fragments: (1) a group of four eighth notes:

and (2) a pair of leaping octaves:

Occurring in each phrase, at different positions in the bar, and in different variations (inversion and others), the fragments create a sense of identity. This identity is enhanced by the recurrence of the same rhythmic values (eighth and quarter notes) throughout Gavotte, and by the symmetry of its four-bar phrases.*

Because it fosters subtle relationships, the group of three contrasting phrases is a sophisticated form, not often found in popular or traditional music. That it does appear, however, and lends itself to the most singable of melodies is shown by the carol "Silent Night," as well as by "A Woman Is a Sometime Thing," from Gershwin's *Porgy and Bess.*

* Compare the techniques of unifying a contrasting period (pages 52–53).

Summary

1. The three-phrase group comprises three phrases joined by the principle of cadential suspense: all cadences are "open" until the last.

2. From now on, a perfect cadence in a key other than the tonic is considered an "open" cadence, because it requires further movement toward a final cadence in the home key.

3. There are three types of three-phrase groups:
   a. Three parallel phrases (a–a′–a″).
   b. Two parallel phrases, one contrasting (a–a′–b) or (a–b–b′).
   c. Three contrasting phrases (a–b–c).

4. Unity in three contrasting phrases is achieved by:
   a. Identity of inner motivic fragments.
   b. A strong over-all melodic curve.
   c. Continuity of harmonic movement.
   d. Persistent accompaniment figures.

V

The
Harmonic
Sequence

Having studied the sequence as a melodic technique, let us turn now to its use in harmony. A *harmonic sequence*, the repetition of a chord pattern on a higher or lower level, often plays an important role in musical development. It has been a valuable compositional device in the Baroque suite, concerto, and fugue, and in the Classical and Romantic sonata and symphony.

The shortest sequence pattern consists of a two-chord progression.

Repetitions of the pattern on different levels form sequences.

Ex. 1   Sequences of a pattern

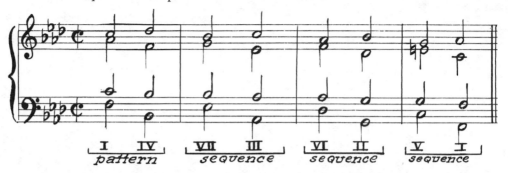

By adding a melodic idea over such a progression and elaborating the texture, Mozart devised graceful melodic-harmonic sequences.*

Ex. 2   Mozart: Sonata, K. 533, last movement

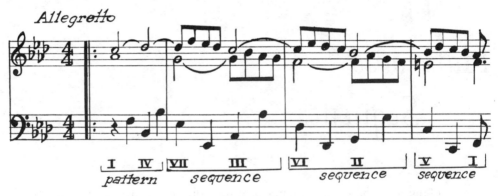

Sequences can be *exact, varied,* or *free.* In an exact sequence all elements of the pattern—melodic, rhythmic, and harmonic—repeat literally on another pitch; in a varied sequence, one or more elements are altered.

Ex. 3   Mozart: Sonata, K. 545

* Note that while the first bar gives the pattern for the harmonic sequences, the pattern for the melodic sequences appears only in the second bar.

In Ex. 3 , a one-bar pattern (*a*) is followed by three sequences (*b, c,* and *d*), each successively a tone lower. The rhythmic unit repeats exactly, as

do the harmonic pattern (two chords of the cycle of fifths) and the melodic idea (a sharply etched broken-chord figure). The sole change is a shift to the upper octave (*c*).* Such a departure from exact repetition makes this a varied sequence; slight as it is, the variation lends charm to the passage and prevents possible monotony.

In free sequences, the chords follow a set pattern, but one or more voices move independently of the pattern.†

Length and Number of Sequences

A sequence pattern varies in length from one half bar to an entire phrase. Note the half-bar pattern in Ex. 4 and the four-bar pattern in Ex. 5.

Ex. 4   Bach: Invention No. 14‡

* To note the value of the octave shift, play measures (*c*) and (*d*) an octave lower.
† See Ex. 19, page 113.

‡ Note that right and left hands both contain their own sequences; in addition, the right-hand pattern is an inversion of that of the left hand, imitating it a beat later.

Ex. 5   Beethoven: Sonata, Op. 53 (*Waldstein*) *

* For another four-bar pattern, see Ex. 26, page 115.

How many sequences are usually found in a phrase? The answer depends entirely on the imagination of the composer; often one suffices to make the point.

Ex. 6   Haydn: Allegro in F

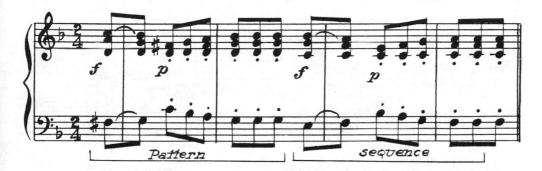

Two sequences are also a common length (Ex. 7). When three consecutive sequences follow a pattern, some variation is generally introduced (Ex. 3). More than three successive sequences can easily provoke boredom unless varied contrapuntally or justified by a dramatic, developmental, or other purpose.*

Functions of the Sequence

Sequences serve a variety of functions, among them:

1. To create directional or traveling motion.
2. To produce a growing tension.
3. To develop a short musical idea into an extended phrase.

These functions are not mutually exclusive; all three may and often do occur in the same phrase.

The Sequence as Directional Movement

The sequence gives music a strong sense of directed movement, because repetition on a higher or lower level enhances harmonic drive. In Ex. 7, the two-bar pattern recurs a third lower at (*a*) and yet another third lower at (*b*). Melody and harmony share the downward movement.

_____
* See Ex. 8 for sequences contrapuntally varied, and Ex. 14 for dramatically motivated ones.

Ex. 7   Chopin: Mazurka, Op. 68, No. 3

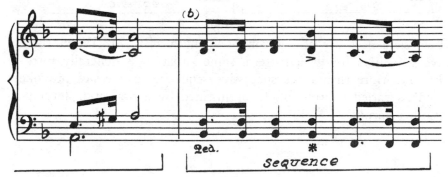

In Ex. 8, the directional drive of bars (c), (d), and (e) is strengthened by two harmonic elements:

1. The cycle of fifths, strongest of root movements.
2. A faster harmonic rhythm in relation to the preceding passage. Note that bars (a) and (b) have one chord each; (c) has two chords—a pattern emphasized by sequences (d) and (e).

Ex. 8   Bach: Invention No. 8

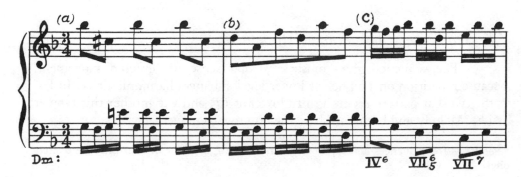

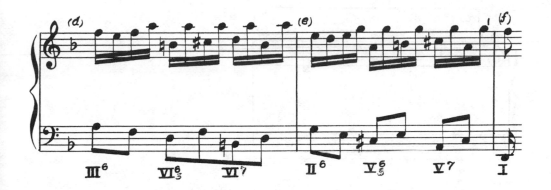

The Modulating Sequence

Directional movement is intensified when a sequence traverses not only several chords but several keys—when, in other words, it becomes a *modulating sequence*. Many of Bach's preludes begin with a relatively stable chord pattern, emphasizing the home key.

Ex. 9   Bach: Prelude No. 5, from *The Well-Tempered Clavier*, Book I

Later in the same Prelude, modulating sequences enhance the sense of movement.

Ex. 10   Bach: Prelude No. 5

Rhythmically as well as melodically, this passage develops the pattern of Ex. 9. The intensifying factors are the modulating sequences, which travel through three keys (B minor, A minor, and G major) in as many bars. Each key is entered through its V; *a modulating sequence usually starts with a dominant-function chord*. (See also Exs. 12 and 26.)

Sometimes a series of sequences covers a wider span. The first movement of Mozart's Symphony No. 40 contains a four-bar phrase that develops through no fewer than six modulating sequences (only two of them shown in Ex. 11, *a* and *b*).

Ex. 11   Mozart: Symphony No. 40, K. 550

Modulating sequences will be considered in further detail later in the chapter.

The Tension-Building Sequence

The second important function of the sequence—to build a growing tension—may be achieved in two ways:

1. Through a series of rising sequences.
2. Through sequences of a fragment in faster harmonic rhythm.

Rising sequences are a time-honored device. The two-bar pattern in Ex. 12 (*a*), repeats one tone higher each time, at (*b*) and (*c*). The V—I progression in each unit produces successive modulations.

Ex. 12   Handel: Minuet in F

The same effect may be accomplished with more elaborate material. In Ex. 13, a two-bar pattern (*a*) repeats in modulating sequences, each time one tone and one key higher. The root movements (a series of falling fourths) lead strongly upward from C major through D minor to E minor. As often happens, the third appearance of the pattern, at (*c*), is varied.

Ex. 13   Beethoven: Sonata, Op. 2, No. 2, third movement

Examples 2–6 and 8–13 have been drawn from Baroque and Classical music; it was in the Romantic period, however, that the tension-building sequence reached its apogee.* The complexity of the harmonies in Ex. 14 exceeds that of the two preceding examples, but the principle—building tension by the rising sequence—remains the same.

Ex. 14   Wagner: *Isolde's Liebestod*, from *Tristan and Isolde*

* See also Exs. 63, pages 287–288, and 33, page 325.

A subtler method of building intensity exists: the sequence of a short melodic fragment in speeded-up harmonic rhythm.

Ex. 15   Bach: Invention No. 14

The motive of Ex. 15, an embellishment of the B flat triad, is one bar long. It is restated at (*a*) and (*b*) over the IV and V chords, reaching an imperfect cadence at (*c*). Here, as so often happens in Bach, the pace quickens. A half-bar fragment of the motive appears (*c*) in a series of rapid sequences over a faster harmonic rhythm (four chords in a bar). The increased melodic and harmonic activity, coupled with the dynamic progression—a cycle of fifths—develops a cool tension in the phrase, leading to a strong half cadence at (*d*).

The Sequence in Phrase Expansion

The third (and possibly most interesting) function of the sequence is to develop a brief idea into an extended phrase. Beginning with a short motive, Baroque composers often proceeded to unfold its possibilities quickly, by means of the sequence.

Ex. 16   Vivaldi: Concerto Grosso, Op. III, No. 6

In Ex. 16, after the vigorous opening statement of the theme, a short motive appears (*a*). Following two repetitions, the motive is extended to a full bar (*b*), and is further repeated in two sequences over a cycle of fifths. The phrase develops in logical fashion.

Ex. 17   Bach: Invention No. 4

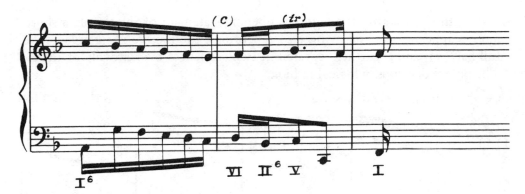

Bach's Invention No. 4 (Ex. 17) starts with a two-bar motive, which is repeated twice in different registers, centering harmonically around the tonic. At (*a*) a variant of the motive initiates a sequence traveling through the cycle of fifths. At (*b*) the motive shifts to the left hand, moving into F major and ending in a perfect cadence at (*c*). Ex. 17 shows how sequence can serve to develop a motive into a widely arching phrase, a strong harmonic movement, and a modulatory progression.*

Sequence Intervals and Patterns

Sequences can best be classified according to the interval at which they recur. A pattern usually repeats (1) one step lower; (2) a third lower; (3) a step higher; or (4) a third higher.

1. The prototype of all sequences repeated *one tone lower* is the cycle of fifths—of which we have already had numerous examples. In a useful variant of the cycle, a sixth chord replaces one triad of the pattern.†

Ex. 18   Cycle of fifths, with alternate sixth chords

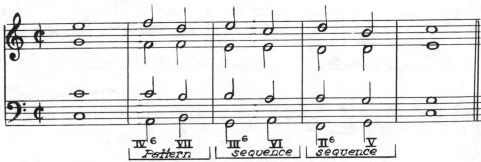

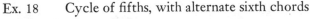

In another variant, the triads of the cycle are replaced by dominant seventh chords, forming a *cycle of secondary dominants* (Ex. 19).‡

* It also provides another example of the contrast between centering motion (from the opening to *a*) and traveling motion (*a* to *c*).

† See also pages 100–101.

‡ See also Exs. 34 and 35, page 21.

When writing sequences with the cycle of fifths, one need not move through the entire cycle. Nor must all voices necessarily follow the pattern of the bass. In Ex. 19, the three upper voices move freely.

Ex. 19   Chopin: Mazurka, Op. 33, No. 3

Another pattern repeated a tone lower is the falling third (Ex. 20).

Ex. 20   Falling-third pattern, repeated a tone below

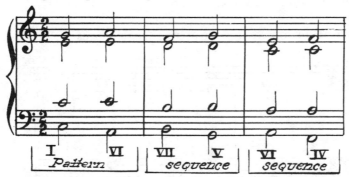

In a Torelli Concerto (Ex. 21), the second chord of this pattern appears in first inversion.

Ex. 21   Torelli: Violin Concerto, Op. 8, No. 8, last movement

2. Among sequences that repeat *a third lower* is the falling fourth (Ex. 22 and also Ex. 7).

Ex. 22   Falling-fourth pattern, repeated a third below

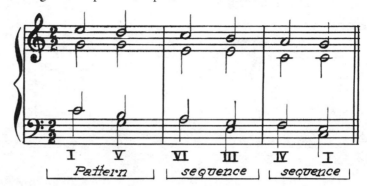

Substitution of a sixth chord for the second triad of the pattern creates a smoothly falling bass line.

Ex. 23   Falling-fourth pattern, with alternate sixth chords

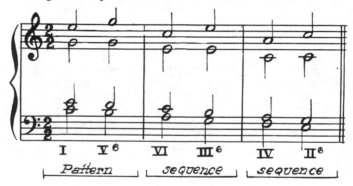

Bach used this sequence in a Gavotte (Ex. 24), in which the chord pattern—as often happens—starts in the middle of the measure and crosses the bar line. A variation, leaping octaves, replaces the flowing bass of Ex. 23.

Ex. 24   Bach: Gavotte, from French Suite No. 5

The falling fifth, like the falling fourth, can also be repeated a third lower—frequently in a modulating sequence.

Ex. 25   Falling-fifth pattern, repeated a third below

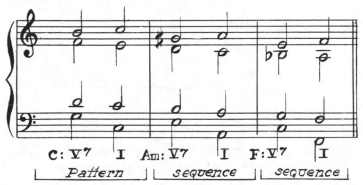

Like other patterns, this one may be embodied in a musical thought far more appealing than the skeletal outline given above. In the Beethoven sonata (Ex. 26), the falling fifth of Ex. 25 is filled in by stepwise motion of the bass. The pattern of two chords in one bar is expanded to a pattern of four chords in four bars, and the entire four-bar pattern is repeated in sequence. The basic plan, however (a falling fifth repeated a third lower), remains the same.*

Ex. 26   Beethoven: Sonata, Op. 10, No. 1

* The suavity and grace contributed by the linear embellishment of a bass pattern reveal once more the interdependence of melody and harmony in actual music.

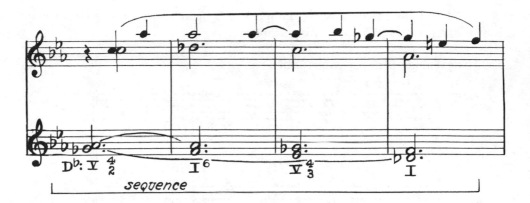

3. A third type of sequence repeats *one tone higher* each time—as in the sequence of falling fourths (Ex. 13). The falling-fifth pattern (written in Ex. 27 as a rising fourth) can also be repeated a tone higher. Beethoven employs this sequence in two successive phrases (Ex. 28): at (*a*) in a two-voice texture, and at (*b*) in three voices.*

Ex. 27   Rising-fourth pattern, repeated one tone higher

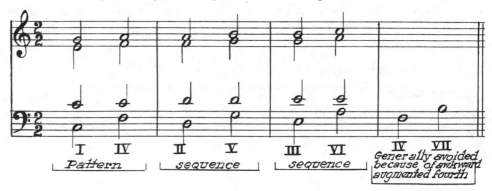

Ex. 28   Beethoven: Sonata, Op. 27, No. 1, last movement

* For other versions of this sequence, see Ex. 12, page 107, and Ex. 34, page 119.

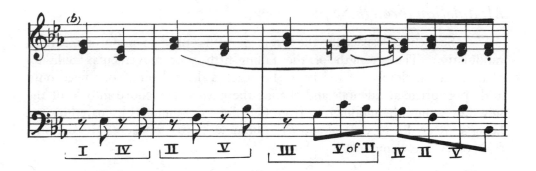

4. Patterns that repeat *a third higher* include the falling second (Exs. 29–30).

Ex. 29   Falling-second pattern repeated a third above

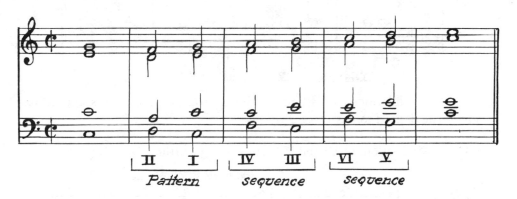

Ex. 30   Weber: Overture to *Der Freischütz.**

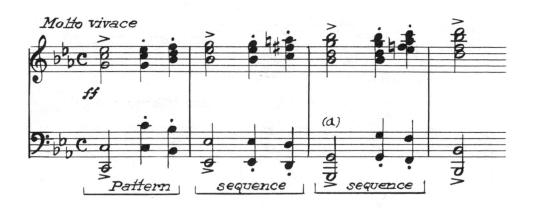

* The drop to the lower octave at (*a*) does not alter the basic plan of this sequence.

Modulation through Sequences

Sequences, especially the cycle of fifths, play an important role in modulation. The strength of the falling-fifth root movements facilitates changes to all closely related keys. To reach a desired tonic, one need only add appropriate accidentals and change the next-to-last chord into V of the new key. Thus, the modulation from C major to D minor is prepared by the latter's lowered 6 (Ex. 31, *a* and *b*). The new V (*c*), replacing the diatonic triad on A, acts as modulating chord.

Ex. 31   Modulation to II by the cycle of fifths

In modulations to VI and V, the appropriate dominants appear just prior to the desired tonics (Exs. 32–33).

Ex. 32   Modulations to VI and V by the cycle of fifths

The versatility of the cycle of fifths explains why it was one of Bach's favorite modulating devices; the momentum it generates served him in countless ways. In Ex. 10, it leads the modulation down one step each time. In Ex. 33, it creates a strong traveling motion, passing quickly through five successive keys.

Ex. 33   Bach: Fugue No. 2, from *The Well-Tempered Clavier*, Book I

Harmonic outline:

When the fifth appears in a rising direction (as a rising fourth), it produces an equivalent energy. The second chord of the pattern becomes a V of the next key (Ex. 34). Bach employed such a modulating sequence in a striking contrapuntal passage (Ex. 35).*

Ex. 34   Modulation with rising fourths, repeated a tone higher

* For a simpler version of this sequence, see Ex. 12, page 107.

Ex. 35   Bach: Fugue No. 2, from *The Well-Tempered Clavier*, Book I

The modulating sequences in Exs. 30–35 do not by any means represent all possible varieties; countless others are to be found in the music of various periods. Sequences were used so often in late Romantic music that most contemporary composers have avoided them. Despite the general disfavor into which they have fallen, examples are nonetheless to be found in contemporary music. For a sequence in Schönberg, see page 392; for one in Hindemith, see page 415.

Summary

1. A harmonic sequence is a chord pattern repeated on a higher or lower level.

2. Sequences can be exact, varied, or free.

3. The pattern of a sequence can vary in length from two chords in half a bar to an entire phrase of four bars.

4. The pattern is usually followed by from one to three sequences. If three or more, the third and subsequent sequences are generally varied.

5. The functions of a sequence are:
   a. To create directional or traveling motion.
   b. To create a growing tension.
   c. To develop a short figure into an extended phrase.

6. Sequences usually repeat:
   a. One tone lower.
   b. A third lower.
   c. One tone higher.
   d. A third higher.

7. The most common sequences are those in the cycle of fifths, utilizing:
   a. Triads.
   b. Triads alternating with sixth chords.
   c. Dominant seventh chords (the cycle of secondary dominants).

8. Other sequence patterns include root movements of falling thirds, falling fourths, rising fourths, and other intervals.

9. Modulating sequences create strong traveling motion. Entry into each successive key is generally made by a V or other dominant-function chord.

10. The cycle of fifths serves as a modulating sequence, when:
    a. Accidentals pertaining to a new key or keys are added, and
    b. The chords immediately preceding the new tonics are V's or other dominant-function chords.

11. Another common pattern in the modulating sequence is the rising fourth, repeated a tone higher each time.

The
Double
Period

Writing an extended composition involves a command of musical form. So long as a melody comprises but two or three phrases, intuition may guide the writer to a happy solution (after all, none of the makers of folk songs ever went to a conservatory). But when the dimensions broaden to include four or more phrases—especially of elaborate or sophisticated material—a need arises for some sort of plan. Without it, diffuseness often sets in, detracting from the unity of the composition.

The Four-Phrase Group

A four-phrase group, as the name implies, consists of a melody in four sections, all of which can derive from a single motive (a-a'-a''-a'''), but with no two exactly alike.* Cadential suspense governs the phrase endings, the perfect cadence being reserved for last.

* For a-a-b-b, see two-part form, page 150; for a-a-b-a, see three-part form, pages 175–177; and for a-a'-b-c, see page 128. Another possible four-phrase pattern, a-b-c-d, is extremely rare, due to the great difficulty of achieving unity among four contrasting phrases.

122

Ex. 36   Lane: If This Isn't Love, from *Finian's Rainbow*

"If This Isn't Love," by E. Y. Harburg and Burton Lane. Copyright © 1946 by The Players Music Corporation. Used by permission of DeSylva, Brown & Henderson, Inc., New York, N.Y.

In this delectable tune, the phrases start on different notes and go their separate ways, but the same motive appears in all four, bringing unity to the song. Unity is further underscored by the over-all melodic curve, a rising wave, with climax at (*a‴*). Note also that in the first three phrases, the climax arrives at the end of the phrase; in the last, it appears at the *beginning*, sharpening the rhythmic drive.

A similar pattern appears in a work of quite different character.

Ex. 37   Beethoven: String Quartet, Op. 59, No. 1

Here, too, only small differences exist among the four phrases; again they are all cut from the same cloth. The rising wave carries the line in one long sweep from beginning to end.

The four-phrase group occurs quite rarely in compositions of the Classical and Romantic periods, and very rarely in music of popular character. At an early date, composers discovered a simpler way of achieving unity in a melody of four phrases—a form called the *double period*.

The Double Period

In the double period, symmetry is the key word. Four phrases divide into balanced periods of two phrases each, the first *period* ending in a half and the second in a perfect cadence. The contrast of suspense and resolution, already observed in a simple period, occurs on a larger scale in the double period.

Ex. 38   The double period

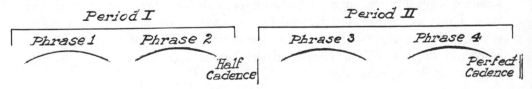

As with its simpler counterpart, the double period exists in two forms: parallel and contrasting.

In the *parallel double period* (by far the more common of the two) both periods begin alike. The second *phrase* of each, however, may either (1) parallel the first or (2) contrast with it.

1. The first type comprises two parallel periods, the second half of each period running parallel to the first (Ex. 39). An old Scotch song (Ex. 40) furnishes an example.

Ex. 39   Parallel double period, first type

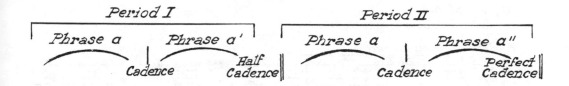

Ex. 40   Scotch song: Flow Gently, Sweet Afton

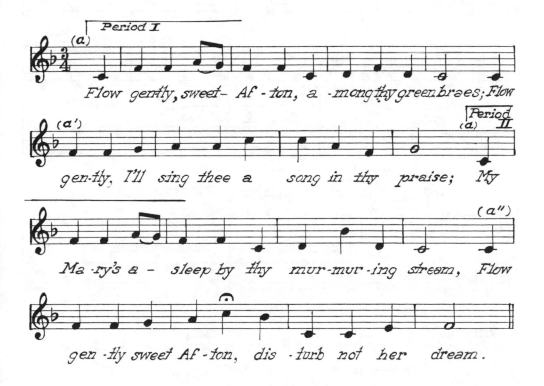

2. The second type of parallel double period employs contrast rather than similarity: each half of the double period forms a contrasting period in itself (Ex. 41).

Ex. 41   Parallel double period, second type

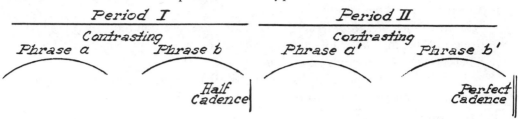

The *b* phrase contrasts with the *a* phrase in each period. The two periods, however, remain parallel, the first ending in a half, the second in a perfect cadence (In Ex. 42, the first period has an unusual ending—an *imperfect* cadence.)

Ex. 42   Beethoven: Sonata, Op. 26.

In Ex. 43, the *b* phrase of Period I is inverted when it reappears (*b'*) in Period II.

Ex. 43   Haydn: Symphony No. 104 (*London*)

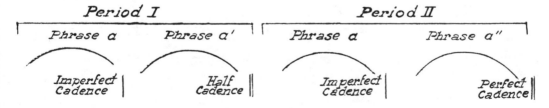

Cadences in the Double Period

As we have seen, the first half of a double period ends in a half cadence, the second in a perfect one. This changes the order of cadences *within each period*. In the first period—a dependent one—the most familiar pattern is: imperfect, then half cadence (Exs. 43–45). The last period closes with the usual perfect cadence.

Ex. 44   Cadences in the double period

Period I		Period II	
Phrase a	Phrase a'	Phrase a	Phrase a"
Imperfect Cadence	Half Cadence	Imperfect Cadence	Perfect Cadence

The Contrasting Double Period

While the parallel double period is by far the most common, occasionally another type appears—the *contrasting double period*. In this type (Ex. 45), the second period, instead of duplicating the first, contains a new melodic idea (*b*). Because of the difficulty of achieving unity in such a form, contrasting double periods are quite rare. "Daisy Bell" illustrates the none-too-logical pattern a–a′–b–c. Despite the disadvantage, however, the old song has survived many a year.

Ex. 45   Dacre: Daisy Bell

Free-Form Patterns

Besides the contrasting double period, even more irregular forms have often appeared in short songs and instrumental pieces. "God Rest Ye Merry, Gentlemen," one of the most popular old English carols, has five phrases, in the pattern a-a-b-c-c′. A Bach chorale (page 198) contains four different phrases, a-b-c-d, and another, *Vater Unser in Himmelreich*, has a splendid melody in six different phrases. Many medieval and Renaissance compositions (see pages 442 and 444, Volume I), folk songs, and short contemporary works (such as those in Bartok's *Mikrokosmos*) reveal free-form designs. In these asymmetrical compositions, the composer's imagination, sense of curve, rhythm, and balance have led to superb melodic results.

Summary

1. In a four-phrase group, all phrases are similar, but no two are exactly alike; the principle of cadential suspense is observed.

2. The double period is the most symmetrical of small forms, containing two periods, each, in turn, containing two phrases. The first period ends in a half cadence, the second in a perfect cadence.

3. In the parallel double period, both periods begin alike. There are two types of parallel double period:
   a. In one (a–a'; a–a''), each *half* of the double period is itself a parallel period.
   b. In the other (a–b; a–b'), each *half* of the double period is itself a contrasting period.

4. In the contrasting double period, the two periods begin differently (a–a'; b–c or some other pattern).

5. Free-form melodies contain irregular phrase patterns, with asymmetrical phrase repetitions (such as a-a-b-c-c') or none.

VI

Harmonization
of Modulating
Melodies

Implied Modulation

Modulation in a melody is generally signalled by accidentals that mark the modulating tone or tones leading to the new key. Sometimes, however, a melody changes key without the use of modulating tones.

Ex. 1   Bach: *Ein' feste Burg ist unser Gott*

In Ex. 1 (*a*), the note B can be harmonized by a diatonic IV, leading either to V or I of the home key.

Ex. 2   Theoretical harmonizations

But such settings lack energy. Bach, who harmonized the famous Lutheran chorale more than once, always accompanied the B by a modulating chord, V of A major (Ex. 3, *a*), followed by the tonic of that key. Since the phrase is rather static melodically (simply moving back and forth between D and A), the harmonic movement added by the modulation is doubly welcome.

Ex. 3   Bach: *Ein' feste Burg ist unser Gott*

A similar modulation to the dominant occurs in *Au clair de la lune*. Its middle section, like the opening phrase of *Ein' feste Burg*, contains no accidentals yet clearly implies a change of key. (To see how important the modulation is, try playing Ex. 4 *without* the C sharp at *a*.)

Ex. 4   French folk song: *Au clair de la lune*

Sometimes, especially in two-part writing, a modulation occurs without change of accidental in any voice. In Ex. 5, which starts in G major, the cadence in D (*a*) leaves no doubt that a modulation has occurred, even though no telltale accidental has intervened.

Ex. 5   Handel: Rigaudon

Modulations can be made from a major key to all closely related keys without accidentals in the melody, provided the approach to the new tonic comes *stepwise from above*. (The mediant key III forms an exception, however; its second step—a modulating tone—does require an accidental before a modulation can take place.) Ex. 6 shows the approach to the tonic of all closely related keys .

Ex. 6   Approach from above to tonic of closely related keys

When a melody modulates without chromatic change, the best place to identify the new key is at the cadence (often the *second* cadence of a piece). The new key generally appears at this point, and must be established by appropriate harmonies.

If the general flow of a phrase seems to imply modulation, try experimenting with the harmonization of its last few notes. Does the last note suggest the tonic of a related key, or perhaps another tone of its I chord? Trial and error will usually reveal the chords leading up to the new tonic.

Let us examine, for instance, the opening of an old English song.

Ex. 7   Thomas Ford: There Is a Ladie Sweet and Kind (1607)

The first phrase ends, obviously, with a perfect cadence in the tonic key.

Ex. 8   There Is a Ladie, trial harmonization of first cadence

The second phrase begins and ends on A; its first five notes, in fact, outline the A minor triad. Assuming a modulation to II, the last five notes suggest an effective cadence in that key.

Ex. 9   There Is a Ladie, trial harmonization of second cadence

Here are the composer's original harmonies. (Note the *tierce de Picardie* in the last bar, Ex. 10.)

Ex. 10   There Is a Ladie, original harmonization

Was nev-er face so pleased my   mind.

What of the modulation in a French Renaissance melody, the *Pavane d'Angleterre?*

Ex. 11   Gervaise: *Pavane d'Angleterre*

While there are no accidentals, the second phrase, starting in F major, leads stepwise downward to a note other than the tonic. It has all the earmarks of a modulation to the relative minor: the last five notes suggest a cadence in D minor (Ex. 12).

Ex. 12   *Pavane*, trial harmonization of second cadence

It suits this passage well, and resembles the sixteenth-century harmonization in five voices by Claude Gervaise.

Ex. 13   Gervaise: *Pavane*, original harmonization

No formula exists to guarantee accurate identification of modulations in melodies lacking accidentals, and for a very simple reason—every melody can be harmonized in several different ways. But perhaps some guidelines have been provided to outline an effective approach.

The Roles of Chromatic Alteration in Harmonization

At first glance it might appear that the presence of chromatic alterations in a modulating melody makes the task of harmonization easier. Don't the accidentals clearly indicate the modulating tones?

Sometimes they do, and sometimes not. As noted in some detail, four different types of chromatic tones can appear in a melody:

1. Chromatic embellishing tones.
2. Raised or lowered scale degrees in minor.
3. Part of secondary dominant chords.
4. Modulating tones.

How do we distinguish accidentals that produce modulations from others? By studying their functions. An accidental can be judged according to its role in the phrase—not only by the modified note but also by the preceding and following notes, as well as the accompanying harmonies, if any. What, for example, is the function of the D sharp in Ex. 14 (*a*)?

Ex. 14   Chopin: Mazurka, Op. 68, No. 2

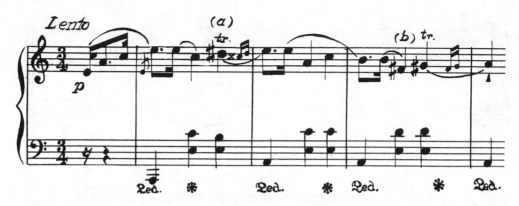

D sharp cannot be a modulating tone; were it so, it would lead to E minor. But the phrase remains clearly in A minor; D sharp is a chromatic embellishing tone. As for the F and G sharps at (b), they are obviously part of the rising melodic minor scale.

Do the accidentals in Ex. 15 lead to modulation?

Ex. 15   Chopin: Mazurka, Op. 68, No. 1

The F sharp in the left hand at (a) presents a less obvious situation. At first glance, it seems to be a modulating tone—part of V_5^6 of G major. But the following chord (b)—V_2^4 of C—points to something different. Leading to V of C, the chord at (*a*) proves to be no modulating chord, but a secondary dominant—V of V—of the home key. The G sharp at (*c*) is a chromatic passing tone.

And what of the chromatic tones in Ex. 16?

Ex. 16   Bach: Fugue No. 16, from *The Well-Tempered Clavier*, Book I

Gm: Dm: V   I⁶   II⁶II V⁶ I

The F sharp at (*a*) is clearly the leading tone of G minor. Examined without relation to the harmony, the C sharp at (*b*) might be interpreted as a chromatic neighboring tone. Observation of the subsequent course of the phrase, however, reveals its function as a modulating tone, 7 of D minor, to which key the music now turns.

By analysis along these lines, the various roles of chromatically altered tones can be identified and an appropriate harmonization discovered.

Successive Modulations—The Modulatory Circle

The melodies studied until now have contained at most one modulation. Many short compositions, however, include more than one—sometimes as many as three or four successive modulations. Before harmonizing melodies of this sort, we must understand the order in which keys generally appear in traditional music: the *modulatory circle*.

When a composition contains several modulations, its first part follows the course already outlined for a single change of key: (1) establishment of the home key; (2) modulation to the second key; and (3) cadence in that key.

It takes a certain amount of time and harmonic energy to establish the original key—the foundation of the entire composition—and then to break away from this key to set up a second one (usually V in major, III in minor). Once the second key is confirmed (usually by a perfect cadence), matters can proceed more swiftly. The third and further keys, if any, can be entered and left more casually. Sometimes the music passes through these keys without a cadence, or with a light, imperfect one. Their role is not so much to contrast with the original key as to keep the harmony in motion, traveling from chord to chord and key to key until the time for the return. The home key is then re-established, as a solid conclusion to the piece.

Ex. 17   The modulatory circle

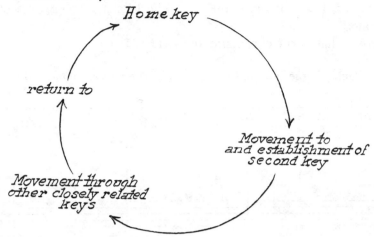

The modulatory circle evolved in music of a certain sophistication. Folk music knows none of it; neither do those traditional songs that contain only one change of key.* Developed in the late seventeenth century, the modulatory circle provides the structural basis for many short compositions, including Bach and Handel suites, Mozart and Beethoven minuets, Schubert, Brahms, and Strauss waltzes, as well as songs of Kern, Gershwin, Porter, and other popular composers.

Until about 1775, modulations moved, for the most part, through closely related keys only.

Let us study the role of the modulatory circle in harmonizing a short Baroque melody for the piano.

Ex. 18   Handel: Gigue, from Suite No. 11

* For example, "Deck the Halls," "Sweet Betsy from Pike," and *Die Lorelei*. The presence of even one modulation shows these songs to be of semi-professional, popular origin rather than true folk songs, which rarely modulate.

No problem exists in harmonizing the first bar, which outlines the home key, D minor. Bar 2 could easily continue in D, except that by looking ahead to (*b*) we note that bar 3 outlines the second key, F major. It would be better to modulate into the new key at (*a*) through its I and V.

Ex. 19   Gigue, sketch 1

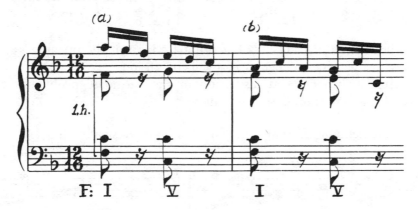

The remainder of the first phrase establishes F major by a perfect cadence (Ex. 18, *c*).

Action begins after the double bar. B natural (*d*) signals a fast move into C major. At (*e*) the I and V of A minor are clearly outlined: the two preceding beats must be used to lead into that key.

Ex. 20   Gigue, sketch 2

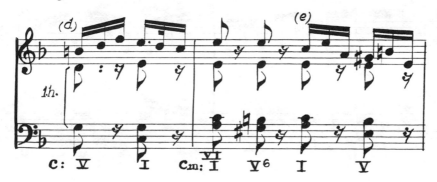

The melodic line in the bar at (*f*), Ex. 18—especially the B natural at (*g*)—shows the phrase remaining in A minor. At (*h*), the V and I chords of G minor produce a fast modulation to that key; and F natural at (*i*) is followed by V and I of F. Since the melody in bar (*i*) is a sequence of (*h*), the harmony logically follows the sequential movement.

Ex. 21   Gigue, sketch 3

The last two bars (*j*, Ex. 18) bring a return of the opening key and melody, with a perfect cadence as a logical conclusion.

After such a detailed discussion of the harmonic problems, let us compare Handel's setting of his own Gigue.

Ex. 22   Handel: Gigue, from Suite No. 11, original version

It becomes quickly apparent that Handel presents no harmonic surprises; the chords he uses are—give or take an inversion or two—the same as those any musician might infer from the given melody.

The texture, however, differs considerably from that of our trial harmonization (Exs. 19–21). In place of the conventional four-part block chords (which might well have struck Handel as too cumbersome for the tripping dance melody) he harmonized more sparingly, in two and three voices. Three-voice chords alternate with broken chords, whose sixteenth-note patterns frequently mirror those of the melody itself (Ex. 22, bar 2, left hand). The *imitation* (echoing effect) adds to the unity and interest of the setting.

Among other subtle touches that add to the interest and fluidity of the harmonization, we find:

1. The bridging of the cadence (Ex. 22, c): while the right hand rests for a moment, the left hand continues the flowing dance rhythm. The same technique is also used at (g) at the cadence in A minor.

2. The melodic curve of the bass: it descends gradually in the first four bars (high D to low F). During the next five bars it forms a wave. In the last two bars, however, there is a headlong descent of two octaves from the highest to the lowest bass tone. Coupled with the downward sweep of the melody, this plunging movement in the bass adds a decisive thrust to the end of the piece.

Knowledge of the modulatory circle is helpful not only in harmonizing melodies but also in writing compositions of more ambitious scope than have been attempted so far. The circle, as we shall see, provides the harmonic foundation for many pieces in two- and three-part form. Following its outline, modulatory action moves not in a straight line away from the home key but *around* and eventually back to it. Shifting from one key to another, it develops an extended traveling motion. Harmonic progression through the modulatory circle is the basis of all developed musical structure.

Summary

1. Some melodies modulate without change of accidental.

2. When the approach to the new tonic is stepwise from above, such modulations can lead from a major key to its V, VI, II, or IV.

3. In modulations without chromatic change in the melody, the best place to identify a new key is at the cadence, where the new tonic generally asserts itself most clearly.

4. Accidentals in a melody may be of four kinds:
   a. Chromatic embellishing tones.
   b. Raised or lowered scale degrees in minor.
   c. Part of secondary dominant chords.
   d. Modulating tones.

5. The role of an accidental in a melody is revealed by analysis of its function, the tones that precede and follow it, and the accompanying harmonies.

6. The modulatory circle outlines the order of modulations in pieces containing more than one change of key. It generally involves the following steps:
   a. Establishment of the home key.
   b. Modulation to and cadence in the second key (usually V in major, III in minor).
   c. Faster, lighter modulations to third and other keys, if any.
   d. Return to and cadence in the home key.

7. Knowledge of the modulatory circle is valuable both in harmonizing melodies that pass through several keys and in writing compositions in more highly developed form.

Two-Part
Form

All the forms studied until now share a common trait: a perfect cadence only at the end. No matter how many phrases a composition may have, if it possesses but one perfect cadence we call it a *sentence* or *one-part form*. One-part forms include the phrase, period, phrase group, and double period.

Governed by the principle of cadential suspense (all cadences incomplete except the last), the sentence is necessarily restricted in length. Such suspense can be maintained for only a limited period: one-part form occurs mainly in children's melodies, folk songs, and short dance tunes.

Early in the history of the dance and the popular song, *two-part* or *binary form* came into being. As the name suggests, it comprises two complete sentences, each with a perfect cadence and full rhythmic stop. The broader structure provides more time for a musical idea to unfold: *two* chains of suspense, followed by *two* resolutions. Originally, two-part form was highly symmetrical, the second part equal in length and balancing the first (an expansion of the symmetry found in the period).

146

Ex. 23   Two-part form

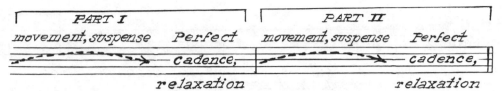

Symmetrical two-part forms have a long history. From "Green-sleeves," a sixteenth-century carol, to "Old Joe Clarke," an American square-dance tune, we find two evenly balanced divisions. Not all two-part forms, however, are symmetrical, as we shall see. Where the parts do not balance, the second is generally longer than the first.

By a convention of the form, the beginning of Part I never recurs literally in Part II. The opening phrase may reappear in another key, in sequence, inversion, or other variation, but never exactly in its original form.*

Types of Two-Part Forms

In the smallest two-part form, each part consists of one phrase. Both phrases are independent, coming to a complete stop (in the melody at least).

Ex. 24   America

Note that both phrases in Ex. 24 have perfect cadences on G. Part II begins differently than Part I, and lasts slightly longer (8 bars instead of 6). Hence, asymmetrical melody.

In a slightly expanded version of the same form, one phrase is repeated—in "Go Down Moses," the first.

---

* The exact return of the opening melody in the latter half of a piece is characteristic of *three*-part form (see pages 174–187).

Ex. 25   Negro spiritual: Go Down Moses

A far more common type of two-part form contains a repeated phrase or a period (often eight bars) in *each* half.

Ex. 26   Bob Farrell (?): Old Zip Coon (1834)

Short, symmetrical two-part form is found in many traditional songs and dance tunes: "Pop Goes the Weasel," "The Irish Washerwoman," "Yankee Doodle," and, in another idiom, the Minuet from Mozart's *Don Giovanni*.*

Examining the patterns of these melodies, we find two broad types: (1) A–A′, in which both parts grow from a single motive; and (2) A–B, in which Part II starts with a new motive.

Parallel Two-Part Form

The first type (A–A′) is most important for further development of two-part form, because it produces a unified structure, despite the varied beginnings of the two parts. The second half of "America" (Ex. 24) starts differently from the first, but its motive

$$| \; \downarrow \; \downarrow \downarrow \; | \; \downarrow. \; \downarrow \downarrow \; |$$

remains the same; a different sound, yet the identical material, making for the unity of the tune.

Contrasting Two-Part Form

In the second type of two-part form (A–B), Part II starts with a fresh idea. The verse-and-chorus pattern, characteristic of many traditional songs and dance tunes, shows the chorus bearing the most important melody. "Old Dan Tucker" and "The Blue Tail Fly" are examples.

* See page 38; for another example of small two-part form, see page 81.

Ex. 27   Minstrel song: The Blue Tail Fly

The A–B pattern is also found in "Old Zip Coon" (Ex. 26), "Pop Goes the Weasel," "Yankee Doodle," and "Greensleeves."

Ex. 28   English Carol: Greensleeves

Although the two sections of a two-part form begin differently, they often end similarly, or even identically. In Examples 25, 26, and 28, the last two bars of Part I are duplicated at the end of Part II. Such parallel endings emphasize the unity of the two parts.

A more sophisticated example of two-part form occurs in a modern theater song (Ex. 29).

Ex. 29   Lane: How Are Things in Glocca Morra? from *Finian's Rainbow*

leap-ing there? —— Does it still run down to Don-ny Cove,? —— Through

Kil-ly-begs, —— Kil-ker-ry and Kil-dare? —— How are things in Gloc-ca

Mor-ra? —— Is that wil-low tree still weep-ing there? ——

—— Does that lad-die with the twink-lin' eye—Come whist-lin' by —— And

does he walk a-way,—Sad and dream-y there not to see me there?—

Part II

—— So I ask each weep-ing wil-low, And each brook a-long the

way, And each lad that comes a-whistlin' "Too-ra-lay," ——

—— How are things in Gloc-ca Morra this fine day? ——

"*How Are Things in Glocca Morra*," by E. Y. Harburg and Burton Lane. Copyright © 1946 by The Players Music Corporation. Used by permission of DeSylva, Brown & Henderson, Inc., New York, N.Y.

In Ex. 29, Part I starts with a standard eight-bar phrase (*a*), repeated at (*b*). Upon repetition, however, the phrase expands at (*c*) and (*d*) to ten bars, ending in a perfect cadence (*e*). Part II, a contrasting B phrase, comprises eight bars, extended at (*f*) to twelve. Thus, in addition to its lyrical melody, "Glocca Morra" is distinguished by an asymmetry unusual in a theater song:

A: 8 + 10 = 18 bars
B: 8 + 4 = 12 bars

Cadences in Two-Part Form

Parts I and II end with perfect cadences, as we have seen. In simpler examples of two-part form, both cadences are in the home key (Exs. 24–26). In more developed music, such as eighteenth- and nineteenth-century suites and idealized dance forms, modulation becomes an important factor. Part I generally ends in the dominant or relative major;* Part II follows the modulatory circle, ending in the home key.

Fully Developed Two-Part Form

A richer development of two-part form occurs in many Schubert dances. Longer than most compositions discussed so far, they move more boldly through the modulatory circle (Ex. 30).

Ex. 30   Schubert: German Dance, Op. 33, No. 1

* In Ex. 30, Part I ends in VI.

Starting with a centering motion in A major, Part I moves into the relative minor, F sharp, at (a), coming to a full stop in that key (b).* Part II immediately begins a traveling motion, passing through the mediant, C sharp minor (c), the major supertonic, B major (d), and the relative minor once more (e). Returning to the home key (f), it ends in a perfect cadence.

Part I forms a parallel period of eight bars; Part II spins a group of phrases out to double that length. The quickly shifting modulations add vitality and interest to the long harmonic line.

The expansion of Part II through the modulatory circle is characteristic of a fully developed two-part form, as is the unity achieved by the continuous unfolding of a single motive. This expansion of Part II reaches its highest development in the Bach suites.

* The imperfect cadence at (b) is exceptional at the end of Part I. The complete rhythmic break, however, is sufficient punctuation to outline the form.

Ex. 31   Bach: Gavotte, from French Suite No. 5

The two-bar motive of Ex. 31 (*a*) appears twice in the first phrase, which ends in an imperfect cadence at (*b*). Without a rhythmic break, the second phrase continues at (*c*), turning to the dominant and ending Part I with a perfect cadence in that key (*d*). As in many two-part forms, each part ends with a double bar and repeat marks.

Part II is twice as long as Part I—a common characteristic of eighteenth-century dance forms. Passing through the modulatory circle, it develops through two more closely related keys. At (*e*), the motive appears, inverted, in the right hand, simultaneously with a fragment of the original form in the left.* At (f) it recurs with varied intervals, moving into E minor. The left hand takes over at (g) with an extended form of the motive, leading to a cadence in E minor at (h)—a cadence bridged by the continuous left-hand rhythm. Another inversion appears in the right hand again at (i), the phrase leading through C major, then back to the key of G. The motive appears for the last time at (j) in the home key, but on different notes and over different harmonies than at the opening of the Gavotte.† An extension leads to the final cadence. With its constant presentation of the motive in new guises and its continuous harmonic traveling, Part II is a development section in miniature.

The analysis of Bach's Gavotte serves a larger purpose than a mere listing of the details of a two-part form. It reveals how a motive making a voyage through the modulatory circle can be repeated over and over and yet hold our interest through constant variation of its melodic and harmonic shapes. Transparent in texture and tight in its organization, the Gavotte reveals the great beauty of structure possible in a two-part form.

Summary

1. Two-part form comprises two sentences, each with a perfect cadence and full rhythmic stop.

2. Small two-part forms are often symmetrically balanced.

3. The smallest two-part form contains only one phrase in each part; but sometimes one part has two phrases.

4. A familiar type of two-part form contains a repeated phrase or period in each half.

5. Parallel two-part form (A–A′) has the same motive in both parts. Part II starts, however, with the original phrase in a melodic variation, another key, or both.

6. In contrasting two-part form (A–B), Part II has a new melody. In popular songs and dances, this appears as a verse and chorus, with the chorus more important melodically.

---

* Or, in other words, the motive is counterpointed *against itself*.
† Were it to appear on exactly the name notes, it would create the feeling of a three-part form—as it does, for example, in Ex. 22, pages 142–143.

7. Both parts of a two-part form often end in similar or identical fashion.

8. In a fully developed two-part form:
   a. One motive is used throughout.
   b. It appears in different keys and variations.
   c. Part II is longer than Part I—sometimes twice as long.
   d. Part II often has the character of a development, with constant motive variation and traveling harmonic motion.

9. Fully developed two-part form generally follows the modulatory circle.
   a. Part I ends in V (III if in minor).
   b. Part II modulates through several or all keys of the circle, ending in the home key.

VII

The
Diminished Seventh
Chord

The history of the diminished seventh chord (VII^{d7}) goes back at least to the eighteenth century. One of its most common roles was as a dramatic chord in opera (Ex. 1, *a*).

Ex. 1   Mozart: Recitative, from *Don Giovanni*, Act II

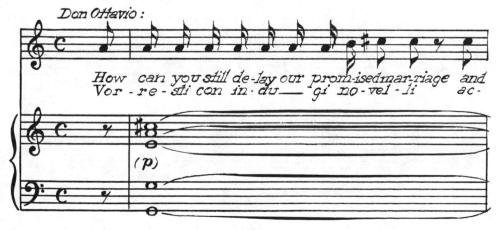

The dramatic effect of the VII^{d7} was later applied to instrumental music.

Ex. 2   Beethoven: Sonata, Op. 109

In Ex. 2, the progression of thinly scored triads and dominant sevenths rising in slow crescendo is capped by a surprise—the nine-voice diminished seventh chord at (*a*). The abrupt changes of harmonic intensity, texture, tempo, and key make this a striking moment.

Structure of the Diminished Seventh

The VII^{d7}, which occurs as a diatonic chord in harmonic minor, is the sole harmonic structure whose intervals are all of the same size*—minor thirds. It generates more tension than any chord studied thus far, for two reasons: not only are three of its tones (root, fifth, and seventh) active ones, but two of its intervals are diminished fifths. These unstable tones and intervals produce a highly active chord.

Ex. 3   Characteristics of diminished seventh chord

Preparation and Resolution

Preparation and resolution of the VII^{d7} are similar to those of other seventh chords. The two least stable intervals, the diminished fifth and seventh, can be prepared as in Ex. 4:

(*a*) Most smoothly, by anticipation in the preceding chord.
(*b*) Quite smoothly, by stepwise movement from tones of the preceding chord.
(*c*) Least smoothly, by leap.

The most common resolution of the diminished fifth and seventh is downward by step to tones of the tonic triad.

---

* Except for the diminished and augmented triads—the latter rarely used in traditional music.

Ex. 4   Preparation and resolution of the VII^{d7} chord

Functions of the VII^{d7}

The diminished seventh chord can be used in a variety of ways:

1. As a dominant-function chord—a darker, more intense form of VII^7.
2. As a secondary dominant, to strengthen movement to V and other degrees.
3. As a chromatic passing chord between triads on adjacent degrees.
4. As a surprise chord in the deceptive cadence and in dramatic situations in opera, oratorio, and instrumental music.
5. As a modulating chord.
6. As a means of creating ambiguous tonality.

The Dominant-Function VII^{d7}

In minor, the VII^{d7} acts as a somber dominant-function chord, often leading to an imperfect cadence on I. Note its use (Ex. 5, *a*) as an accented embellishment of the tonic triad, to emphasize the word "gloomy." But since the bass movement 7—1 lacks the decisiveness of a falling fifth, the progression VII^{d7}—I usually occurs during the course of a composition rather than at the end.

Ex. 5   Gluck: *Ah! dans ce bois*, from *Orfeo*, Act I

Influenced by the dramatic style of Gluck, Beethoven frequently employed the VII^{d7} as a dark-hued dominant. The diminished seventh appears in Ex. 6 (*c*) both as a broken and as a block chord; at (*b*) with one of its voices (the fifth) omitted; and at (*a*) in second inversion.

Ex. 6   Beethoven: Sonata, Op. 10, No. 1

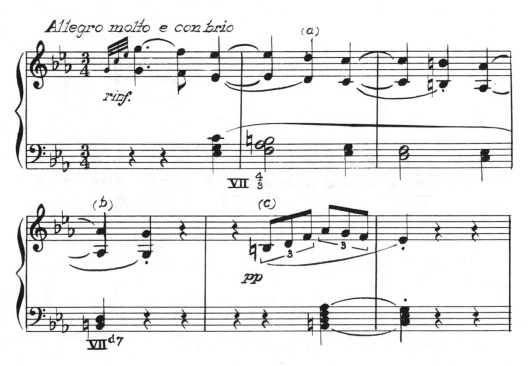

VII^{d7} as a Secondary Dominant

In another role, the diminished seventh acts as a secondary dominant chord, creating a strong drive to the dominant. In Ex. 7 (*a*), VII^{d7} of V leads powerfully to V.*

Ex. 7   Mozart: Fantasy in C minor, K. 475

I$^6_4$ can be interposed between the VII^{d7} of V and V, expanding the cadence.

Ex. 8   Mozart: *The Magic Flute*, Act I

Like V, the VII^{d7} also serves as a secondary dominant of II, III, IV, and VI. Through its greater instability, it intensifies the drive to each of those degrees.

---

* Beethoven created a dramatic effect by *starting* his Sonata, Op. 111, with the progression VII^{d7} of V—V (see Ex. 42, page 334, Volume I).

Ex. 9   VII^{d7} as secondary dominant

In the opening of Bach's B Minor Mass (Ex. 10), we find a most expressive deceptive resolution of the VII^{d7}; instead of leading to the tonic, it resolves (*a*) to VII^{d7} of IV.

Ex. 10   Bach: *Kyrie*, from the Mass in B minor

The Passing-Chord VII^{d7}

The VII^{d7} of V (Ex. 11, *a*) frequently appears as a chromatic passing chord between IV and V, sharpening the movement to the half cadence.

Ex. 11   Beethoven: Sonata, Op. 2, No. 1

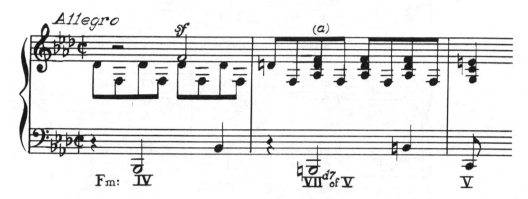

The VII^{d7} also acts as a passing chord between I and II (Ex. 12, *a*). Similarly, it occurs between V and VI (Ex. 13, *a*).*

Ex. 12   Mozart: Quintet for Clarinet and Strings, K. 622

Ex. 13   Mozart: Sonata, K. 333

* For other passing-chord VII^{d7}s, see Ex. 9, page 165.

VII^{d7} as a Surprise Chord

In another of its functions, the diminished seventh appears as a "surprise" chord in the deceptive cadence, in place of the expected tonic (Ex. 14, *a*).

Ex. 14   Bach: Toccata and Fugue No. 3, for Clavier

It appears with even greater force at dramatic moments in opera and oratorio, especially after a series of triads. A famous example is the scene in Gluck's *Orfeo* in which the hero turns around to look at his wife, violating the commandment and causing her death (Ex. 15, *a*).*

Ex. 15   Gluck: *Orfeo*, Act II

* For similar dramatic uses, see pages 160, 243–244, and 298.

In the late nineteenth century the VII^{d7} served so often for operatic surprises that it eventually became melodramatic. It is used today mainly in parodies of old-fashioned style.

VII^{d7} as a Modulating Chord

In one of its most important roles, the diminished seventh acts as a modulating chord, leading directly into a new key in much the same manner as a V or V^7. The third movement of the Schumann Piano Concerto (Ex. 16) starts in A major, enters C sharp minor through that key's VII$\frac{4}{3}$ (*a*), and B minor through its VII^{d7} (*b*).

Ex. 16   Schumann: Piano Concerto, Op. 54 third movement (condensed)

When serving as a modulating chord, the VII^{d7} sometimes resolves to V of the new key before proceeding to the new tonic. Starting in E flat, the phrase in Ex. 17 uses the VII$^6_5$ of C minor (*a*) to make a feint in the direction of that key (which, however, never arrives). At (*b*) the VII$\frac{4}{2}$ serves to enter D major, followed at (*c*) by V, at (*d*) by VII$\frac{4}{3}$, and, finally, at (*e*) by I^6 of D. The V clarifies and reinforces the modulatory action of the VII^{d7}.*

* See also Ex. 30 (*c*) and (*d*), pages 152–153.

Ex. 17   Beethoven: Sonata, Op. 13 (*Pathétique*)

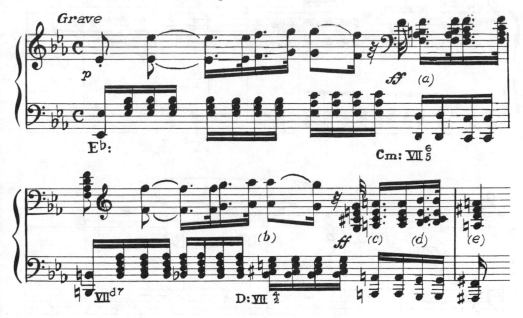

The new key can also be entered by the diminished seventh acting as a secondary-dominant VII^{d7} of V (Ex. 18, *a*). Followed by the new V (*b*), the progression has a strong modulating drive.

Ex. 18   Beethoven: Symphony No. 5, Op. 67

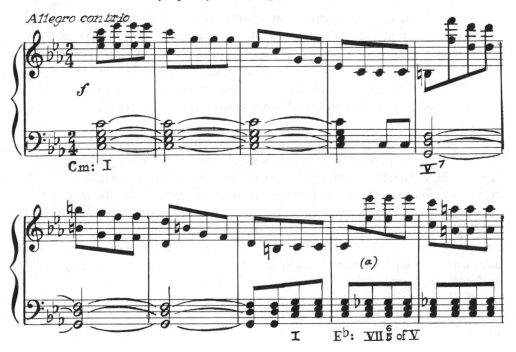

VII^{d7} and Ambiguous Tonality

In the last and perhaps most distinctive of its roles, the diminished seventh serves to produce a vague or ambiguous tonality. Tonality is the very foundation of traditional music; the composer's first concern in writing a piece has almost always been to establish a key. To obscure or negate the tonality was, therefore, a *coup de théatre*—a dramatic stroke. As employed by Bach, Beethoven, Wagner, and other masters, it often created a powerful contrast.

One of the most effective ways of obscuring the tonality is to introduce three different diminished sevenths in a row. The multiple meanings of these chords temporarily destroy the sense of a key center and of a definite harmonic direction. Passages containing such harmonic ambiguity often appear in the development section of a sonata or symphony, providing a striking antithesis to the clear tonality of earlier and later sections. When the music returns to a clear tonal statement after the obscurity produced by the diminished sevenths (as in Ex. 19, *a*), the effect is one of emerging from darkness into light.*

* For another example of consecutive VII^{d7}'s, see Ex. 20, Volume I, page 401 (last 2 bars).

Ex. 19   Beethoven: Sonata, Op. 2, No. 3

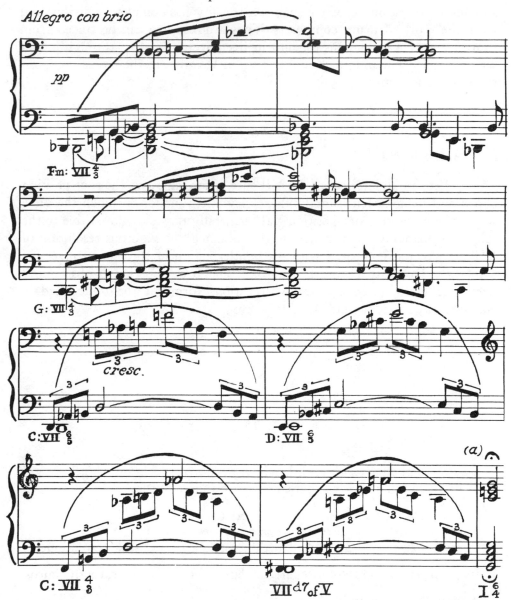

Diminished sevenths also serve to produce a sense of ambiguity, mystery, or darkness in introductory sections to large dramatic compositions —as in the opening of Haydn's *Creation* ("representation of Chaos": "And the earth was without form and void, and darkness was upon the face of the deep"). They produce a similar effect in the slow introductions to sonatas, quartets, and symphonies, setting the stage by contrast, as it were, for a clear, vigorous allegro to follow.* Romantic composers sometimes created broader

* See, for example, Haydn's *Surprise* Symphony and Beethoven's Sonata, Op. 111 (page 334, Volume I).

areas of tonal ambiguity by means of VII^{d7} and other ambivalent harmonies. In contemporary music, as we shall see, tonality has completely disappeared from the work of many composers. Thus a direct line can be traced from short sections of ambiguous tonality in Beethoven (Ex. 19), through longer sections in Chopin and much longer ones in Wagner, to the atonal compositions of Schönberg.*

Inversions of the VII^{d7}

Because all intervals of the VII^{d7} are of the same size, the root-position chord and its inversions sound alike. They also function in much the same way, except that the root-position VII^{d7} generally possesses more drive to the following harmony. Note in Ex. 16, for instance, the vigorous resolution of VII^{d7} (*b*) to I as compared with the gentler action of the second inversion VII$^{4}_{3}$ (*a*). To create a more flowing bass line, a composer will often move from one inversion to another with various forms of the tonic triad in between (see Ex. 6, page 163).

Summary

1. The diminished seventh chord, which occurs as a diatonic chord on VII in harmonic minor, is composed of three minor thirds.

2. It is a highly active, unstable chord because:
   a. Its root, fifth, and seventh are active tones.
   b. It contains two diminished fifths which urgently seek resolution.

3. Its preparation and resolution are similar to those of other seventh chords.

4. The VII^{d7} functions as:
   a. A somber dominant-function chord on VII.
   b. A secondary dominant, sharpening the approach to V and other degrees.
   c. A chromatic passing chord between triads on adjacent degrees.
   d. A substitute for the tonic in the deceptive cadence.
   e. A surprise chord in a dramatic context.
   f. A modulating chord.

* For Chopin, see Ex. 61, page 285; for Wagner, Ex. 63, pages 287–288; and for Schönberg, pages 406–407.

5. The VII^{d7} serves in modulation:
   a. As a dominant-function chord, leading directly into the new key.
   b. As a dominant-function chord, followed by V, and then I, of the new key.
   c. As a secondary dominant, VII^{d7} of V, of the new key, leading to the new V and I.

6. Three different consecutive VII^{d7}'s can produce a passage of tonal ambiguity, which contrasts with passages of clear tonality.

7. Inversions of the VII^{d7} sound exactly alike and serve similar functions. One inversion can progress to another, either directly or through a form of the tonic chord.

Three-Part
Form

With *three-part form* we arrive at one of the most universal of all musical structures. Unlike the novel and the drama, which move onward from start to finish, music tends to be a circular art, departing from and often returning to the beginning. Listeners take pleasure in this return—or *reprise* or *recapitulation,* as it is variously called. Perhaps the evanescent nature of sound patterns accounts for our pleasure in hearing them again after an interruption. At any rate three-part form, with its characteristic recapitulation, appears in a wide range of compositions, from the simplest nursery rhyme to lengthy symphonic movements.

The plan of three-part, or *ternary,* form is:

Part I	*Part II*	*Part III*
Statement	Contrast	Return

The essence of the form lies in the contrast between its middle and outer sections. Whether Part II differs from Parts I and III in melody or in structure is unimportant; it is the sharpness of the contrast that counts.

174

Cadences in Three-Part Form

The different sections of three-part form are commonly set off by strong cadences:

At the end of Part I: perfect cadence (in home or related key).
At the end of Part II: half cadence in home key.
At the end of Part III: perfect cadence in home key.

Part I usually ends in a full rhythmic stop. Part II serves not only as contrast but as a springboard for the return. It ends, therefore, in a half cadence leading back to the original theme and key, often without pause. Almost universally, Part III ends with a perfect cadence in the home key.

Types of Three-Part Forms

The smallest three-part form, found in nursery rhymes and folk songs, has one phrase in each part (A–B–A).

Ex. 20   French song: *Ah, vous dirai-je, maman*

More commonly, Part I consists of a repeated phrase or a period. The A–A–B–A pattern (a description we shall presently have cause to modify), occurs in countless traditional and popular songs, such as "Oh Susannah" and "Old Man River," and in an equal number of eighteenth-, nineteenth-, and twentieth-century sonata and symphony themes, from Haydn's *Surprise* Symphony (Ex. 22) to the *Intermezzo Interrotto* of Bartók's Concerto for Orchestra.*

* For the opening phrase of the Bartók, see *Workbook*, Volume I, page 87.

Ex. 21   Mozart: Sonata, K. 331

In Ex. 21, Part I of the theme ends with a perfect tonic cadence. In Ex. 22 it ends in the dominant.

Ex. 22   Haydn: Symphony No. 94 (*Surprise*), slow movement

Note, in Ex. 22, that each *half* of the three-part form is repeated—Part I by itself, then Parts II and III together. Also that Part III is a varied sequence rather than a literal repetition of Part I.

The A–A–B–A pattern sometimes develops considerable length. The conventional popular song lasts thirty-two bars—if in fast tempo, sixty-four or even longer.*

The Structure of Part II

As already suggested, the formula A–A–B–A is not always an accurate symbol of three-part form. The letter B implies a new melodic idea, which, to be sure, frequently appears. Sometimes, however, the contrast is simply one of tonality—Part II consists of A in a new key. And often, the contrast is one of *structure:* motives of Part I reappear in Part II, organized differently—in new rhythms, harmonies, or textures, or interwoven with contrasting material.

Part II, therefore, can take three forms:

1. A transposition of A (Part I) into another key (A′).
2. A new melody (B).
3. A, or part of it, in a new structure (A′).

Part II as Transposition of Part I

Transposition of Part I provides a simple way of obtaining contrast— a change of key. The new key, a common characteristic of Part II, is occasionally sufficient in itself to provide the basis of a middle section, especially if it also includes a change of mode.

---

* As in Porter's "Begin the Beguine."

Ex. 23   Chopin: Mazurka, Op. 68, No. 2

Since Part II (Ex. 23, *a* to *b*) simply presents A in a different key, let us call it A′ rather than B, and the entire form A–A–A′–A.*

Part II as a New Melody

More familiar is the middle section that contains a new melody.

Ex. 24   Beethoven: Minuet in G

* This analysis does not include the repeats, which in no way alter the structural basis of the composition.

Part II of the Minuet sounds a fresh note: neither in rhythm nor interval does it resemble Part I. Middle sections of this kind, however, are rather infrequent. (Note, incidentally, that, like Ex. 22, Part III begins as a sequence, not a literal repetition of Part I—therefore, A' rather than A.)

Part II as a New Structure

Far more common are those middle sections that at first seem completely new but on closer study reveal their derivation from some fragment of the A section.

Ex. 25   Musette, from *The Notebook of Anna Magdalena Bach*

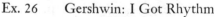

Part II of Ex. 25 sounds new: its key, intervals, and rhythm appear quite distinctive. When examined closely, however, some of its motivic elements prove to be derived from Part I. The new melody at (*c*) is seen as a transposition of the fragment at (*b*); the left hand adds unity by continuing the rhythmic figure of the opening. Even the interesting sixteenth-note rhythm at (*d*) springs not out of the blue but from the figure at (*a*), shifted from the second to the first beat. This is a B section; but its motivic links to A are undeniable.

Sometimes the melody of Part II will alter the intervals but not the rhythms of Part I. (Compare Ex. 26, *a* and *b*.)

Ex. 26   Gershwin: I Got Rhythm

Another and more subtle example can be found in a Brahms melody. The rhythm of the B section (Ex. 27), reproduces that of A, although the notes themselves are quite different.

Ex. 27   Brahms: Violin Concerto, Op. 77, second movement

Part II as a Development Section

In the discussion of two-part form, we have seen that Part II can form a miniature development section, presenting the motives of Part I in new shapes, often asymmetrical and freshly conceived.

In three-part form, Part II can follow a similar design, contrasting with Parts I and III not so much in melody as in its new, more closely woven structure.

Ex. 28   Brahms: Waltz in A flat, Op. 39, No. 15

The melody of Part II (Ex. 28), although derived from the opening,
does not merely duplicate it. Its phrase lengths are tighter—a two-bar

grouping (*c*) repeated twice, instead of the two four-bar groupings of Part I. Its rhythm, also drawn from the opening, becomes more insistent and concentrated: with the pattern (*x*) eliminated, motive (*a*) appears five times in succession. And although the melodic curve in both parts is a rising wave, the highest tessitura and the over-all climax of the entire piece (*d*) occurs in Part II, emphasizing the greater intensity of that section.

Harmonically, Part II is likewise more intense. Whereas the first part consists mostly of calm, flowing triads, the second contains seventh chords, including two secondary dominants that press actively forward. A suspension (*e*) just before the *reprise* adds to the growing tension. Finally, the harmonic rhythm is faster and the root movements stronger than in the opening section. Clearly, for all its modest size, Part II has the feeling of development.

Ex. 29   Beethoven: Menuetto, from Sonata, Op. 2, No. 1

Similar in broad outline to Ex. 28, the Menuetto (Ex. 29) reveals a greater subtlety of techniques, befitting its role as a sonata movement.

Part I opens with two motives (*a* and *b*), forming a short phrase. Repeated a third higher in the relative major (*c*), it is extended to eight bars, closing on a new little fragment (*d*). After the cadence, we hear the fragment once more as a codetta.*

Part II, the development, reveals a more complex structure than that of the Brahms Waltz. Starting once more with phrase (*a*), it utilizes only the first motive, omitting the second (*b*). Dissonant diminished seventh chords, contrasting with the simpler harmonies of Part I, modulate quickly from A flat to B flat minor, creating a traveling motion. The phrase now concentrates on fragment (*d*), repeated three times in succession in a mysterious *pianissimo*. Suddenly at (*e*) an explosive rush of *fortissimo* eighth notes leads swiftly down to the V of the original key (*f*) and into the return of Part I (*g*).

Only fourteen bars long, Part II illustrates some typical techniques of development. It presents fragments of the original material, recombined: bits of the head joined to bits of the tail and stretched out of their first shape to form a new shape. Another characteristic is the fitfulness of the harmonic motion: the phrase rushes forward, stops, and plunges ahead again. Its groupings are irregular, its harmonic rhythms broken and unpredictable. Avoidance of the home key produces a tonal contrast with Parts I and III. A development section usually contains more chromaticism and greater freedom of modulation than the outer sections of a composition. Part II ends on a half cadence, leading to the *reprise* in the home key.

The evolution of a new phrase from previously dispersed fragments typifies the organic process of development. Short as it is, Part II of the Menuetto serves as a prototype of more ambitious development sections in larger forms.

Variation in Part III

Part III, as we have already seen, does not always repeat Part I literally. Minor variations—not great enough to make the first theme unrecognizable—are fairly common in the return. Motive (*a*) appears in Ex. 29 in the left hand instead of the right (*g*). Motive (*b*) disappears, being replaced by a restatement of motive (*a*) in the right hand an octave higher (*h*). Repeated in a series of strongly accented descending sequences, it leads to a sudden return of fragment (*d*). A brief codetta, echoing the end of Part I in *pianissimo*, brings the section to a close. Note that Part III does not modulate as did Part I; it starts and ends in the home key.

* A segment added after the cadence is termed a *coda*—or, if very short, as in the present case, a *codetta*.

Compared with the opening section, Part III is taut and concentrated. Aside from the first three notes (the *head* of the motive), all the rest has been reworked; the original ideas are there, but in a new guise. Such variation—an index of Beethoven's questing mind—provides a distinctive close to the developed three-part form.

Summary

1. Three-part form comprises three divisions: statement, contrast, and return.
   a. Part II contrasts with Parts I and III.
   b. Parts I and III begin alike.

2. The cadences are:
   a. Part I—perfect cadence (in home or related key), with full rhythmic stop.
   b. Part II—half cadence (in home key), often without pause.
   c. Part III—perfect cadence (in home key).

3. The smallest three-part form has one phrase in each part.

4. The small three-part form—far more common—has two phrases or a period in Part I, a phrase each in Parts II and III (A–A–B–A).

5. Small three-part forms vary in length from sixteen to more than sixty-four bars.

6. Part II may be constructed in three different ways:
   a. Transposition of Part I into another key (A').
   b. A new melody (B).
   c. A new structure, based on the initial motive or phrase (A').

7. When Part II contains a new melody, the latter is often related to A by an inner identity of motive fragments, or rhythm.

8. Part II often has the structure of a small development section, in which various motives, phrases, fragments, or rhythms of Part I appear:
   a. In melodic, rhythmic, or harmonic variation.
   b. In different keys.
   c. In different (usually faster) harmonic rhythm.
   d. In shorter or longer phrase lengths.
   e. In asymmetrical construction, if Part I has been symmetrical.
   f. In different textures and levels of harmonic intensity.

9. Part III can be a varied rather than literal repetition of Part I; but the variation does not extend so far as to conceal the return of the original motive.

Chorale Harmonization

Once the analyses have been made and the rules studied, what, after all, determines anyone's choice of chords in harmonizing a melody? The answer can only be: the expressive quality conceived by the writer. Like the poem entitled "Thirteen Ways of Looking at a Blackbird," there are many ways of looking at a melody, depending on one's skill, background, and imagination.

Diversity of Harmonic Styles

The old German chorale melody *Vater unser in Himmelreich* (Ex. 1) was variously harmonized by many composers over a period of some two hundred years.

189

Ex. 1   Chorale melody: *Vater unser in Himmelreich*

A century before Bach, Samuel Scheidt harmonized it this way:

Ex. 2   Scheidt: *Vater unser*

Still writing in the old modal style, Scheidt accompanied the melody by a group of independent lines rather than by a series of block chords. Concerned more with the interplay of voices than with root movements or the need to emphasize a tonality, the composer produced a gentle setting. Its voices flow along without creating a sense of vigorous forward movement; the chords follow each other—they do not *progress* one to the other.

Scheidt was little concerned with the strong establishment of a key. The tonic triad (D minor) has little more prominence than other chords. Where one might expect a perfect cadence—the point (*a*) at which the melody first comes to rest on D—the harmony ignores the expectation: a IV chord appears under the note, and the phrase continues without pause. Although the melody shows D to be the tonic, it is unclear from the accompanying voices whether the scale is an Aeolian mode on A or a Dorian or Aeolian mode on D. In this music, tonality was still slightly vague.*

What a different harmonic world we enter with Bach's setting of the same melody.

Ex. 3   Bach: *Vater unser in Himmelreich*

Abandoning modal style, Bach affirms a strong sense of tonality. The chords in Ex. 3 do not merely accompany the melody; they stress its tonal foundations. Thus D minor, firmly established by the perfect cadence at (*a*), receives further emphasis from the half cadence at (*b*). Each melodic tone is supported by a full chord, and the harmonies drive vigorously forward from one chord to the next. Instead of the equality of all four voices found in Scheidt, melody and bass become most important, the inner voices having less interest. Under the influence of functional chord progression, the free-flowing lines of Ex. 2 have been shaped in Ex. 3 into clear-cut, balanced phrases. A comparison of the two examples shows how a change in harmonic style can alter the quality and impact of a melody.

Simple and Complex Harmonizations

But it is not only in the contrast between two composers that differences in harmonic style are revealed. As we have seen, Bach himself often made different harmonizations of the same chorale. *O Ewigkeit, du Donnerwort* exists in two Bach harmonizations of contrasting character. Comparison of Exs. 4 and 5 reveals the subtle variations of a master harmonist.

---

* Compare the gliding quality of Scheidt's harmony with the linear progressions of some twentieth-century music (see pages 350 and 356).

Ex. 4   Bach: *O Ewigkeit, du Donnerwort*

Gm: II$\frac{4}{3}$ III^6 VII$^{\sharp7}$ of V V

The harmonization in Ex. 4 is sturdy and calm. The chords chosen—largely diatonic triads, with emphasis on the primary degrees—suggest a mood of serene resignation, an effect strengthened by the repeated perfect and half cadences in the home key. The first three phrases, moreover, are almost entirely diatonic, with but one chromatic alteration, at (*a*). Only in the fourth phrase (at the words "Then with our anguish let us bend") does a dissonant chromatic progression appear, heightening the tension. Note the chromatic descent of the bass (*b*), which underlies four extremely dissonant chords—a sudden change in harmonic style underscoring the bitterness of the text. Note that Bach carries the dissonant texture through the entire phrase; he does not merely introduce one dissonant chord to emphasize a single word.*

Note also that linear and contrapuntal impulses—particularly the contrary motion between tenor and bass at (*b*)—override the normal direction of dissonance resolution, adding to the tension of the phrase.† Especially distinctive are the progression of II$_3^4$ to an augmented III and the latter's extraordinary resolution to the VII^{d7} of V. The final phrase returns to the style of primary chords and diatonic flowing lines, which re-establishes the mood of the opening.

Ex. 5   Bach: *O Ewigkeit, du Donnerwort*

---

* Such literal musical illustration of a single moment (known in today's movie music as "Mickey mousing") was foreign to the spirit of chorale harmonization. The broad changes in mood from one *phrase* to another are related to the type of musical-dramatic characterization discussed in Chapter XI, especially pages 297–302.

† This is but one instance of many in which the desire for good contrapuntal motion leads a composer to disregard traditional harmonic resolutions. Melodic impulses, in other words, overcome harmonic ones.

The second harmonization (Ex. 5), a setting of another verse of the chorale text, presents an approach so different that it would be difficult to recognize it as by the same composer were we not already familiar with Bach's wide stylistic range. In place of the primary harmonies of the first

Ewigkeit (Ex. 4), reflecting submission and serenity, the second strikes a darker, more agitated tone—undoubtedly a reflection of the differences in text between the two versions.

The voice leading alone is extraordinary. In the first three bars, the bass mounts an octave and a sixth, from its lowest to its most intense high register. Two octave leaps are suddenly followed, at (*a*), by a pair of dissonant chords (at the word "thunder").* The chord at the first cadence is strange: a VI with two roots, two thirds, and no fifth, producing a harsh, ominous sound. At (*b*), the bass once more leaps down an octave and up again, then descends in a long falling wave, reaching its starting point at (*e*). The second phrase contains a number of dissonances; by contrast, the third is relatively quiet.

Now comes a dramatic change. Despite the tradition that forbids too many wide leaps in any one voice, the bass (which had already made four octave jumps) rises a major tenth, at (*f*), drops a diminished fifth, at (*g*), and surpasses itself with three octave leaps in one bar (*h*). Obviously, Bach was prepared to fling the rules aside when moved by a need for intense expression.

Embellishing tones, too, play their part in the plan. Note the suspensions at (*a*) and (*d*) and the harshly accented passing note in the bass at (*c*). Bitter harmonies add to the intensity of the treatment: seventh and diminished seventh chords and secondary dominants, which contribute a sense of urgency.

Compare the two harmonizations of *O Ewigkeit, du Donnerwort* bar by bar and chord by chord and notice the variety of Bach's harmony. Other chorales with multiple harmonizations will also repay careful comparison, among them *Herzlich thut mich verlangen, Jesu, meine Freude, Christ lag in Todesbanden,* and *O Welt, ich muss dich lassen.*

Problems of Harmonization

Study of the chorales provides an excellent review of the harmonic procedures we have investigated thus far. Harmonization of chorale melodies, followed by a comparison with Bach's settings, remains an unsurpassed method of acquiring a rich and varied harmonic vocabulary.

Procedure in chorale setting follows that of previous harmonizations.† However, since chorales are characterized by their numerous and sharply defined cadences, the cadence points become a matter of special concentration. From the viewpoint of the over-all structure, the various cadences not only contrast with each other but also build a continuous

---

* Albert Schweitzer, among others, pointed out the correlation of text and harmonic style in Bach's music. See also pages 297–298.

† See pages 173–176 and 319–322 of Volume I, and 131–139 of this volume.

harmonic line throughout the whole chorale. Note, incidentally, Bach's fondness for the II$^6_5$ (rather than the IV) as the subdominant chord in the cadence.*

Preliminary sketching of the cadences should make clear the form of each chorale; awareness of the form is basic in harmonizing a melody. Two patterns appear again and again in the chorale: two-part form and the phrase group.

In the chorale, Part I of a two-part form generally ends with a perfect tonic cadence. The cadences of Part II are varied, with the perfect cadence in the home key reserved, wherever possible, for the last. The phrase group may have as few as three or as many as seven or eight cadences. Harmonic variety becomes especially important when two successive phrases end on the same melody note.

Ex. 6   Bach: *Gott sei gelobet und gebenedeiet*

It would be tedious to harmonize both cadences with the tonic of G.

Ex. 7   *Gott sei*, trial harmonization

How much fresher is Bach's setting, which pauses first on III of C (an unusual cadence chord) and then on I of G.

* See pages 437–438 of Volume I.

Ex. 8   Bach: *Gott sei*

The Lord be prais - èd O the Lord be bless - èd.
Gott sei ge - lob - et und ge - be - ne - dei - et.

C: VI⁶ II⁶ III   G:V   I

In harmonizing a chorale, start with block-chord style.

Ex. 9   Bach: *Meine Seele erhebet den Herren*

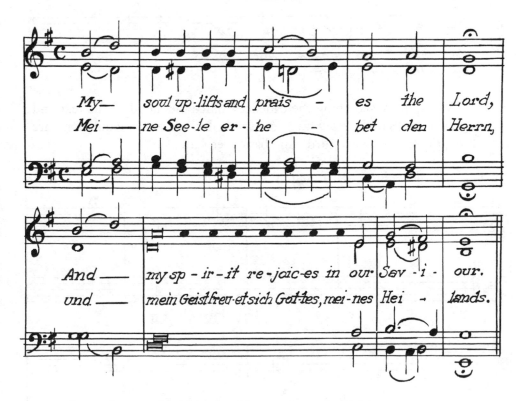

My__ soul up-lifts and prais - es the Lord,
Mei __ ne See-le er - he - bet den Herrn,

And __ my sp - ir - it re - joic-es in our Sav - i - our.
und __ mein Geist freu-et sich Gottes, mei - nes Hei - lands.

Later, harmonizations should contain embellishing tones to promote greater melodic interest in all the voices, achieve a more fluid rhythm, and add needed harmonic accents or variations.

Steps in Chorale Harmonization

For the first steps in chorale harmonization, let us start with the melody of Ex. 10. Sing the melody and the words.

Ex. 10   Bach: *Ich dank dir schon durch deinen Sohn*

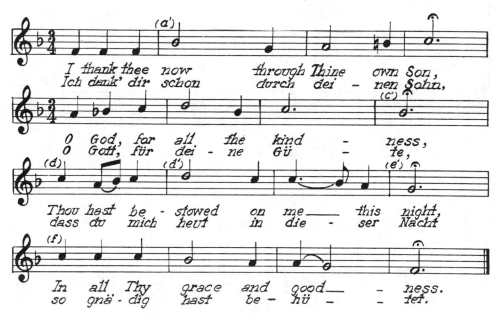

We begin by sketching the cadences. Since the mood of the text and melody expresses simple reverence, no unusual chords or modulations are called for; the cadences are sturdy and basic, yet varied.

Ex. 11   *Ich dank dir:* trial harmonization, sketch 1

Continuing as with earlier harmonizations, we now map out the bass line, striving for simplicity.

Ex. 12   *Ich dank dir*, sketch 2

The sketched-in bass moves largely stepwise, sustaining the quiet mood of text and tune; several leaps are introduced, however (including two octave jumps at *c* and *d*), to lend variety to the line. Note that in two instances (at *a* and *e*) sketch 2 shows some small alterations of sketch 1 (Ex. 11) in the interest of a more flowing bass. Remember that sketches are *meant to be changed* in the course of work.

At the third stage of harmonization, inner voices and embellishing tones are added, again with emphasis on flowing lines.

Ex. 13   *Ich dank dir*, sketch 3

For the final sketch of the harmonization (Ex. 13), minor changes in the bass line have once more been made, to promote greater fluency and interweaving of voices. At (*b*) the E flat in the bass has been deleted in order to re-establish the tonic key of F for a moment, before modulating to B flat. At (*c*) passing tones have been added in the bass to achieve a more flowing rhythm; they have also been added at (*d'*) and (*e*). The last note in the bass has been shifted down an octave. Although low F had already appeared for a moment at (*d*), the general downward motion of the bass in the last phrase leads more logically to the final low tonic.

The harmonization completed, the last step is to compare it with the version by Bach, carefully noting the differences.

Ex. 14   Bach: *Ich dank dir schon durch deinen Sohn*

Here are the salient points that emerge from a comparison of the Bach harmonization (Ex. 14) with that of Ex. 13:

1. There is but a single octave leap in the bass, in bar 2; it adds energy at the very opening of the chorale.
2. Low F appears only once in the entire harmonization, as the very last note. Its climactic effect is stronger than in Ex. 13, where it occurs twice.
3. The high note of the bass line (A) is reserved for the last phrase (f), again producing a stronger climax. From the high A the bass has a more graceful curve and a more clearly directed motion down to the final low tone.
4. The II⁷ chord at (a′) enriches the harmonic color of the phrase.
5. At (d) the V is used to re-enter the key of F, adding harmonic motion at that point.
6. The rhythm of the tenor line is more flowing just before and at (c′).
7. A suspension in the tenor provides harmonic variety at (d′), and another in the alto adds rhythmic suppleness at (e′).
8. Finally, the inner voices have more interesting melodic curves and greater rhythmic variety throughout.

No one can duplicate the mastery of Bach in chorale harmonization; nor is that the object. The study serves to stimulate the flow of harmonic and linear ideas and to solidify previously acquired techniques. A good chorale harmonization never merely "obeys the rules"; it can and should be the product of taste and imagination.*

Summary

1. A chorale melody can be harmonized in various styles. Different harmonizations alter the feeling and impact of a melody.

2. In Bach's chorale harmonizations:
   a. Tonality is strongly emphasized.
   b. Each melody note is usually supported by a four-voice chord.
   c. Root movements between the chords are mainly strong.
   d. Movement is strongly directed toward the cadences.
   e. Soprano and bass have the most interesting lines; alto and tenor, while smooth and flowing, are often of lesser melodic interest.
   f. Harmonic style varies from calm, diatonic, and consonant to agitated, chromatic, and dissonant.
   g. Differences in harmonic style and technique are often suggested by the text.
   h. Linear and contrapuntal movement of the voices sometimes overrides the normal direction of dissonance resolution.

3. The steps in harmonizing a chorale are:
   a. Sing the melody with its text.
   b. Study the text and decide on the general character of the harmonization.
   c. Sketch the cadence chords.
      i. Let the cadence plan indicate the form of the chorale—whether a phrase group or a two-part form.
      ii. Vary the cadences, observing the principle of cadential suspense wherever possible.
   d. Write the entire bass.
   e. Complete the harmony in block-chord style.
   f. Rewrite, introducing embellishing tones in the interests of better melodic and rhythmic flow, harmonic accents, and communication of the mood of the text as a whole.

---

* For a satirical modern style of chorale harmonization, see the Great Chorale in Stravinsky's *Story of a Soldier* (page 59 of the miniature score).

Harmonic
Generation
of Melody

We have seen how melody can arise from a short harmonic pattern. The process goes beyond the limits of a phrase: in certain larger compositions, too, the bass and harmonies are sometimes created first, the melody afterward. The practice of fitting melody to a given bass dates back as far as the Renaissance *passamezzo antico*—a standard bass formula over which each composer wrote his own setting.* In the Baroque, repeated chord patterns took the form of the *ground bass*, *chaconne*, and *passacaglia*, each repetition giving rise to another melodic or contrapuntal variation.† Contemporary jazz

* See Reese: *Music in the Renaissance* (New York, 1954), page 524.

† For these forms, see Green: *Form in Tonal Music* (New York, 1965). Well-known examples include Bach's *Crucifixus*, from the B minor Mass, his Passacaglia in C minor for Organ, and his Chaconne in D minor for Solo Violin.

performances also frequently start from a given set of harmonies (generally those of a popular song), which the player uses as the framework for rhythmic and melodic improvisation. In a wide variety of musical styles, therefore, harmony comes first, melody later.

Writing Melody to a Given Progression

What kind of phrase can be written, for example, over this progression?

Ex. 15   Chord progression as the basis of melody

Gm: I   IV⁶   VII   III   VI   II⁶   V

Such a series of chords is scarcely distinctive: it will quickly be recognized as a variant of the cycle of fifths. A familiar Baroque progression, it served Handel as the framework for a stately passacaglia. Here are the theme and three of the fifteen melodic variations devised by the composer.

Ex. 16   Handel: Passacaglia, from Suite No. 7

While retaining the same basic chords, Handel altered the bass somewhat from variation to variation, root positions being interchanged with first inversions and passing tones added to secure a more varied bass line.

In his *Six Easy Variations on a Swiss Song*, Beethoven kept to a given chord progression and melody, making free variations of both. The eleven-measure bass that serves as starting point is shown in Ex. 17.

Ex. 17   Beethoven: *Six Easy Variations on a Swiss Song* (bass line)

Here are the theme and first three variations. Note the different rhythms used—quarter notes in the theme, triplets in the first variation, dotted eighths and sixteenths in the second; and flowing eighth notes in the third.

Ex. 18   Beethoven: Six Easy Variations

In Variation I, the flowing rhythm interweaves gracefully between right and left hands; there are slight embellishments of both melody and harmony.

In Variation II, the left hand has a new contrapuntal melody against the right.

Var. 2

Variation III introduces a change of mode, new variations in the bass line, and a change of texture (three voices instead of two).

Writing a Two-Part Form over a Given Progression

Certain Baroque suites utilize the same chord progression as the basis for several movements; while the harmonies remain constant, melody and rhythm change in each variation.

Consider the following harmonic framework for a two-part form of twelve bars.

Ex. 19   Harmonic framework for two-part form

* In Baroque music, Part I sometimes ends with a half cadence.

What kind of melodic line can be created over such a harmonic framework? Once more Handel provides an answer.

Ex. 20   Handel: Variation 1 (first part), from Suite No. 3

Note:

1. The flowing melody in sixteenth notes.
2. The smooth bass line, which adds a few subtle variations to the given progression.
3. The melodic curves, which form two arches:
   a. In the melody, low point at (*a*), high point at (*b*), low point at (*e*).
   b. In the bass, with high and low points (*f* and *g*, respectively) placed differently from those of the melody.
4. A harmonic embellishment—a passing secondary dominant, V of IV, at (*a*), which adds movement and elegance to the line.
5. The syncopations of the inner voice starting at (*b*), which add rhythmic variety and tension.
6. The broken rhythms in the left hand at (*c*), which give further variety to the texture.
7. The thinning down of the texture to two voices at (*d*)—a surprise at the cadence.

Various Melodic Possibilities over the Same Bass

The opening measures of the other variations written by Handel over the same harmonic framework show different melodic, rhythmic, and textural figurations over a given bass.

Ex. 21   Handel: Beginnings of Variations 2, 3, 4, and 5

Close examination of other examples of ground bass, chaconne, and variations will disclose many of the techniques composers have developed for writing harmony and melody over a given bass. Among works well worth study are "Dido's Lament" from Purcell's *Dido and Aeneas*, Bach's Chaconne for Solo Violin and the *Crucifixus* from his B minor Mass, Mozart's Variations on *Ah, vous dirai-je, maman*, and Beethoven's Variations on *Nel cor più non mi sento*, his Thirty-Two Variations, and the last movement of his Symphony No. 3. More recent examples of simple variation techniques include Bartók's *Ballad* from *Fifteen Hungarian Peasant Songs*, and the piano solo arrangements by Gershwin of his own songs, in *The Gershwin Song Book*.

Summary

1. In certain compositions, the harmony forms the starting point; the melody derives from it. Examples of such compositions are the *passamezzo antico*, ground bass, passacaglia, and chaconne.

2. When the bass or a given chord progression serves as the basis for a set of variations:
   a. Different melodies are written over the same progression.
   b. Different rhythms and textures are employed in successive variations.
   c. Sometimes the bass line is varied while the basic harmonies are maintained.

3. Variations over a given bass are often written in two-part form.

IX

Ninth Chords

The dominant ninth is a five-voice chord consisting of a V^7 with an additional third. It has two forms, major and minor:

Ex. 1   Dominant ninth chords

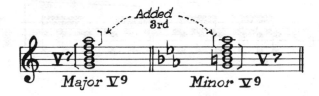

Used occasionally during the eighteenth century, the ninth chord was exploited more freely during the nineteenth, becoming a familiar element of Romantic music and, later, a hallmark of Impressionism in the twentieth century.

Functions of the Ninth Chord

The dominant ninth serves:

1. To harmonize the sixth degree, as an embellishment of the fifth.
2. As a richer, more colorful form of dominant chord.
3. As a dominant chord with greater tension and expressive quality.

Often the ninth appears as an accented neighboring tone, approached from and returning to 5 (Ex. 2, *a*).

Ex. 2   Beethoven: Sonata, Op. 13 (*Pathétique*), second movement

The richness of the ninth chord attracted Romantic composers, who were especially sensitive to harmonic color. The ninth resolves downward, even when the chord changes (Ex. 3, *a*).

Ex. 3   Schubert: Waltz, Op. 50, No. 8

Compare the rather chaste use of the ninth in Schubert with Franck's emphasis on its rich sonority.

Ex. 4   Franck: Violin Sonata in A major

The Minor Ninth

Just as a minor second is more dissonant than a major one, the minor ninth has more bite in *forte* and more expressive quality in *piano* than its major counterpart. Compare the rapid alternation of the two forms in *forte* (Ex. 5).

Ex. 5   Beethoven: Sonata, Op. 14, No. 1

Chopin frequently made use of the melancholy quality of the minor ninth, introducing it without preparation.

Ex. 6   Chopin: Mazurka, Op. 63, No. 2

The poignancy of the interval is further enhanced by the open position of the chord. Compare, incidentally, the effect of the minor ninth (*a*) with the blander major ninth, at (*b*).*

Placing the ninth at the peak of a phrase, as in Ex. 7 (*a*), highlights its colorful quality.

Ex. 7   Schubert: Waltz, Op. 9b, No. 17

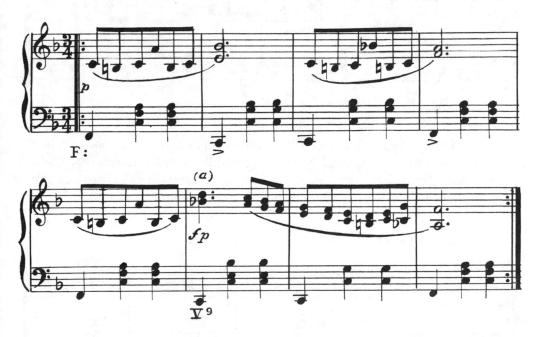

Voice Leading

In four-part harmony, one voice of the ninth chord must be omitted —generally the fifth, a tone least essential to the distinctive quality of the chord.

* For Bach's use of the minor ninth, see page 243; for Schubert's, page 312.

Ex. 8   Positions of the ninth chord

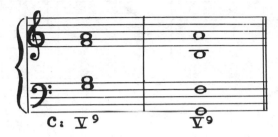

The ninth generally appears in the upper voice, where its special color is heard most clearly. Even when introduced in an inner voice (Ex. 9, *a*), it is usually placed at least a ninth above the root.

Ex. 9   Chopin: Mazurka, Op. 6, No. 3

Setting the ninth closer to the root changes it into a second, altering its characteristic quality. Such voicing (generally avoided during the traditional period) produces the suggestion of a *tone cluster*—a twentieth-century sonority favored by Henry Cowell and other contemporary composers.*

Ex. 10   Modern voicing of the ninth chord

By the time the ninth came into general use in the early nineteenth century, the traditional concern for preparation and resolution of dissonances had abated somewhat. Composers began to resolve the ninth by leap to another voice of the V chord (Exs. 4 and 11, *a*).

* See pages 397–398.

Ex. 11   Schubert: Hark, Hark the Lark

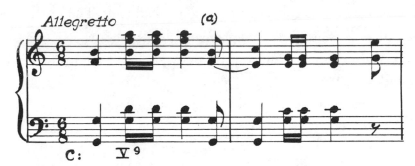

Resolution of the ninth can be embellished or delayed in the same way as that of the seventh (Ex. 12, *a*). Note the preparation of the ninth as a suspension—its earliest use.*

Ex. 12   Bach: Fugue No. 5, from *The Well-Tempered Clavier*, Book II

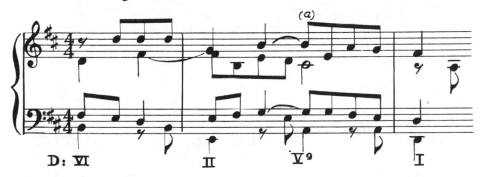

Inversions

Inversions of the ninth chord usually have the ninth on top (Exs. 13–16).

Ex. 13   Inversions of the ninth chord

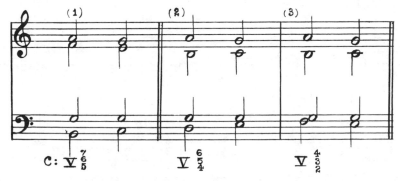

* See pages 394–395, Volume I.

Although they are rather infrequent, these inversions, when sensitively scored, add subtle color variations to the harmony. The first inversion ($V^6_{5\ 3}$...) $(V^{6}_{5}{}^{7}_{3})$ occurs in Brahms' First Symphony (Ex. 14); the second $(V^{6}_{4}{}^{5}_{})$, in a Schubert Waltz (Ex. 15); and the third $(V^{6}_{4}{}^{3}_{2})$, in an unusually dissonant Haydn work (Ex. 16).

Ex. 14   Brahms: Symphony No. 1, Op. 68, second movement

Ex. 15   Schubert: Waltz, Op. 33, No. 2

Ex. 16   Haydn: Sonata No. 7, in D

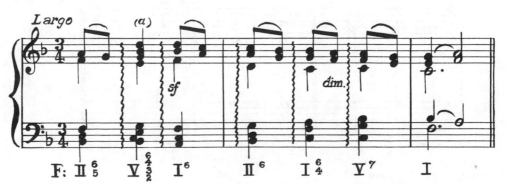

Since the ninth does not occur in the bass in traditional style, neither does its fourth inversion. It does appear occasionally, however, in twentieth-century music. Here is an interesting fourth inversion from an early work of Schönberg:

Ex. 17   Schönberg: *Verklärte Nacht*, Op. 4

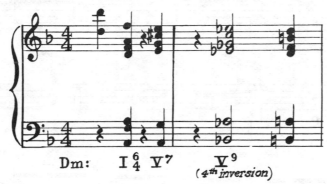

Dm: I_4^6 V^7 V^9
                        (4th *inversion*)

The Ninth Chord as a Secondary Dominant

Like the V, V^7, VII, and VII^{d7}, the V^9 may also act as a secondary dominant, V^9 of V (Ex. 18, *a*).

Ex. 18   Schubert: *Valse Sentimentale*, Op. 50, No. 2

c:

(a)

V^9 of V   V V^9

A more richly colored example—V⁹ of II in third inversion—occurs in a Schumann piece (Ex. 19, *a*).

Ex. 19   Schumann: *Arabeske*, Op. 19

Other Ninth Chords

Toward the end of the nineteenth century, composers began to experiment with the use of ninth chords on degrees other than V. If sevenths can be used on other steps, why not ninths? In Ex. 20 (*a*) we find a II⁹, which resolves to V.

Ex. 20   Debussy: *La fille aux cheveux de lin*, from Preludes, Book I

In the song *Après un rêve*, by Gabriel Fauré, the IV⁹ and VII⁹
appear.*

Ex. 21   Fauré: *Après un rêve*

* For the characteristic use of parallel ninth chords in twentieth-century music, see Exs.
12, page 349, and 33, page 400.

Summary

1. The V⁹, a five-voice chord, consists of V⁷ with an added third.
   a. The major V⁹ has an added major third.
   b. The minor V⁹ has an added minor third.

2. The functions of the V⁹ are:
   a. To harmonize the sixth degree.
   b. To serve as a richer, more colorful dominant chord.
   c. To serve as a dominant chord with greater tension and expressive power.

3. The ninth can be prepared in the previous chord, or it can enter without preparation.

4. The ninth is generally resolved:
   a. By step downward.
   b. By leap to another voice of the V⁷ chord.

5. The minor ninth is more dissonant in *forte* and more poignant in *piano* than the major ninth.

6. In four-part harmony:
   a. One voice, generally the fifth of the chord, is omitted.
   b. Traditionally, the ninth appears at least a ninth above the root.
   c. In contemporary writing, the ninth may be written closer to the root, forming a tone cluster.

7. In traditional style, the first, second, and third inversions are used. The fourth inversion appears only in twentieth-century music.

8. The V⁹, like V⁷ and VII^d7, can serve as a secondary dominant.

9. In twentieth-century music, ninth chords appear on degrees other than V.

Broader
Aspects
of Rhythm

Earlier in our discussion, melodic rhythms were analyzed and reference was made to the broader implications of rhythm in music. What are these implications?

In its broadest sense, rhythm refers to the movement and pacing of a composition, its slow or swift flow, the pattern of its progress from the first note to the last. Thus, rhythm exists in a variety of forms:

1. Melodic rhythm.
2. The rhythm of melodic climaxes.
3. The rhythm of accompanying figures.
4. The rhythm of phrase lengths.
5. Harmonic rhythm.
6. The rhythm of harmonic intensities.

We have seen how melodic rhythm creates symmetry or freedom in a melody and moderate or rapid motion in a composition.* Let us examine other ways in which rhythm propels the music.

The Rhythm of Melodic Climaxes

A melodic climax, as already noted, often serves as a point of crowning interest in a phrase.† When a work contains more than one phrase, it may have two or more melodic peaks. The spacing of these peaks produces a special rhythmic effect: the rhythm of melodic climaxes.

This rhythm, like other kinds, can be symmetrical or asymmetrical; it can be emphasized for cumulative power or deliberately underplayed.

Symmetrical climaxes are often found in compositions having two equal divisions, such as a parallel period. The appearance of the climaxes in similar positions in the phrase enhances the feeling of symmetry. We find melodic peaks just before the end of both phrases in the theme from Mozart's Sonata in D (page 29). The parallel phrases culminate in parallel high points (with the second generally higher than the first), producing symmetrical climaxes.‡

A different rhythmic pattern arises when the high note is repeated at irregular distances during the phrase.

Ex. 22   Bach: Sinfonia, from Partita No. 2

* See Volume I, pages 150ff and 277–282.
† See Volume I, pages 94–98.
‡ See also Handel's Sarabande, pages 363–364, Volume I.

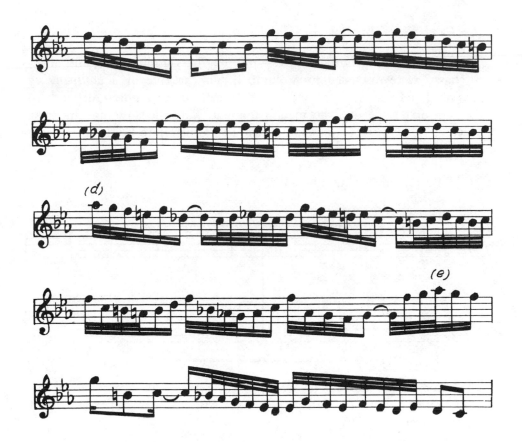

In Ex. 22, high A flat appears five times, always on a different beat and after a different space of time:

1. At (*a*), on the second half of the second beat.
2. At (*b*), on the third beat.
3. At (*c*) again, on the third thirty-second note of the fourth beat.
4. At (*d*), on the first beat.
5. At (*e*), on the fourth thirty-second note of the fourth beat.

Such deliberate irregularity in the rhythm of the climaxes produces a feeling of unpredictability, adding freshness to the long-line melody.

Underplaying the climactic tone by frequent repetition occurs in des Prés' *Ave verum* and Schubert's *Heidenröslein* (pages 444 and 450 of Volume I). In both melodies the high note, appearing at irregular intervals, is sounded gently rather than driven home vigorously. The entry of the peak tone at uneven distances helps to de-emphasize its climactic effect, making it simply a note slightly more prominent than others.

The forceful reiteration of the climax tone soon after its first appearance, however, is a rhythmic device that generates tension and excitement, as we have seen.*

* Pages 97–98, Volume I.

The Rhythm of Accompanying Figures

Several accompanying figures—jumping bass, rolling bass, and alternating bass—were discussed in Volume I, but the role of *accompanying rhythm* has barely been mentioned.* The momentum of a phrase depends to some extent on the speed of the accompaniment. Thus the slow movement of Beethoven's *Sonata Pathétique* starts with a sixteenth-note figure in the left hand.

Ex. 23   Beethoven: Sonata, Op. 13 (*Pathétique*), second movement

Later in the movement, the phrase is repeated, accompanied by sixteenth-note triplets. The change in pace due to the livelier left-hand rhythm is obvious.

Ex. 24   Beethoven: Sonata, Op. 13

In some compositions, accompaniment rhythm remains unchanged. In others, quickening or slowing down the rhythmic values of an accompaniment figure during the course of a phrase serves to intensify or relax the rhythmic feeling. The third movement of Beethoven's Sonata, Op. 14, No. 1, opens with a lively melody accompanied by running eighth-note triplets. After three and a half bars, the accompaniment changes to quarter and half notes, leading to a more expansive ending of the phrase.

* On the use of accompanying rhythm to unify two contrasted passages, see page 50 and Ex. 22, page 54, of this volume.

Ex. 25   Beethoven: Sonata, Op. 14, No. 1

The Rhythm of Phrase Lengths

Phrases vary in character, from complete freedom to strictly balanced symmetry.* Going beyond the structure of individual phrases, what is the effect of joining phrases of different length and rhythmic design?

The difference of phrase lengths in an asymmetrical period can produce a rhythmic and emotional intensification.† An irregularly con-

* See pages 277–281, Volume I.
† See Exs. 25 and 26, pages 75–77.

structed three-phrase group, such as Handel's Largo from *Xerxes* (page 94) creates a sense of fluid movement.

Varying phrase-length rhythm becomes a still more important force in two- and three-part forms whose second section provides an intensification of the ideas stated in the first. The Gigue from Handel's Suite No. 11 is a case in point.

Ex. 26   Handel: Gigue, from Suite No. 11

Part I of the Gigue consists of a symmetrical four-bar phrase. In Part II the phrases become irregular and shorter, adding tension to the movement. The four-bar pattern of Part I is first compressed into three bars, then into two fragments of one bar each (*h* and *i*), ending finally in a return of the opening motive, extended to two bars. The irregular quality of the second section contrasts sharply with the regularity of the first.

Such uneven phrase lengths, following a symmetrical opening, are typical of a development section.* When expanded beyond the confines of a small two- or three-part form to the wider dimensions of the sonata or symphony, varied phrase-length rhythms provide an important means of structural contrast.

* On this point, review pages 182–186.

Harmonic Rhythm

The rate at which chords change in a bar or in a group of bars has been called harmonic rhythm.* But rapid or slow change of harmony is not in itself an index of musical activity; Baroque music generally contains faster harmonic rhythms than does Classical music, yet one is not necessarily more energetic than the other.

When a fixed harmonic rhythm persists throughout a phrase or section of a composition, the tendency is toward regular movement. In traditional styles, the harmonic rhythm generally emphasizes the meter of the piece. Bach chorales illustrate a change of chord on every beat, sometimes twice during a beat.† A Chopin waltz (page 17) shows change in each bar, and a prelude by the same composer (pages 240–241), change every two bars.

Harmonic rhythm becomes a more potent force when it varies from one to another section of a composition or even within a single phrase. The opening of Beethoven's Ninth Symphony presents a dramatic example of a sudden quickening of harmonic rhythm in the course of a phrase.

Ex. 27   Beethoven: Symphony No. 9, Op. 125

---

* Walter Piston was among the first to use this term. For prior discussion, see Volume I, pages 86, 323, and 375.

† See page 191.

The famous opening chord of the Ninth Symphony—an empty fifth which hangs suspended for fourteen bars—gives way (*a*) to a second chord, which holds for five bars. Then the rhythm suddenly explodes (*b*) into a series of two chords per bar. The effect (in which the harmonic changes are, to be sure, reinforced by other musical elements) is a famous one, and justly so.

In his first sonata (page 385, Volume I), Beethoven used a technique similar to that of the Ninth Symphony, speeding up the harmonic rhythm at the very outset. The phrase starts with a pattern of one chord for two bars. This pattern is repeated, then cut to one chord in a bar, and finally to two chords per bar. Although on a far more modest scale than in the Ninth Symphony, the rhythmic contraction is similar.

Increasing tension by speeding up the harmonic rhythm at the end of a phrase is another technique used by many composers. In the Bach Invention (page 109), a rhythm of one chord per bar is sustained for three bars; then there are four chords in a bar. A similar quickening appears in Schubert's Ecossaise (page 245) and Clementi's Sonatina (page 40).

Relaxing tension by slackening the harmonic rhythm is another well-known device often found toward the end of slow movements, in a "dying away" effect. Beethoven, ever an innovator, introduced it at the beginning of the last movement of his Sonata, Op. 14, No. 1 (page 233). The exciting opening rhythm of four chords per bar suddenly drops (in bar four) to one and two chords per bar, leading to a placid cadence. The opposite of the usual pattern of change, it takes the listener by surprise and proves as effective as speeding up the harmonic rhythm.

Yet the replacement of a fast by a slow harmonic rhythm, or even by no chord change at all, need not necessarily cause a loss of excitement. Insistent repetition of the dominant chord, if coupled with other energizing elements, can produce a remarkable increase in tension.

Ex. 28   Beethoven: Sonata, Op. 13 (*Pathétique*), last movement

The harmonic rhythm slows down at (*a*) from two chords per bar to one chord in eight bars. Through the long sweep of the rising-wave line, however, and its sudden downward rush, the intensity builds to the last note.*

* See also Jan La Rue: "Harmonic Rhythm in the Beethoven Symphonies," *The Music Review*, Vol. XVIII, No. 1 (February 1957).

Tempo and Harmonic Rhythm

A further aspect of harmonic rhythm concerns its relation to tempo. To the eye, a chord is a chord, whether it lasts a considerable time or passes in a split second; to the ear, however, sustained harmonies carry more weight than those that change quickly. In slow or moderate tempo, each harmonic formation is heard as a separate chord. Beyond a certain speed, the ear no longer recognizes a quickly changing series of chords as separate harmonies. In fast and very fast tempos, one tends to hear only the most strongly accented chord or chords in a bar.

Ex. 29   Schumann: *Symphonic Etudes*, Op. 13

In this *presto possibile*, the eye sees two or three different chords in every bar; at such speed, however, the ear catches only one or at most two of the chords in a bar as they flash by. The rest register simply as melodic resultants—lightly touched passing or changing chords, part of the linear movement. The harmonies actually heard in the Schumann piece are:

Ex. 30   Schumann: Chords as heard

One must be careful never to analyze harmonic rhythm (or any other musical element, for that matter) only by the eye; the ear remains the basic and final judge. The harmonic outline in Ex. 30 represents the harmonic rhythms more accurately than does one in which every sixteenth note is identified as a separate chord.*

The Rhythm of Harmonic Intensities

Chopin's Prelude in A major moves for eleven bars in a regular alternation of tonic and dominant, while the melody repeats a simple motive.

Ex. 31   Chopin: Prelude, Op. 28, No. 7

* For another passage in which a similar analysis would be appropriate, see Ex. 42, page 28.

At (*a*) the phrase rises to a peak, where the high tone is repeated. At (*b*) the texture expands to nine voices, and a secondary dominant, V⁷ of II, suddenly appears. All these elements contribute to the climax; but the intrusion of a rich chromatic chord into the simple tonic-dominant progression of I and V is the most telling: it creates a point of harmonic intensity that stands out sharply from the rest.

Harmonic intensity, illustrated here, is an enhanced activity, power, or color imparted to a phrase by a chord or group of chords more complex in structure or function than those that have preceded. In the Chopin piece it occurs at one point only, and comes as a delightful surprise.

Such intensity can be entirely lacking in a phrase—in Scheidt's *Vater unser* (page 190), for example. It can, on the other hand, permeate an entire composition, as in the Sarabande from Bach's English Suite No. 6 (page 23), with its many tense, active chords. In either case, the harmonic intensity remains fairly constant.

When, however, the level of harmonic intensity *varies* in the course of a composition or a passage, increasing, decreasing, or forming some other pattern, we speak of a *rhythm of harmonic intensities*. Schubert's Ecossaise (page 245), for example, starts with a low-intensity pattern of alternating V and I chords. After eight bars, the tension rises in a series of secondary dominants, which, appearing in rapid succession, lend a sense of exciting movement to the phrase. Each chromatic chord adds cumulatively to the effect of the preceding ones, building a rhythm of mounting tension.

Harmonic intensity can be developed in various ways, by the use of (1) strong root movements, (2) dissonant chord structures, (3) dissonant embellishing tones, (4) quickened harmonic rhythm, (5) chromatic chord structures and movement, (6) modulation—or by several of these together.

Such methods are most effective when they contrast with their opposites: strong root movements with moderate ones, chromatic chords following diatonic ones, a modulation or a group of modulations after a long diatonic passage, and the like.*

Differences in harmonic intensity often occur near the end of a phrase or a composition—the natural point for a climax. Such terminal heightening of tension is frequently found in the last of a group of phrases or the second half of a two-part form. When a composition contains a development as its middle section (e.g., Part II of a three-part form), the highest intensity can occur there rather than near the end. In other cases, the rhythm of harmonic intensities is irregular and varies in its pattern from work to work.

1. Intensity produced by a series of *strong root movements* can be noted near the beginning of many Baroque compositions. Passages from Bach and Vivaldi (pages 109–112) illustrate a common harmonic practice of the period: the tonality, established in the first bars by the I—IV—V—I progression, is then re-affirmed more forcefully by a cycle of fifths; vigorous root progressions produce a stronger harmonic drive.

2. *Dissonant chords* following consonant ones effect a similar heightening. In Ex. 32, the music moves along smoothly in a succession of simple diatonic triads and seventh chords.

Ex. 32   Bach: Prelude No. 5, from *The Well-Tempered Clavier*, Book I

G:

* It is obvious that music lacking harmony—Oriental music, Gregorian chant, and certain types of contemporary music—cannot employ these means of producing intensity and contrast.

Gradually the harmony grows more complex. In Ex. 33, a pedal point, a minor ninth, diminished seventh chords, and a series of tense suspensions lead to a dissonant climax (*a*). Two more dissonant diminished sevenths (*b*) and (*c*) precede the final cadence. The gradual change from consonance to dissonance produces a marked intensification at the end of the work.

Ex. 33   Bach: Prelude (continuation)

3. *Dissonant embellishing tones* add harmonic spice to a phrase. In the last movement of Beethoven's Sonata, Op. 2, No. 2 (page 107), the accented neighboring tones in bars 2 to 5 and the accented passing tone at (*d*) contribute a rhythmic stress to the phrase, adding to its harmonic intensity.*

4. Quickening the *harmonic rhythm*, already amply illustrated, is another important means of enhancing the intensity of a phrase.

* See also the intensity of the dissonant embellishing tones in Bach, Ex. 5 (*c*) and (*d*), pages 193–194; and Haydn, Ex. 16, page 224.

5. *Chromatic chords* serve to increase the harmonic tension, especially following diatonic ones. Chopin's Mazurka, Op. 33, No. 3 (page 22) starts with four bars of tonic and dominant. In an abrupt change, a cycle of secondary dominant sevenths fills the next four bars. Their dynamic quality heightens the harmonic energy of the phrase.*

6. The power of *modulation* to increase harmonic tension has been shown in numerous examples, from Monteverdi to Brahms; the more abrupt the modulation, the more telling the effect. Thus, the sudden key change in Monteverdi's *Orfeo* (page 36) is more forceful than the gradual one in Mozart's *Magic Flute* (pages 46–47). Traveling motion—especially swiftly traveling motion—heightens the energy of a phrase.

Interplay of Rhythmic Techniques

We have studied individual methods of producing intensity; the most important aspect of this study, however, concerns their synthesis. In most compositions, melodic, rhythmic, and harmonic patterns of intensity are interwoven in various ways. When two or more coincide exactly and recur at regular intervals, a *symmetrical rhythm of intensities* is produced (Ex. 34).

Ex. 34   Schubert: Ecossaise, Op. 18a, No. 1

* A similar contrast appears in Beethoven, Ex. 60, page 283. The alternation of passages in diatonic and chromatic harmony is an important compositional technique.

In the second part of Schubert's Ecossaise, short motive fragments, fast harmonic rhythms, and secondary dominants dovetail precisely. Spaced at shorter intervals than in the first part, the pulse of intensities beats faster, more vigorously, and with perfect symmetry.

Bar	Motive fragments	Harmonic rhythms	Bar	Secondary dominants
9 10	2 bars long	[1 chord per bar [1 chord per bar	9 10	V of II
11 12	2 bars long	[1 chord per bar [1 chord per bar	11 12	V of IV
13 14	2 bars long	[1 chord per bar [1 chord per bar	13 14	V of VI
15 16	2 bars long	[1 chord per bar [1 chord per bar	15 16	

On the other hand (and this forms one of the most interesting of musical relationships), melodic and harmonic methods of producing intensity can be used simultaneously, but in *different* rhythms. Their nodal points, instead of coinciding, overlap. Stresses, appearing at different points, form a cross-weaving pattern rather than a neatly symmetrical one.

By interweaving various rhythmic techniques, a composer such as Bach reveals the subtlety of his thought. The second part of the Gavotte from his French Suite No. 5 (pages 154–155) contains three parallel rhythmic currents: (1) phrase-length rhythms, (2) harmonic rhythms, and (3) the rhythm of modulations.

While the phrase lengths divide into symmetrical four-bar patterns befitting a formal dance movement, the harmonic and modulatory rhythms follow two different asymmetrical plans. By outlining them, we can see the interweaving and contrast of the three types of rhythm:

Bar	Phrase-length rhythms	Harmonic rhythms	Bar	Modulatory rhythms
9		1 chord per bar	9	D major
10		1 chord per bar	10	
11		3 chords per bar	11	E minor
12	End of phrase	[1 chord for 3 bars	12	
13			13	
14		]	14	
15		2 chords per bar	15	
16	End of phrase	1 chord per bar	16	Perfect cadence in E m.
17		1 chord per bar	17	C major
18		2 chords per bar	18	G major
19		[1 chord for 4½ bars	19	
20	End of phrase		20	
21			21	
22		]	22	
23		3 chords per bar	23	
24	End of phrase	1 chord per bar	24	Perfect cadence in G

A careful study of this outline, together with a re-examination of the Bach Gavotte, discloses the independence of the three parallel rhythmic streams. Through the linking of such parallel streams, Bach produces an artistic interplay that makes the Gavotte a masterpiece of its genre.

Summary

Rhythm in the broadest sense includes six types of movement:

1. Melodic rhythm—the pattern of time values in a melody.

2. The rhythm of melodic climaxes—the spacing of the peak tones, which can be:
   a. Symmetrical.
   b. Irregular and asymmetrical.

3. The rhythm of accompanying figures, which:
   a. Remains constant during an entire composition.
   b. Speeds up, creating an intensification.
   c. Slows down, creating a relaxation.

4. The rhythm of phrase lengths, which:
   a. Remains constant throughout a composition, producing rhythmic symmetry.
   b. Changes from one phrase to another, producing an irregular design.

5. Harmonic rhythm, which:
   a. Remains constant throughout a composition.
   b. Speeds up, heightening the tension.
   c. Slows down, producing a relaxation.

6. The rhythm of harmonic intensities—the patterns of heightened harmonic activity.
   a. They are produced by:
      i. Strong root movements.
      ii. Dissonant chords.
      iii. Dissonant embellishing tones.
      iv. Quickened harmonic rhythm.
      v. Chromatic chords or movements.
      vi. Modulations.
   b. They can increase, following contrasted techniques:
      i. Near the end of a work.
      ii. At the beginning.
      iii. In the middle of a work, as in a development section.
      iv. Irregularly.

7. The various types of rhythm can be organized:
   a. To coincide, producing a symmetrical rhythm of intensities.
   b. To overlap, with their nodal points appearing in different places, and forming a cross-weaving pattern of intensities.

X

Borrowed and Altered Chords

Ever since the Renaissance, chromaticism has enriched the expressive possibilities of music. Melody and harmony have been closely linked in the process, horizontal impulses often being transformed into vertical tensions. Throughout the centuries, new types of chromatic linear motion have given rise to new harmonic structures: *borrowed chords* in the late Renaissance, *altered chords* in the Baroque and Classical eras,* and more complex chord formations in the Romantic and modern periods.

* Several unusual examples of altered chords appear in Renaissance music. See Koechlin: *Traité de l'Harmonie*, Volume II, page 119; and Miller: *The Augmented Sixth Chord: Its Historical and Theoretical Origin*, in *Journal of Musicology*, I (1939), page 17.

Modal Mixtures and Borrowed Chords

A simple way of introducing chromatic color to a major or minor key is through *modal mixture*—the use in one mode of tones or chords borrowed from another. Thus a chanson in D major by the French Renaissance composer Claude le Jeune contains the lowered 6, a step characteristic of D minor.*

Ex. 1   Claude le Jeune: *Qu'est devenu ce bel oeil*

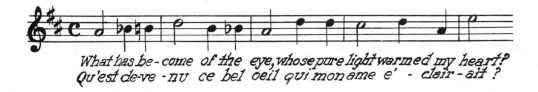

What has be-come of the eye, whose pure light warmed my heart?
Qu'est de-ve -nu ce bel oeil qui mon ame e' - clair-ait ?

Harmonization of this step requires the use of a *borrowed chord*—a harmony characteristic of minor but used in major. Ex. 2 (*a*) shows the minor IV appearing in a major key. Followed by the *major* IV (the normal chord on that degree), it produces an expressive coloration. Further examples of chromaticism involving borrowed chords are found at (*b*) and (*c*); at (*d*) minor I is followed by major I. These harmonic changes result from free melodic motion.

Ex. 2   le Jeune: *Qu'est devenu ce bel oeil*

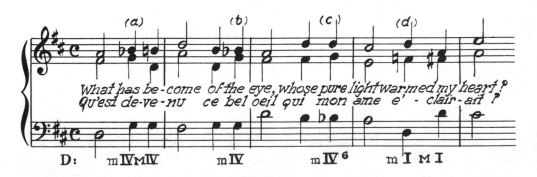

What has be-come of the eye, whose pure light warmed my heart?
Qu'est de-ve-nu   ce bel oeil qui   mon ame e' - clair-ait ?

D: mIV MIV   mIV   mIV⁶   mI M I

In Renaissance-Baroque practice, minor compositions, as we have seen, often close with a major triad (the *tierce de Picardie*). Although this practice became obsolete after 1750, the interchange of tonic triads between major and minor modes—not only at the end but also during the course of a

---

*Intermixture of what were later to become the major and minor modes was common in late Renaissance music. It was not again until the nineteenth century that major and minor were so freely mingled.

composition—was characteristic of eighteenth- and even more of nineteenth-century music. Thus in Ex. 3 (*a*), a G minor triad appears in the middle of a G major passage, producing a typically Brahmsian warmth.

Ex. 3   Brahms: Symphony No. 2, Op. 73, third movement

Alternation of major and minor tonics produces a color change that is a hallmark of Romantic style.

Ex. 4   Schubert: Impromptu, Op. 90, No. 1

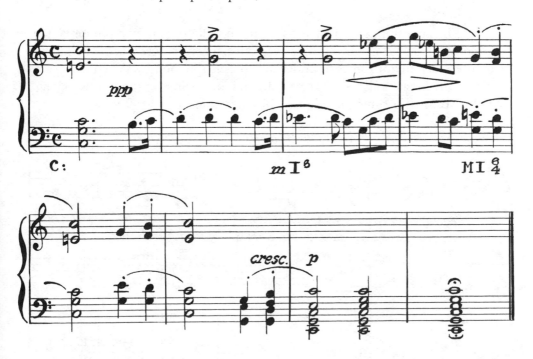

Sometimes the interchange of major and minor tonics, occurring at the start of a composition, provides a strikingly dramatic opening.

Ex. 5   Brahms: Symphony No. 3, Op. 90

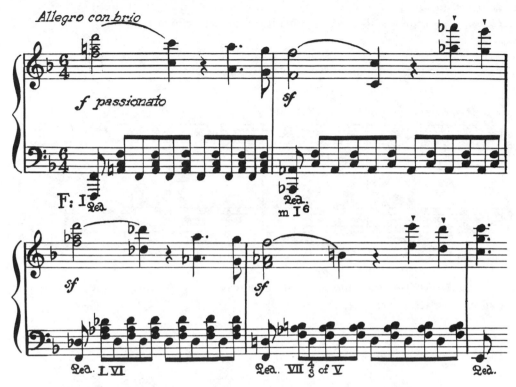

The appearance of a major I in the middle of a minor phrase is not very common and thus all the more effective when it does occur. Schubert often used such major tonics to underline contrasts in mood. "When my heart speaks in my breast" (Ex. 6) has a somber minor setting; at the words "I sing so gaily," the major tonic introduces a brighter color.

Ex. 6   Schubert: *Muth*, from *Die Winterreise*

Another modal borrowing—the use of lowered 6 in major—led to the appearance of a number of borrowed chords in that mode, among them the minor IV and lowered (major) VI, the diminished II and VII[r], and the minor V[9].

Ex. 7   Borrowed chords containing the lowered 6

Harmonies containing the lowered 6 in major—especially minor IV—enrich the harmonic color, sometimes suggesting a tinge of melancholy. Ex. 8 shows the minor IV at the beginning of a phrase in major; Ex. 9, in the middle of a phrase; and Ex. 10, at the cadence—a position where its darker color is particularly telling.

Ex. 8   Beethoven: String Quartet, Op. 135

Ex. 9   Schumann: *Papillons*, Op. 2

Ex. 10   Brahms: Symphony No. 3, Op. 90, second movement

In Romantic music, modal mixtures often have poetic implications. Thus minor IV appears twice in Schubert's *Morgengruss*, underscoring changes in mood. The song begins with the young poet breezily greeting the miller's daughter. When he says, "Do you resent my words so much, does my glance disturb you?" the first minor IV suggests a change of key (Ex. 11, *a*), and the second, a darker color in the original key (*b*). As the poet shrugs off the rebuff, "Well, then I'll go along," the carefree major of the opening returns (*c*).

Ex. 11   Schubert: *Morgengruss*, from *Die Schöne Müllerin*

For his song *Ständchen* ("Serenade"), Schubert relied on the opposite type of borrowing—that of a major IV in a minor key—to suggest a reverse change of mood, from dark to bright.

Ex. 12   Schubert: *Ständchen*

The lowered 6 also appears in major as part of another borrowed chord: the lowered VI. Schubert used it in an imaginative chamber-music setting.

Ex. 13   Schubert: Quintet, Op. 163

Lowered VI also occurs as a passing chord (between the diatonic VI and V), in Haydn's *Clock* Symphony.

Ex. 14   Haydn: Symphony No. 101 (*The Clock*), last movement

Another borrowed chord arising from lowered 6 is the diminished II. Used in first inversion, it produces a subtle harmonic inflection (Ex. 15, *a*).

Ex. 15   Schubert: *Lachen und Weinen*

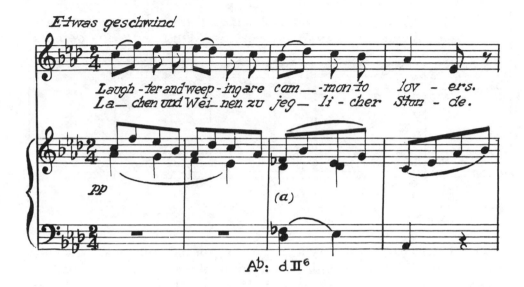

Still other borrowed chords result from the use of lowered 6 in major —VII^{d7} (Ex. 16) and V^{m9} (Ex. 17).

Ex. 16   Schubert: *Erlkönig*

Ex. 17   Schubert: *Rastlose Liebe*, Op. 5, No. 1

Modal mixtures can vary in extent from the inflection of a single note or chord (Ex. 17) to the coloring of an entire phrase. Example 18 contains three borrowed chords in four bars: VII$_3^4$ at (*a*), II$_5^6$ at (*b*), and VII^{d7} at (*c*).

Ex. 18   Schubert: *Wanderers Nachtlied*, Op. 96, No. 3

Example 19 shows an entire phrase in major colored by modal mixtures: minor IV at (*a*), lowered II⁶* at (*b*), and minor I at (*c*). (This passage can also be regarded as a temporary change from major to minor mode.) Note the expressive contrast that follows when the phrase is repeated in pure C major (*d* to *e*).

Ex. 19 Beethoven: Sonata, Op. 53 (*Waldstein*)

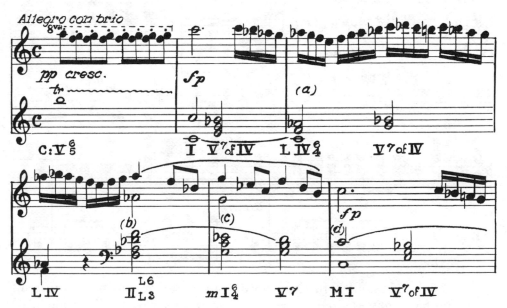

*For the lowered II, see page 273. For another example of modal mixtures, see Ex. 5, page 309.

$$\text{IV}^6_4 \qquad \text{V}^7 \text{of IV} \qquad \text{IV} \qquad \text{II}^6 \qquad \text{I}^6_4 \ \text{V}^7 \qquad \text{I}$$

Diversions and Widened Tonality

Besides using harmonies taken from the opposite mode, Romantic composers sometimes inserted into a phrase chords borrowed from more distant keys, thereby widening still further the bounds of tonality. Thus Berlioz, in his *Fantastic* Symphony, starts a phrase (Ex. 20) in G minor. As if to emphasize the wild, nightmare aspect of his theme (the movement is entitled *March to the Gallows*), the harmony shifts suddenly to the tonic of D flat—the distance of a tritone. It oscillates between the two chords, ending on G minor.

Ex. 20   Berlioz: *Fantastic* Symphony, Op. 14, fourth movement

Such intrusion of foreign chords into a passage can be considered, from another angle, as a temporary *diversion from a key*. Unlike a modulation, such a passage does not establish another tonality. Formerly, diversion from a key, no matter how brief, was labeled a "passing modulation." More

recently, the term "modulation" has been applied only to key changes sustained for a certain length of time and confirmed by a strong cadence. Chromatic harmonies not leading to a definite modulation are now seen as *part of the home key.* In this expanded concept of tonality, *a key includes foreign as well as diatonic chords.* We no longer consider the appearance of even the most distant harmonies as necessarily a modulation; often such harmonies simply represent movement from the diatonic center to the chromatic outer regions of a key.

Thus, in the middle of a G major melody from Wagner's *Die Meistersinger,* four chords borrowed from F major suddenly appear (Ex. 21, *a* to *b*). There is no real modulation; the diversion finished (at *c*), the music proceeds calmly in the home key, as before.*

Ex. 21   Wagner: *Die Meistersinger,* Act II

* In Ex. 13, bars 3 to 6 can be considered a diversion from C major.

The Largo from Dvorak's *New World* Symphony contains borrowings from two different keys in one phrase. Starting in D flat, the harmony turns to I⁶ of G major (*a*), back to I of D flat (*b*), to I of B flat (*c*), and, finally, to a cadence in D flat. The chromatic motion of the upper voices binds the progression together. Imaginative borrowings of this kind from various keys enrich the color and harmonic content of a phrase.*

Ex. 22   Dvorak: Symphony No. 5 (*From the New World*), Op. 95, second movement

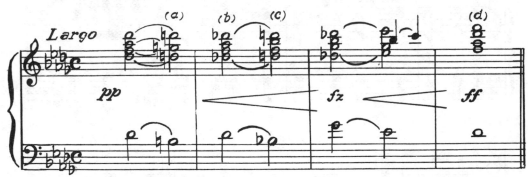

Secondary Tonics and Tonal Regions

The widening of tonality by the use of borrowed chords leads to the concepts of secondary tonics and tonal regions. We have already studied the harmonic enrichment added by secondary dominants. In larger compositions (sonatas, quartets, and symphonies) the reiteration of secondary dominants

* When such distant borrowings or diversions occur by leaping instead of by stepwise movement, they are referred to as *escaped chords*. For further discussion of expanded tonality, see pages 350–353.

sometimes gives rise to *secondary tonics*—tonal centers other than I, around which the harmony circles for a time, without modulating.* Beethoven's First Symphony provides an example.

Ex. 23   Beethoven: Symphony No. I, Op. 21

* This concept is related to Schenker's *Tonikalisierung* (see *Neue Musikalische Theorien und Phantasien*, Vienna, 1906, page 337).

In Ex. 23, phrase (*a*) stresses the I; (*a'*) a secondary tonic on II; and (*a"*) the V, followed by a return to the tonic. We call the basic chord of (*a'*) a secondary tonic on II rather than merely a II chord because it is preceded several times by V of II and forms a temporary *tonal region* on that degree—without modulating. Seen in the proportions of a long movement, Ex. 23 contains no change of key, forming instead a broadly arching perfect cadence I—II—V—I in C major. The secondary tonic on II gives a stronger emphasis to the supertonic element than would be provided by a simple II chord.

Tonal regions extend beyond diatonic secondary tonics to areas centering around borrowed and altered chords, forming a still broader concept of tonality. In Beethoven's *Waldstein* Sonata (Ex. 19), the first phrase quoted stresses the tonic minor region of C major; in the excerpt from *Die Meistersinger* (Ex. 21), the diversion to F major (*a* to *b*) stresses the subtonic region of G. Going still further afield, Beethoven's second *Rasumovsky* Quartet (Ex. 24) enters the region of lowered II*—a daring diversion from the center of E minor to the periphery of that key right near the beginning of the composition. Beethoven's free use of such remote tonal regions in an opening statement opened the door to the further expansion of tonality by the Romantics and, later, by contemporary composers.

Ex. 24   Beethoven: String Quartet, Op. 59, No. 2

* Or Neapolitan sixth (see pages 273–279).

Altered Chords

Modal mixtures and borrowings are one aspect of chromatic harmony. Another is represented by *altered chords*—chords that include chromatic tones not found in either the major or minor modes of a given key. The chromatic tension embodied in such a structure creates a strong drive toward the next chord; altered chords are, therefore, among the most active of harmonies. One of the most important is the *augmented sixth chord*.

The Augmented Sixth Chord

We have noted the half-step motion from the bass of minor IV^6 down to V as characteristic of the half cadence in minor.* Baroque composers found they could produce a still sharper drive to the half cadence by chromatically raising the root of the IV^6 in an upper voice. The interval formed—an augmented sixth—lent its name to the resultant chord (Ex. 25). Note the tension produced by the unstable interval and the sense of release when it resolves outward to the octave. In this wedge-like progression, one voice rises, the other falls, both by half-step (Ex. 25 and 26, *a–b*).

* See Ex. 38, page 303, Volume I.

Ex. 25   Origin of the augmented sixth chord

Ex. 26   Gluck: Overture to *Iphigenia in Aulis*

The augmented sixth chord is most smoothly prepared by stepwise motion (Ex. 26, *a*), but sometimes one of the two voices forming the sixth arrives by leap (Ex. 27, *a*). In resolving, the chromatic tones move in the direction of their alteration: the raised 4 continues upward, the lowered 6 down. The third voice moves to the neighboring 7; in a four-voice setting, the fourth voice always doubles the tonic, resolving by step to 2 or by leap up to 5 (Ex. 27, *a*).

Ex. 27   Beethoven: Symphony No. 5, Op. 67

When the augmented sixth chord appears in major, the wedge-like chromatic movement of the outer voices to V is still more striking (Ex. 28, *a*).

Ex. 28   Beethoven: Sonata, Op. 13 (*Pathétique*), last movement

Sometimes the chord's intensity is heightened by the simultaneous appearance of the diatonic and altered forms of the 4, producing an expressive cross-relation (Ex. 29, *a*).

Ex. 29   Beethoven: Sonata, Op. 10, No. 1, last movement

The A6 chord occurs in three different forms: *Italian, German,* and *French* sixths (Ex. 30).

Ex. 30   Italian, German, and French sixths

The Italian sixth is a first-inversion triad, whose fourth voice always doubles the fifth of the chord (Ex. 30). The German sixth has four different voices (root, third, fifth, and augmented sixth) and a richer sonority. In order to avoid parallel fifths, this form of augmented sixth chord often resolves to I$^6_4$ followed by V (Ex. 31, *a*), rather than directly to V.

Ex. 31   Mozart: Overture to *Don Giovanni*

Late Romantic composers, less concerned about such matters than were earlier masters, calmly accepted the resolution with parallel fifths (Ex. 32, *a*).

Ex. 32   Franck: Symphony

Sometimes the German sixth is written with a raised 2 instead of a lowered 3, making the resolution to I$^6_4$ more logical (Ex. 33).

Ex. 33   Resolution of German sixth

The French sixth, containing an augmented fourth as well as the augmented sixth, embodies a still greater tension and drive than do the Italian and German forms.

Ex. 34   French sixth

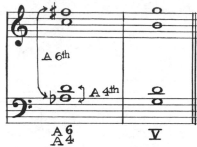

In his A minor Sonata (Ex. 35), Mozart makes use of the German sixth (*a*), then, a few bars later (*b*), the V and French sixth, repeating these two chords to hammer away at the half cadence.

Ex. 35   Mozart: Sonata, K. 310

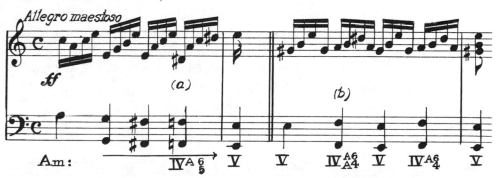

The differences among the three forms of augmented sixth are not of basic importance; being variations of a basic pattern, they often appear interchangeably. In Ex. 36, we again find the German sixth (*a*), followed briefly by the French sixth (*b*), the alteration resulting simply from a melodic movement. The two chords serve exactly the same function—to drive vigorously to the dominant (*c*).

Ex. 36   Chopin: Mazurka, Op. 30, No. 1

The augmented sixth chord appears most commonly as a form of IV⁶, but sometimes it occurs on another degree, as a $V^{A6}_{A4\atop3}$ (second-inversion V^7 with lowered fifth).

Ex. 37 $V^{A6}_{A4\atop3}$ with lowered fifth

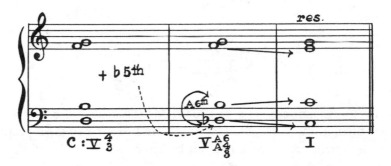

As shown in Ex. 37, the lowered fifth of the V^7 in second inversion produces an augmented sixth between bass and leading tone: the bass drives strongly downward, the 7 upward. Besides adding color to the V chord (Exs. 38–40), the lowered fifth sharpens its movement to the tonic. (The chord is sometimes referred to as the "flatted fifth" chord.)

Ex. 38   Beethoven: Sonata, Op. 31, No. 3

Ex. 39   Schubert: Quintet, Op. 163, last movement

Ex. 40   Brahms: Symphony No. 4, Op. 98, fourth movement

In addition to its cadential functions as IV^{A6} and $V^{A6}_{A4 \atop 3}$, the augmented sixth chord also plays an important role in modulation to distant keys—as we shall see in Chapter XI.

The Neapolitan Sixth Chord

The *Neapolitan sixth chord* consists of a II^6 with chromatically lowered root and fifth. Like the augmented sixth, the Neapolitan chord has a subdominant function, leading generally to the dominant. Both lowered tones resolve downward, and the bass (the only tone usually doubled) moves up to 5.

Ex. 41   The Neapolitan sixth chord

Since the lowered 2 and 6, characteristic of the Neapolitan sixth, are diatonic steps in the Phrygian mode,* it has been suggested that the chord represents a mixture of the Phrygian with the more modern modes. In any event, it occurs in both minor and major, adding to each mode the distinctive color of the lowered 2. Compare, in Ex. 42, the first statement of a phrase containing a diatonic II⁶ (*a*) and its repetition with the Neapolitan II^L6 (*b*).

Ex. 42   Mozart: Sonata for Violin and Piano, K. 377, second movement

When II^L6 resolves to V⁷, the fifth of the latter is usually omitted to avoid a cross-relation. On the other hand, this resolution often produces the interval of a diminished third (Ex. 43, *a–b*), imparting a characteristic flavor to the melody.

* See page 123, Volume I.

Ex. 43   Beethoven: Sonata, Op. 27, No. 2 (*Moonlight*)

Sometimes—especially in dramatic music—a composer prefers the deliberate clash of the cross-relation (Ex. 44, *a*).

Ex. 44   Weber: *Der Freischütz*, Act I

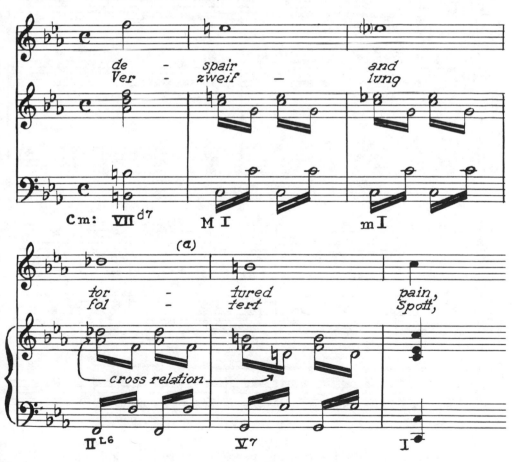

Although the Neapolitan sixth generally resolves to V, another chord is frequently interposed. Most familiar is the progression II^{L6}—I_4^6—V, with I_4^6 serving as an accented passing chord (see Ex. 19, *c*). Another harmony often interpolated between II^{L6} and V is the VII^{d7} of V. Since the bass of II^{L6} lies on 4, its rising chromatic motion is logical and effective.

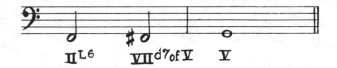

$$II^{L6} \qquad VII^{d7}\text{of}V \qquad V$$

This progression frequently occurs at dramatic moments in opera (Ex. 45, *a*) and in narrative songs, where its strong drive to the cadence provides vigorous harmonic action.

Ex. 45   Mozart: *The Magic Flute*, Act II

Note, in Ex. 46, the contrast between the two unstable chords, II^{L6} and VII^{d7} of V, and the two strongly tonal chords, V^7 and I. The former underscore the lines of the text expressing the father's uncertainty; the latter, his discovery of the child's death.

Ex. 46   Schubert: *Erlkönig*

Gm: II^{L6}   VII^{d7} of V   V^7   I

Other resolutions of the Neapolitan sixth lead to I⁶ (Ex. 47) and V⁹ (Ex. 48).

Ex. 47   Mozart: Sonata, K. 284, last movement

Dm: II^{L6} I⁶   VII⁶

Ex. 48   Beethoven: Sonata, Op. 90

When, in the Romantic period, altered chords functioned with greater freedom, the Neapolitan II, used until then mainly in first inversion, began to appear also in root position. As in so many other areas, Beethoven foreshadowed the Romantics in this respect as well. Note in Ex. 49 the resolution of the Neapolitan root-position triad (LII) to V⁶. The diminished third, often characteristic of melodic progressions involving the II^{L6}, now appears in the bass (*a*).

Ex. 49   Beethoven: Sonata, Op. 31, No. 2, last movement

In minor especially, the lowered II is frequently preceded by a lowered VI, which has the effect of a secondary dominant (Ex. 50). Such use of altered chords serves to broaden the tonal boundaries of a key.

Ex. 50   Chopin: Prelude, Op. 28, No. 20

Most commonly found in minor, the Neapolitan root-position chord sometimes appears in the major mode as well.

Ex. 51   Brahms: Intermezzo, Op. 119, No. 3

The Augmented Fifth Chord

The history of Romantic music is the record of a constant search for more intense means of expression, and consequently for ever new forms of chromatic harmony. In addition to modal mixtures, borrowed triads, and augmented and Neapolitan sixth chords, the early Romanticists began to experiment with the *augmented fifth chord*.

Identical in structure with III of harmonic minor, the A5 chord is formed in major by chromatically raising the fifth of a major triad (usually I or V). Because the perfect fifth played such a fundamental role in traditional music, alteration of that interval was considered a drastic step, to be undertaken only after careful preparation. At first the augmented fifth occurred as a chromatic passing tone, rising from 5 to 6.

Ex. 52   Schumann: *Fabel*, from *Fantasiestücke*, Op. 12

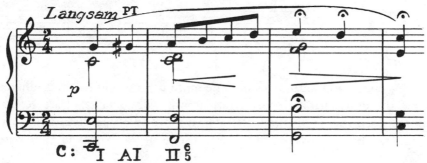

Sometimes the augmented fifth appears over a I⁶—usually as a passing chord between I and IV (Exs. 53–54).

Ex. 53   Augmented I⁶ as passing chord

Ex. 54   Schumann: A Little Study, from *Album for the Young*, Op. 68, No. 14

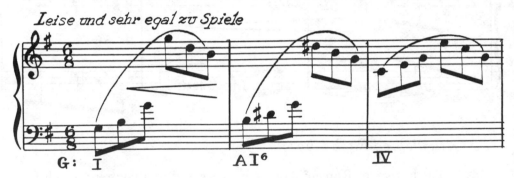

In the normal resolution of the A5 chord, the augmented fifth resolves upward a half step and the root of the chord down a falling fifth. Ex. 54 shows the progression AI⁶—IV, and Ex. 55, AV⁶—I.

Ex. 55   Brahms: Piano Concerto No. 2, Op. 83

As chromatic harmonies became more common in the mid-nineteenth century, the conventions regarding their use were relaxed. Late Romantic composers used the augmented fifth chord more freely; it became a favorite of Wagner, who employed it in the weird song of the Norns (Ex. 56) and in the theme of Siegfried's unearthly love of Brunnhilde (Ex. 57). Note in the latter that the augmented fifth on V does not resolve directly to I, but, with its bass descending chromatically, passes through VII^7 of V and V$^4_2$ before reaching I^6.

Ex. 56   Wagner: Prelude to *Götterdämmerung*

Ex. 57   Wagner: *Siegfried*, Act III

Liszt was even more daring in his use of augmented triads, introducing them in a parallel chromatic series. The opening of his *Faust* Symphony anticipated twentieth-century practice in its freedom of harmonic movement and the deliberate vagueness of its tonality.

Ex. 58   Liszt: A *Faust* Symphony

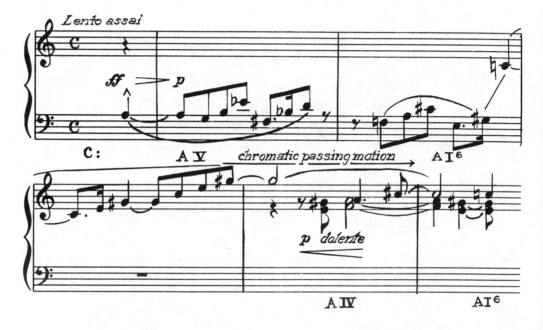

It was but a step from such consecutive augmented triads to their completely free use in the whole-tone scale—a procedure we shall consider in Chapter XII.

Linear and Free Chromaticism

In the last years of the nineteenth and the first years of the twentieth century, chromatic harmony became increasingly more complex. Composers vied with each other in creating highly charged harmonic textures, made up largely of altered and borrowed chords moving in irregular resolutions. Altered triads, seventh chords, and ninth chords now appeared in such concentration as to make traditional methods of analysis based on diatonic functions almost irrelevant. Highly chromatic music, while still maintaining links to the past, gradually became emancipated from reliance on root movement as a basic force. In many works of Wagner, Strauss, Franck, and Mahler, motion is generated by the linear progression of voices and by the search for variation of color and texture rather than by the connection of block chords. Chromatic music becomes most intelligible when viewed as the product of *moving lines and changing colors.*

Linear chromaticism was already at work in Beethoven.*

Ex. 59   Beethoven: Sonata, Op. 13 (*Pathétique*)

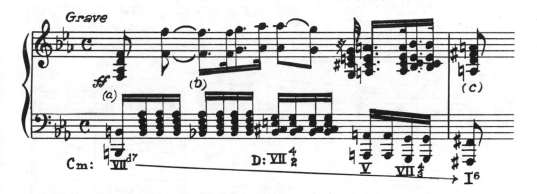

According to traditional analysis, the second chord (Ex. 59, *b*) would be labeled V⁷ of E flat. But this chord neither arises from nor leads into that key. A more logical view reveals the V⁷ as a passing chord, resulting from the linear chromatic motion of the outer voices. The bass descends step by step from B natural (*a*) to F sharp (*c*), and the harmony moves from C minor to D major. The chord at (*b*) is an interim stage, deriving entirely from the chromatic progression of the bass.

Chromatic contrary motion in the outer voices often gives rise to harmonies of considerable color and complexity.

Ex. 60   Beethoven: Variation 15, from *Diabelli* Variations, Op. 120

* For still earlier examples, see Ex. 1, page 305, and the Claude le Jeune example in *Workbook,* Volume II, Chapter X, Exercise 20.

After eight bars of almost elementary C major, the upper and lower voices of Ex. 60 suddenly begin a diverging chromatic movement (*a*). The slow ascent of the soprano and descent of the bass in half steps produces a series of dark, wandering harmonies, moving apparently into distant flat keys and furnishing an abrupt change from a light-hearted to a distinctly somber mood. Yet no modulation takes place, for no second key is ever established. The chromatic passing chords produce a temporary tonal ambiguity: the key becomes indefinite and the harmonic direction obscure.* Suddenly, the confusion is dispelled (*d*), and diatonic C major reappears as sweetly as though it had never been interrupted.

As in Ex. 59, there is little point in labeling each of the chromatic chords with a specific chord symbol. Identifying the harmony at (*b*), for instance, as I$^6_4$ of B flat minor (the traditional approach) casts no light on its function or character.† This and the other chromatic chords between (*a*) and (*d*) are more accurately viewed as passing harmonies resulting from linear chromatic motion of the outer voices.

---

* Similar to the tonal ambiguity produced by diminished sevenths (pages 170–172).

† Chord-by-chord labeling makes even less sense at (*c*), which conventional analysis might describe as "V$^4_2$ of B major, with enharmonic spelling of the alto and tenor"— truly an artificial description of a chord that is simply a result of chromatic motion of the outer voices.

In Ex. 61 the progression derives from the falling chromatic bass line, which leads broadly from the IV$^6_4$ at (*a*) to the V^7 at (*d*), passing through a series of chromatic chords on the way. (Note especially *b* and *c*.) A subtle harmonist, Chopin developed suspense by avoiding the tonic at the outset,* keeping the harmonic motion fluid and the key uncertain until the phrase attains a clear tonal statement at the half cadence (*d*).†

Ex. 61   Chopin: Mazurka, Op. 17, No. 4

Example 61 also illustrates another common technique of chromatic harmony—the retention of the common tone while one or two other voices of a chord move by half step, creating a different harmony. Thus, just before (*c*), the D sharp in the left hand repeats over the barline (enharmonically changed to E flat)‡ while the two lowest voices move downward chromatically, producing a radical change of chord.

* Beethoven and the Romantics after him often sought for such tonally vague openings, beginning a composition on chords other than I. See Exs. 20 (page 15), and 58 (page 282); also Ex. 42, page 334, Volume I.

† For other examples by Chopin of falling chromatic movement, see page 326 of this volume and 11 of Volume I.

‡ For enharmonic change, see page 307.

In the famous "sleep" motive from Wagner's *Die Walküre*, linear chromaticism and fluid tonality attain the utmost freedom. Following two broadly convergent lines,* the phrase starts in E major (Ex. 62, *a*), leads through a series of varied chromatic colors in a shifting, indefinite tonality, which becomes definite only at the return to the original chord (*b*). Flowing chromaticism suggests here a dream-like vagueness—a lovely musical image of the stage action, in which the god casts a spell of sleep over his daughter.

In this type of passage, harmony serves almost entirely for the creation of mood; functional chord progression ceases to exist.† Yet there is no uncertainty of movement; the clear, converging lines of soprano and bass carry the music inevitably forward. The emergence of a definite key at the end of the phrase is most satisfying after the prevailing tonal vagueness.

Ex. 62   Wagner: Sleep motive from *Die Walküre*, Act III

---

* The outline beneath Ex. 62 disregards octave shifts.

† Thus foreshadowing a basic characteristic of twentieth-century harmony (see page 349).

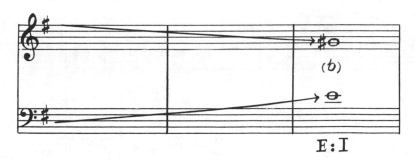

E:I

While viewing chromatic progressions as the product of free linear motion, we cannot overlook differences in the structure of the chords employed. In Ex. 62, triads and their inversions form the core of the harmony, with a few altered seventh chords to bind the phrase together. Compare the lucidity of such harmonies with the tense, intricately woven textures of another chromatic composition, the Prelude to *Tristan*.

Ex. 63   Wagner: Prelude to *Tristan and Isolde*

Apart from a chord-by-chord analysis of Ex. 63 (and many have been made detailing the chromatic complexities of this celebrated work), we gain deeper insight into the nature of the composition by charting its broad harmonic movement. We might begin an over-all view of the harmonic plan by noting that the opening bars suggest the key of A minor, although (as in Ex. 61) the A minor triad is nowhere stated. The V⁷ of that key (*a*) resolves not to its tonic but to the V⁷ of C (*b*), and then to the V⁷ of E (*c*)—a series of modulations by rising thirds. The latter chord is stressed by repetition.

At (d) the harmony moves back toward A minor, but, deflected in its course by a deceptive cadence, turns toward D minor at (e). Again a cadence is interrupted, at (f), by the chromatic ascent of the bass, which leads finally to the first tonic cadence of the entire work—the I of A *major* (at g). Notice how carefully Wagner avoided making even this cadence too definitive: it occurs on the second half of the bar, and the top line contains a chromatic suspension which, resolving upward on the fifth eighth note, keeps the movement fluid. Constant avoidance of the perfect cadence is a basic harmonic characteristic of *Tristan*.

It is worth noting that the tonal pattern in the first 24 bars of *Tristan* moves from the tonic key A minor to E, the dominant (at c); through D minor, the subdominant (at e); finally reaching an imperfect cadence in A (at g). The plan I–V–IV–I is a broad affirmation of the central tonality A minor. What Orlando di Lasso did in four chords, and Bach in four bars, Wagner expanded to 24 bars. Thus, beneath all the chromatic complexities of *Tristan*, there lies a solid framework of tonality, conceived on a large scale.

Compared with Ex. 62, the harmonies of the *Tristan* Prelude are complex and close-textured, including a high proportion of seventh and ninth chords embellished by chromatic appoggiaturas and suspensions. Together with the distinctive melodic figures, they brought the chromatic style to a height of intensity and emotional power. *Tristan* remains to this day the unsurpassed masterpiece of chromaticism.

Once their chords are analyzed, the chromatic compositions of Wagner, Strauss, Mahler, and other late Romantic composers are best studied in broad harmonic lines. Seen in perspective, they represent a turning point in the evolution of musical thought, when traditional harmony was about to give way to the new concepts of twentieth-century music—the subject of Chapters XII and XIII.

Summary

1. Modal mixtures and borrowings are tones and chords of one mode used in another.

2. Borrowed chords include:
   a. In major—the minor I and IV, dII, lowered VI, V^{m9}, and VII^{d7} (all borrowed from minor).
   b. In minor, the major I (borrowed from major).
   c. Chords borrowed from more distant keys.

3. Modal mixtures vary in extent from a single tone or chord to an entire phrase.

4. Tonal diversions involve temporary emphasis on tonal centers outside the key; they widen the tonality.

5. Secondary tonics are scale degrees other than I, preceded by reiterated secondary dominants, without involving modulation.

6. Tonal regions are secondary areas of a key, based on secondary degrees, borrowed or altered chords.

7. Altered chords are those containing chromatic tones not found in the diatonic modes of a key.
   a. They add drive and color to the harmony.
   b. Most commonly used are the augmented and Neapolitan sixths and the augmented fifth chord.

8. The augmented sixth chord (A6) contains that interval in its structure.
   a. Its three forms are the Italian ($^{A6}_3$), German ($^{A6}_5$), and French ($^{A6}_{A4}$) sixths.
   b. It occurs mainly as the IV^{A6} and V^{A6}_{A4}.
   c. The A6 chord is prepared:
      i. Traditionally, by stepwise motion to the altered tones.
      ii. In free style, by the leap of one voice.
   d. Its voices resolve in the direction of their alteration; the chord resolves:
      i. IV^{A6} to V, V^7, or I^6_4.
      ii. V^{A6}_{A4} to I.

9. The Neapolitan sixth (II^{L6}) is a II^6 with lowered root and fifth.
   a. It resolves to V, V^7, I^6_4; irregularly to VII^{d7} of V.
   b. The sixth and third resolve downward, the bass up.
   c. The Neapolitan chord also occurs in root position (lowered II), resolving usually to V^6.

10. The augmented fifth chord (A5) is a triad with a chromatically raised fifth.
    a. It occurs mainly on I and V in major.
    b. Traditionally, the augmented fifth is prepared and resolved by rising chromatic motion; the bass generally resolves to the fifth below.
    c. In free style, it can be approached by leap.
    d. In late Romantic and modern styles, parallel augmented triads can appear in a series.

11. In linear and free chromaticism, chromatic chords result from moving lines and changing colors rather than from functional root movements.
    a. Altered and borrowed chords often resolve freely.
    b. Harmonic progression is to be viewed in broadly linear fashion from one tonal point to another, rather than from one chord to another.
    c. A broad tonal framework often underlies the complexities of chromatic chord structure.

Dramatic Sources
of Harmony
and Melody

The word "dramatic" has been freely used throughout these volumes, as have "mood," "tension," "contrast," "development," and "climax." While important to some extent in all the arts, they have particular relevance in the drama—to which music, as we have seen, has often been closely related. The close association of music with the theater has led to the rise of great musical forms: directly, opera, the overture, and ballet music; and indirectly, the passion, the oratorio, the cantata, and the symphony.

Dramatic motivations played a large part in the development of harmony. The birth of opera was contemporary with the flowering of the chordal technique; early opera composers adopted accompanied melody as a basic dramatic style. Since their theatrical interests led them to concentrate mainly on melody and harmony, their contributions were inevitably large in both areas. The needs of the drama led to the evolution of certain techniques that, appearing first in theater music, later entered the mainstream of the musical language.

291

Mood, tension, contrast, development, and climax—basic forces in the theater—penetrated from words and action into the structure of melodies sung onstage and of harmonies played as accompaniment.* Analysis of these dramatic elements involves a summary of virtually our entire discussion.

Mood in Melody and Harmony

"Setting the stage" by an appropriate musical mood is the first step in a musico-dramatic work. The opening chords of any opera, musical comedy, motion picture, or ballet score suggest the character of the action to follow. From the first measures the audience quickly knows whether it is to be plunged into a comedy, a tragedy, a romantic drama, or an opera with an exotic locale. Compare the gaiety of *The Marriage of Figaro* Overture with the bleakness of the Prelude to *Boris Godunov*. Both start with unaccompanied melodies; but Ex. 64, in the major mode, is fast and scintillating; Ex. 65, in Aeolian mode, is slow and somewhat somber.

Ex. 64   Mozart: Overture to *The Marriage of Figaro*

Ex. 65   Moussorgsky: Prelude to *Boris Godunov*

* The drama was not, of course, the sole generator of these forces in music. Religious, poetic, dance, and other functions have also played important roles.

Lest the contrast of Exs. 64 and 65 be construed simply as a difference in the style of two composers, a similar diversity can be found in two works by the same man. The opening of Wagner's *Die Meistersinger*, with its straightforward C major harmony and sturdy block-chord progression (*a*), announces a story of robust characters from the German past, the Mastersingers of Nuremberg.

Ex. 66   Wagner: Prelude to *Die Meistersinger von Nürnberg*

The chromatic melody and harmonies of the *Tristan* Prelude, on the other hand, presage the tense drama of the two Wagnerian lovers.

Ex. 67   Wagner: Prelude to *Tristan and Isolde**

* See also the longer excerpt on pages 287–288.

Differences of mood in dramatic music are developed by differences of mode, interval, melodic curve, motive, rhythm, tempo, harmonic structure and intensity.

Tension and Contrast in Melody and Harmony

Melodic tension can be created by a rising wave or sequence, dissonant embellishing tones or intervals, or the substitution of irregular for regular rhythms or phrase lengths. Harmonic tension results from the appearance of dissonant chords, faster harmonic rhythms, abrupt modulations, or heavy in place of light textures.* The use of tension-producing melodic and harmonic techniques helps to develop the heightened moods characteristic of dramatic music.

Contrast arises from the juxtaposition of musical opposites. Differences in characterization are emphasized by differences in melodic style. In *Carmen,* for example, the insinuating chromaticism of Carmen's music† contrasts with the naïve diatonic phrases of Micaela; and in *Porgy and Bess,* the sliding intervals of Sportin' Life's "It Ain't Necessarily So" contrasts with the diatonic blues melody of Porgy's "Bess, You Is My Woman Now."

Rhythm, too, serves as a means of dramatic differentiation. Contrasts between characters, scenes, or situations are underscored by the opposition of fast and slow tempos, calm and exciting rhythms, regular and irregular phrase lengths, or rising and falling melodic curves. A sharp dramatic reversal often calls forth an abrupt shift of rhythm, melody, or harmonic intensity. Thus, the moment when Tosca discovers her lover's murder is signalled by sudden alterations in tempo, key, dynamics, texture, and other elements. In the theater, dramatic contrast is the source of musical contrast.

Harmonic contrasts also contribute to dramatic characterization: in Wagner's *Tannhäuser,* the simple triads of the Pilgrim's Chorus as opposed to the lush chromatic chords of the Venusberg music; or the contrast of keys in Monteverdi's *Orfeo*—straightforward E major for the Messenger's factual narration, dark G minor for Orfeo's despairing outcry.‡

* On this point, review pages 240–245. A continuous play of tension is an important element in a harmonic progression, as in a drama. The resolution should not come until the very end—in a play, the final curtain; in a harmonic progression, the perfect cadence.

† As in the "Habañera," page 21, Volume I.

‡ See page 36.

Development in Dramatic Music

Development is the essence of drama. Without changes of mood, situation, and the relationship of characters, a play or opera becomes static and ceases to hold our interest. In the musical theater, development includes progress not only of the story but also of its musical embodiment. When a character moves from devil-may-care gaiety to tragic downfall—as does Don Giovanni, for example—his music evolves from transparent melodic and harmonic patterns into darker, more intricate ones. Thus, in Act I of the opera, Don Giovanni's "Champagne" aria has a triadic melody and the simplest of chords.

Ex. 68   Mozart: *Finch' han dal vino*, from *Don Giovanni*, Act I

Toward the end of the opera, when the hero confronts the awesome stone figure of the Commander, his song becomes more violent, its harmonies more intense.

Ex. 69   Mozart: Finale, from *Don Giovanni*, Act II

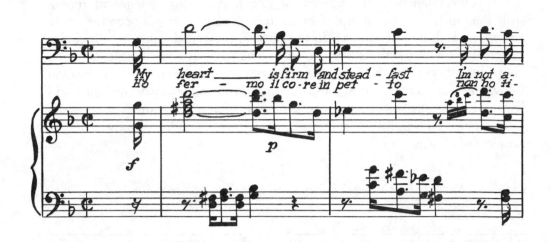

Development of character and situation have led opera composers to corresponding musical developments.* Masters of dramatic music have been masters of the techniques of development: Monteverdi, Purcell, Mozart, Wagner, Verdi, Puccini, and Berg in opera; Schütz, Bach, Handel, and Honegger in oratorio, passion, and cantata; Tchaikovsky and Stravinsky in ballet music; Walton and Prokofiev in film music.

* Compare the discussion of musical development as such, pages 182–186.

Climax in Dramatic Music

The culmination of every dramatic score is a convincing climax. Like a good melody, a good play and a good opera often have not one but a series of climaxes, graded in steadily mounting steps, with the highest near the end.*

As with contrast and development, specific musical techniques serve to build a climax; among them are melodic high points, heightened harmonic intensities, faster tempos and rhythms, abrupt modulations, tightened or expanded phrase lengths, and fuller textures. Several or all of these techniques appear in such climactic scenes as the death of Boris, the murder of Carmen, the burning of Valhalla in Wagner's *Götterdämmerung*, the death of Wozzeck, and the departure of Porgy for New York. The composer marshalls all his forces—the utmost intensity of melody, rhythm, harmony, and texture—to achieve the final climax of a musico-dramatic work.

Dramatic Techniques in Instrumental Music

As already noted, musical techniques originating in the theater soon found their way into choral and instrumental music. Bach used sudden harmonic contrasts, sharp changes of rhythm and dynamics, and abrupt modulations in dramatic and abstract compositions alike. In *The St. Matthew Passion*, when Pontius Pilate asks whom to set free, Jesus or the robber Barabbas, the High Priests answer "Barabbas!"; after the simple musical setting of Pilate's question, the sudden outburst of the crowd on a *fortissimo* diminished seventh chord in a foreign key is electrifying.

Ex. 70   Bach: *The St. Matthew Passion*

*Quiet endings, like those of *Boris Godunov* and *Wozzeck*, provide exceptions that prove the rule. Their understatements are ironic.

More intimate but not different in kind is a dramatic contrast in one of the preludes from *The Well-Tempered Clavier*. After a long two-voice passage in flowing sixteenth notes, the movement is suddenly halted by a ten-voice diminished seventh chord over a dissonant pedal (Ex. 71, *a*).

Ex. 71   Bach: Prelude No. 5, from *The Well-Tempered Clavier*, Book I*

Abrupt changes from consonant to dissonant harmony, from flowing to arrested rhythm, or from light to heavy texture create the same effect whether they occur in Bach's instrumental works or in his dramatic music.

Beethoven, many of whose sonatas and symphonies have an intrinsically dramatic structure, often employed the methods of a stage composer in constructing his purely instrumental compositions. Think of the long drum roll in the transition between the third and fourth movements of the Fifth Symphony, and the entry of the trombones on the C major triad; or of the ferociously dissonant chord ushering in the last movement of the Ninth Symphony (Ex. 72, *a*). What is more theatrical than the sudden intrusion of the baritone recitative (*b*) in that movement?

* For the measures preceding this passage, see pages 242–244.

Ex. 72   Beethoven: Symphony No. 9, Op. 125, last movement

An objection may be made, however, that the Ninth Symphony is virtually a dramatic work—scarcely the standard symphony. What then of the *Tempest* Sonata, written many years earlier?

Ex. 73   Beethoven: Sonata, Op. 31, No. 2 (*Tempest*)

In this purely instrumental work, Beethoven changes tempo twice in ten bars; he switches from the running eighth notes of the Allegro to a sustained dissonant chord at Adagio, and then, in an abrupt modulation, to a serene C major at Largo. The contemplative recitative (*a*) forms a striking contrast to the agitation of the preceding passage. The similarity in dramatic quality to the Ninth Symphony recitative is unmistakable.

We need not labor the point; dramatic techniques are imbedded in the structure of such instrumental works as Mozart's Fantasy in C minor, Berlioz' *Fantastic* Symphony, Tchaikovsky's *Romeo and Juliet* Overture, many compositions of Schönberg and Stravinsky, Shostakovich's Fifth Symphony and Ives' Fourth, and Bartók's Concerto for Orchestra.

They appear in smaller instrumental compositions as well. To name only three, climax, contrast, and mounting tension occur in even the shortest pieces. The sudden appearance of a secondary dominant at the peak of Chopin's Prelude in A major (page 240) illustrates the first element, and the abrupt rise in harmonic intensity in the second half of Schubert's Ecossaise (page 245) illustrates the other two.* Taken in perspective, dramatic structure has been one of the great forces in the evolution of Western music, whether in large or small, theatrical or instrumental forms.

---

* Mounting tension and climax are further illustrated in Brahms' Waltz in A flat, pages 182–183.

Summary

1. The drama has had an important influence on music, on the evolution of melodic and harmonic techniques and of such forms as opera, oratorio, passion, and symphony.

2. Dramatic elements, such as mood, tension, contrast, development, and climax, have penetrated from words and action into melodic and harmonic techniques.

3. Mood is expressed musically through the choice of certain intervals, modes, rhythms, melodic curves, harmonic structures, and levels of intensity.

4. Tension is advanced in dramatic music by such melodic techniques as the use of unstable intervals, asymmetrical phrases, and quicker motive repetition; and by such harmonic techniques as faster harmonic rhythm, abrupt modulation, and the use of dissonant chords.

5. Contrast is developed through the opposition of various tempos, textures, rhythms, modes, and harmonic structures.

6. Development is expressed by denser textures, more complex harmonies, tighter phrase lengths, more active rhythms, and the like.

7. Climaxes are built by graded harmonic intensities, faster harmonic rhythms, the use of melodic high points, tightening or expansion of phrase lengths, and combinations of these techniques.

8. Originating in the theater, musico-dramatic techniques entered the mainstream of musical practice, becoming an inherent part of many abstract compositions in small and large forms.

XI

Modulation to Distant Keys

Distant modulations, often identified with Romantic music, were already known in the late Renaissance, as witness the works of Monteverdi, Marenzio, Claude le Jeune, and others. From the start, such modulations were associated with the expression of intense, highly personal emotions. In a madrigal of Gesualdo da Venosa, printed in 1611, the words "I die, alas! from my pain" were set to music modulating rapidly from C sharp major to A minor.

Ex. 1   Gesualdo da Venosa: *Moro Lasso*

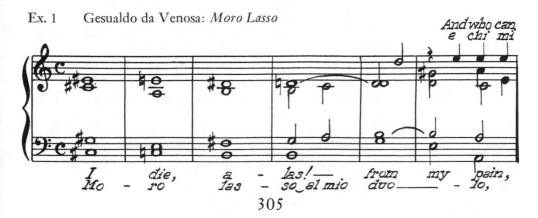

When, in the Baroque period, major-minor harmony developed into a highly formal system, close modulations became the rule. Modulations to distant keys occurred only in exceptionally dramatic moments in opera and oratorio* and in instrumental fantasias—compositions of a free, improvisatory character.† The Classical period saw the reappearance of distant modulations, in the development sections of certain Haydn and Mozart compositions; later they became a basic element of Beethoven's technique. Romantic music derived much of its color and intensity from a wide modulatory freedom.

Degrees of Distance

Distant keys are those separated by more than one accidental from the home key. Modulations vary in distance, their force often increasing with the number of sharps or flats added. Modulatory distance is measured by the *circle of fifths*.‡

Ex. 2   Circle of fifths

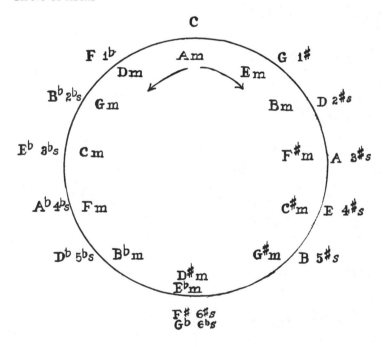

It is apparent from Ex. 2 that the modulation C to E (four sharps distant) is a more decisive step than the one from C to D (only two sharps away). Similarly, a change of key from C to B flat (a distance of two flats)

---

* See Ex. 1, page 36.

† Outstanding among Baroque fantasias are the Bach Chromatic Fantasy and his Fantasy in G minor for Organ. For a distinguished Classical example, see the Mozart Fantasy in C minor, pages 327–328.

‡ Not to be confused with the *cycle* of fifths (see page 227 of Volume I).

does not carry as much weight as one from C to D flat (five flats away). The furthest modulation leads diametrically across the circle of fifths, a distance of six sharps or flats—for example, from C to F sharp or G flat.

Modulations may move in the sharp (clockwise) or flat (counterclockwise) direction. Those crossing the bottom of the circle—F sharp–G flat—often require *enharmonic change**—notation of the same tone in a different manner. (For example, F sharp is the enharmonic equivalent of G flat; and B flat, of A sharp.)

One can modulate to distant keys in various ways, by the use of:

1. Pivot chords—diatonic or borrowed triads.
2. Pivot tones.
3. Diminished seventh chords.
4. Altered chords.
5. Sequences.
6. Chromatic bass motion.
7. Abrupt leaps into the new key.

Let us examine each method in turn.

Modulation by Diatonic Triad

A major key shares diatonic pivot chords with only four distant keys: (1) the major supertonic, (2) the major subtonic, and (3 and 4) the relative minors of both. In each of these modulations, there are two pivot chords (marked with asterisks in Ex. 3).

Ex. 3   (a) Pivot chords between major key and its major supertonic

(b) Pivot chords between major key and its major subtonic

* See Ex. 9, page 311, and Ex. 16, page 315.

Modulation by these pivot chords is quite rare. When it does occur (Ex. 4), it follows the four traditional stages: (1) establishment of the home key (*a*), (2) motion through a pivot chord or chords (*b*) and (*c*), (3) entry into the new key (*d*), and (4) cadence confirming the new key (*e*).

Ex. 4   Dvorak: *Carnival* Overture, Op. 92

Modulation by Borrowed Chord

Borrowed chords frequently serve as pivots in distant modulations from major. Minor I and IV and lowered III and VI are particularly valuable as pivots to keys in the flat direction. A change from major to its *parallel minor*—C major to C minor, for example—requires only a shift to the minor tonic, followed by a cadence. In Ex. 5, a minor tonic (*b*) replaces the major one (*a*). Such an interchange of mode is especially common in Schubert and Brahms.

Ex. 5   Schubert: *Gute Nacht*

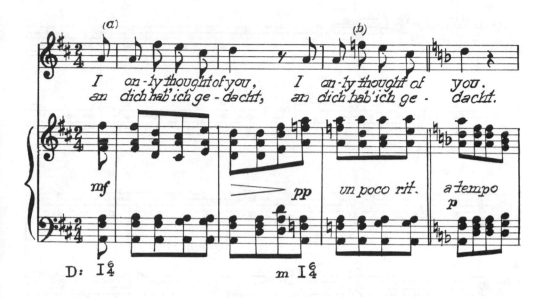

The minor I also serves in modulating to lowered III—in Ex. 6 from C to E flat major, and in Ex. 7 from B to D major. The borrowed chord is marked (*a*) in both examples.

Ex. 6   Schubert: *Valse sentimentale*, Op. 60, No. 2

Ex. 7   Beethoven: Symphony No. 9, Op. 125, last movement

Another modulatory pathway opened by the minor tonic leads from major to its lowered VI: from F to D flat in Ex. 8 (the pivot chord is marked *a*).

Ex. 8   Beethoven: Symphony No. 3 (*Eroica*), Op. 55

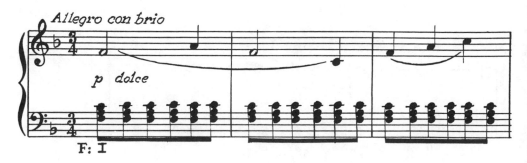

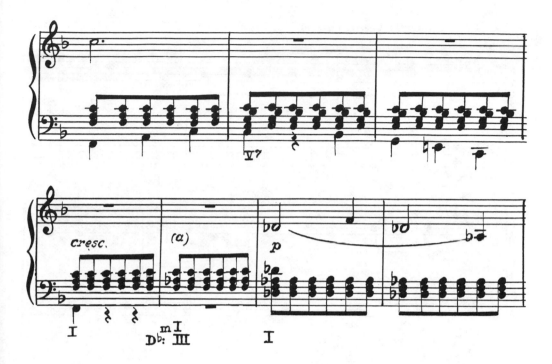

Modulation to lowered VI involves a move of four steps in the flat direction. In Ex. 10, the music shifts (*a*) from A flat to the theoretical key of F flat. To avoid a key with double flats in its signature, Schubert substituted the enharmonic equivalent E major, as shown in the diagram (Ex. 9).

Ex. 9   Circle of fifths, with enharmonic change

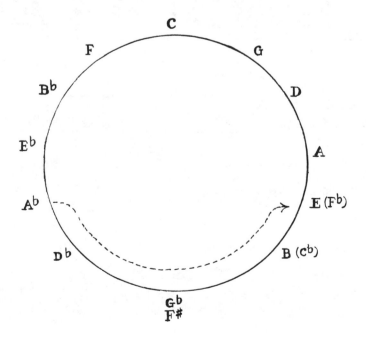

Ex. 10   Schubert: Waltz, Op. 9a, No. 2

Minor IV is most useful in modulations to keys in the flat (counter-clockwise) direction. Ex. 11 shows its role as a pivot chord leading to lowered VI, and Ex. 12, to lowered III.

Ex. 11   Beethoven: Sonata, Op. 106 (*Hammerklavier*)

Ex. 12   Chopin: Mazurka, Op. 50, No. 1

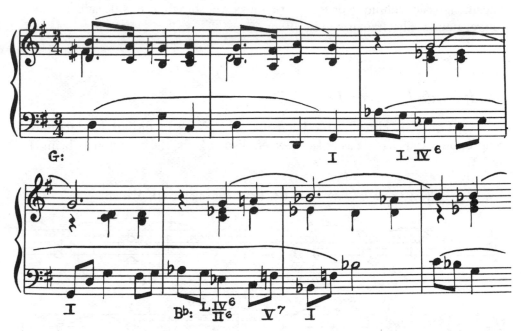

Borrowed chords are rarely used as pivots in minor. Two chords characteristic of major—major IV and V—already exist as variable triads in the minor mode. Major I, when followed by V, can produce a modulation to the *parallel major* key, which creates a brightening of mood.*

Ex. 13   Schubert: *Gräzer* Waltz, Op. 91a, No. 9

* The major I also appears in minor as V of IV. See page 4, 1 (*c*), and page 87, Ex. 15 (*d*).

Modulation by borrowed chords, previously a dramatic device, became a basic technique of Romantic music (as shown in Exs. 12 and 13), no longer necessarily dramatic in its effect.

Modulation by Pivot Tone

Thus far, chords have been the sole pivots in distant modulations. Single tones can also act as links between distant keys, the commonest being 1 and 3.

Ex. 14   Pivot tones leading to L VI, L II, and major III, VI, and VII

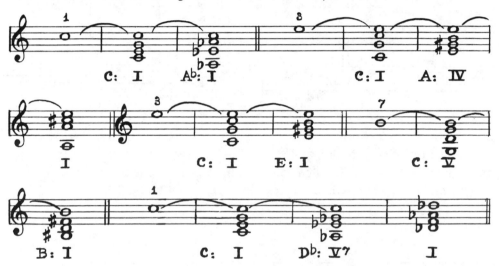

The tonic, harmonized as 3 of lowered VI, forms a link between I and L VI. Thus 1 of D major, sustained over the double bar (Ex. 15), becomes 3 of B flat (L VI of D). With this tone as pivot, the music moves abruptly into the new key. Such modulations usually occur at cadences and at large form divisions—in Ex. 15, between Parts I and II of a three-part form.

Ex. 15   Chopin: Mazurka, Op. 33, No. 2

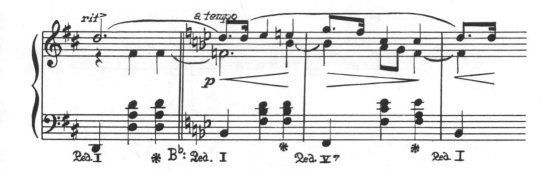

A pivot tone, like a pivot chord, can serve in enharmonic as well as other modulations. Ex. 16 shows the tonic of D flat (*a*) sustained over the double bar and changed enharmonically into C sharp (*b*), 3 of A major.

Ex. 16   Chopin: Mazurka, Op. 7, No. 4

Another pivot-tone modulation leads to the major VI—a key with three sharps more than the original. In this modulation, 3 of the home key acts as pivot, becoming 5 of the new key. In Ex. 17 we find B, 3 of G major (in an inner voice at *a*), changed into 5 of E major, at (*b*).

Ex. 17   Schubert: *Hommage aux belles Viennoises*, Op. 67, No. 1

When 3 of a major key becomes 1 of another, a modulation is made to the major III, a key with four added sharps. In Ex. 18 (*a*), the change leads from A to C sharp major.

Ex. 18   Schubert: *Valse sentimentale*, Op. 50, No. 5

In the distant modulations discussed so far, 1 and 3 of the home key have assumed different roles in the tonic triads of other keys. The 1 can also become a new 7; such a change leads to lowered II, a key with five flats more than the original. In Ex. 19 (*a*), 1 of C major is re-harmonized (*b*) as 7 of D flat, producing a rapid modulation to that key.

Ex. 19   Chopin: Mazurka, Op. 24, No. 2

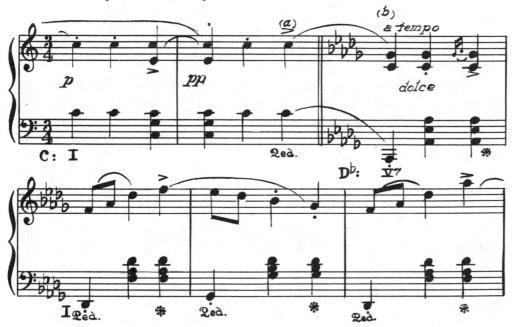

Note that the pivot tone in Ex. 19, instead of being sustained in the same part, shifts from the upper to a middle voice. Such octave displacements are quite common in modulation; they do not impair the pivot function of a tone linking two keys.

Modulation by Diminished Seventh Chord

The diminished seventh chord has already appeared as a modulatory link between closely related keys. It serves equally well in distant modulations, mainly through the use of enharmonic changes. Because the component intervals of the VII⁷ are all of the same size, one tone of the chord can easily assume the role of another; by a simple change in spelling, the third, fifth, or seventh can become the root of a VII⁷ in another key. Thus if we change the notation of the seventh of the VII⁷ of C minor from A flat to G sharp, it becomes the *root* of the VII⁷ of A minor.

Ex. 20   Enharmonic change in VII^d7

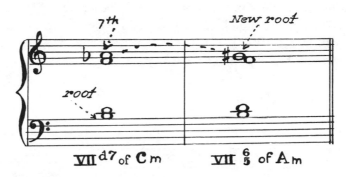

Through such enharmonic changes the VII^d7 can lead into distant keys. The chords at (a) and (b) in Ex. 21 are identical in sound. By appearing first in one notation (as VII^d7 of C minor) and then in another (as VII^d7 of A minor) the chord reveals its *multiple meaning* and its role as a modulating chord.

Ex. 21   The VII^d7 as enharmonic modulating chord

At the beginning of the development section of Beethoven's Sonata *Pathétique* (Ex. 22), the VII⁴₂ of G minor appears at (a). With one of its notes enharmonically changed from E flat to D sharp, it is transformed into VII⁴₂ of E minor (b), opening the path into that key.

Ex. 22   Beethoven: Sonata, Op. 13 (*Pathétique*)

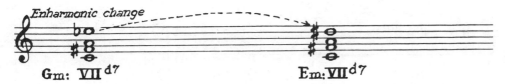

Enharmonic change of *all four* tones of the VII^{d7} (Ex. 23, *a*) provides a modulatory link between F sharp and E flat major.

Ex. 23   Beethoven: Sonata, Op. 106 (*Hammerklavier*), third movement

Instead of leading directly to I of the new key, the enharmonically changed VII^{d7} often moves first to V of that key. In Beethoven's *Eroica* Symphony, VII^{d7} of V of E flat is sounded for four bars (Ex. 24, *a*). After three bars of other harmonies, the same chord returns (*b*) acting now, however, as the VII^{d7} of D flat, and resolving first to V (*c*), then to I of that key.

Ex. 24   Beethoven: Symphony No. 3 (*Eroica*), Op. 55

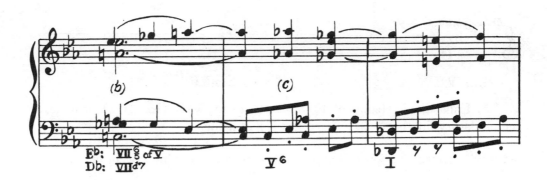

The ambiguity of the diminished seventh chord is frequently exploited for its suspense value. In Ex. 25, the music has just left the key of G.
The VII^{d7} at (*a*) appears in an intermediate area, where its tonality is unclear.
To which key will it lead—F minor? A flat? D minor? From the mere
reiteration of the chord, one cannot tell. Beethoven draws out the uncertainty
for 26 bars (only 16 shown here), until, by changing one note (*b*) he arrives
at a totally unexpected chord and key: V of B major.

Ex. 25   Beethoven: Symphony No. 4, Op. 60

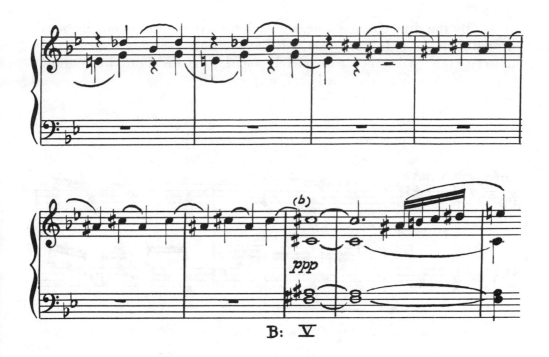

B: V

Modulation by Altered Chords

Altered chords are among the most striking means of modulation to distant keys, especially to those keys one half step (or five sharps or flats) away from a home tonic. Most commonly used are the augmented and Neapolitan sixth chords. Since the German sixth and V⁷ are identical in sound, one can be substituted for the other—a simple change in spelling being sufficient to lead into a new key. Thus in Ex. 26, the V⁷ of F, repeated with changed spelling (B flat = A sharp), becomes an augmented sixth chord, leading (*a*) into E major.

Ex. 26   Mozart: Sonata, K. 310

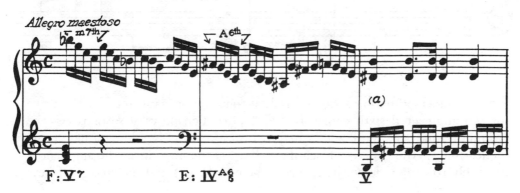

By the change of one note, a diminished seventh can become an augmented sixth chord. In Ex. 27 (*a*), VII^{d7} of II creates a sense of suspense and mystery (the tonality being completely vague); the A6 chord, by contrast (*b*), points directly to the new key, C major.

Ex. 27   Beethoven: Symphony No. 5, Op. 67, second movement

The modulating action of a pivot tone can be reinforced by the drive of the augmented sixth chord. In Ex. 28 (*a*) Tchaikovsky sustains A—the common tone between F and A major. Instead of simply adding a new tonic beneath it (in the manner of Schubert, Ex. 18), he introduces the augmented sixth chord, emphasizing the entry of the new I$_4^6$ (*b*) and the change of key.

Ex. 28   Tchaikovsky: Symphony No. 4, Op. 36, third movement

The Neapolitan sixth also serves in modulations to keys one half step above or below the home key. In modulating upward, a chord appearing first as a Neapolitan sixth (Ex. 29, *a*) is followed by its own dominant (*b*), and then becomes a new tonic (*c*). In modulating downward, a chord that starts as the tonic of F (Ex. 30, *a*) assumes the role of a Neapolitan sixth, resolving through a dominant chord (*b*) to the new tonic E major (*c*).

Ex. 29   Beethoven: Sonata, Op. 2, No. 2, second movement

Ex. 30   Beethoven: Sonata, Op. 14, No. 1, last movement

Distant Modulations through Sequence

The cycle of fifths, one of the strongest of modulating sequences, leads to distant as well as to closely related keys.* In such modulations, chromatic changes can be introduced, if necessary, with each chord of the cycle.

Ex. 31   Distant modulation by the cycle of fifths

Through one set of accidentals, the cycle leads to flat keys (Ex. 31, *a*); through another, to sharp keys (Ex. 31, *b*). Since each chord of the modulating cycle acts as the dominant of the next, the progression can lead almost anywhere. Example 32 shows a modulation from B flat major to the doorstep of C flat major.

* Compare pages 118–119.

Ex. 32   Chopin: Mazurka, Op. 67, No. 2

By similar addition of accidentals, other modulating sequences can also lead to distant keys. In Ex. 5, page 102, the first sequence appears in a key one tone (two flats) below the original pattern. In Ex. 14, page 108, each sequence appears in a key a minor third (three flats) above the preceding one.

Altered chords are also used in more complex modulating sequences, characteristic of late Romantic music. In Ex. 33 sequential modulations lead from V of A major (a) through V of B (b) and V of C sharp (c), to V of E flat major (d)—a distance of six accidentals in two bars! Note that these modulations occur without touching on the tonics of their respective keys— a technique characteristic of Wagner in his *Tristan* period.

Ex. 33   Wagner: *Tristan and Isolde*, Act I

Progressions such as those of Ex. 33 border on another method of leading to distant keys: modulation by chromatic bass movement.

Modulation by Chromatic Bass Movement

Another technique of distant modulation involves chromatic movement of the bass, often producing a fluid, ambiguous tonality. In Ex. 34 (*b* to *e*), the harmony consists of a series of chromatically falling seventh chords, connected by various altered tones. Masking the tonality for five bars, the chords reach a cadence in F minor, re-establishing the original key (*f*).

Ex. 34   Chopin: Mazurka, Op. 68, No. 4

When the first phrase of Ex. 34 is repeated, starting at (*g*), the bass again falls chromatically; but instead of returning to the original key, it leads first to V (*h*), and then to I of A major (*i*). Chromatic bass motion thus produces a distant modulation, from F minor to A major.

Brahms provides a simpler example of chromatic bass movement, leading from B minor to its subdominant.

Ex. 35   Brahms: Capriccio, Op. 76, No. 2

Sometimes a chromatic falling bass extends over a considerable distance. Note in Ex. 5, page 102, that each bass tone is held for two bars; seven bars are needed to get from C to A natural. In Ex. 36 the chromatic bass changes once in a bar. Falling a perfect fourth in seven bars, it touches on D major, F minor, C major, E flat minor, and B major, ending in G—quite an extraordinary tonal journey for an eighteenth-century composer!

Ex. 36   Mozart: Fantasy in C minor, K. 475

(Chord symbols in Ex. 36 are given for identification only; they do not imply modulation to all the keys touched on.)

Modulation by Leap

The final technique of distant modulation involves leaping into a new key without benefit of pivot chord or tone. Such abrupt modulations often have dramatic impact; they generally appear right after a cadence, where they will be most noticeable. In Ex. 37, a phrase cadences in D major; abruptly, the melody leaps into F major, continuing in that key.

Ex. 37   Beethoven: Sonata, Op. 31, No. 1

Abrupt modulatory leaps also occur at the end of a *section* of a composition. In Ex. 38, Part I of the waltz ends in A major; abruptly, Part II starts in F.*

Ex. 38   Schubert: *Hommage aux belles Viennoises*, Op. 67, No. 6

* For an abrupt modulation in the *middle* of a phrase, see Ex. 1, page 36, and Ex. 73, pages 301–302.

Where sudden modulations occur, a link can be provided by half-step motion of the melody or bass. Thus, the melodic movement D—D sharp (Ex. 39, *a*) serves as a binding element for the abrupt change from G to B major. Example 40 shows a half-step movement of the bass leading from I of A flat (*a*) to V⁷ of C (*b*).

Ex. 39   Beethoven: Sonata, Op. 106

Ex. 40   Chopin: Mazurka, Op. 33, No. 3

A series of half-step movements by two voices in contrary motion can also serve as a binder in distant modulation. Ex. 41 (*a*) shows a double chromatic progression from V of A flat minor to V of B minor.*

Ex. 41   Chopin: Mazurka, Op. 33, No. 4

* Compare the non-modulating linear chromaticism discussed on pages 283–284— especially Ex. 60.

Side-slipping is still another technique of abrupt modulation. While progressing normally, a phrase (Ex. 42) suddenly slides up or down one half step in parallel motion, continuing in a key seven sharps above or seven flats below the original key.

Ex. 42   Bizet: Gypsy Song, from *Carmen*, Act II

Underscoring the wild, shifting movements of Carmen's dance, the music, starting in F sharp major, suddenly drops into F (Ex. 42, *a*). (The change is emphasized by an abrupt alteration of dynamics from *pp* to *f*.) Returning to F sharp (*b*), the phrase slips down once more to F (*c*), reflecting the mercurial temperament of the heroine.

Summary

1. Distant modulations are those between keys whose signatures differ by by more than one accidental.

2. Such modulations are often associated with strong emotional expression.

3. The greater the number of sharps or flats dividing the two keys, the more forceful the modulation. The distance between keys is measured by the circle of fifths.

4. Enharmonic change is an alteration in the notation of a given tone, as from A flat to G sharp.

5. Diatonic chords can act as pivots between keys separated by two sharps or flats.

6. Borrowed triads, especially minor I and IV and L VI and L III in major, and major I in minor, serve as pivots in distant modulations.
   a. In major, minor I and IV lead to modulations in the flat direction.
   b. In minor, major I leads to the tonic major.

7. Single tones can also act as pivots in distant modulations.
   a. The 1 can lead to L VI and L II.
   b. The 3 can lead to the major VI and III.
   c. A pivot tone can shift from one voice to another.
   d. The spelling of a pivot tone can be changed enharmonically.

8. VII^{d7} serves as a pivot chord in distant modulations, by enharmonic change of one or more of its notes.

9. Altered chords serve as pivots.
   a. The A^6 chord, through its identity in sound with the V^7, can lead to a key one half step below.
   b. The Neapolitan sixth can lead to keys one half step above or below.

10. Sequences can lead to distant modulations.
   a. The cycle of fifths leads to the most distant keys, when an accidental is added to each successive chord.
   b. Repetition of a pattern one tone lower makes possible modulations to keys two flats lower each time.
   c. Repetition a minor third above makes possible modulations over a distance of three flats at a time.
   d. Modulations with altered chords can create radical changes of key.

11. Chromatic bass motion can lead to distant keys.

12. Abrupt modulation by leap may be made:
   a. Without any pivot chord or tone.
   b. With melody or bass progressing by half step.
   c. By side-slipping—sudden sliding into a new key one half step away.

Function
and Form

One of the problems of student and composer alike is to find a framework on which to build musical ideas. When melody and harmony are germinating but have not yet taken shape, determining the form sometimes poses a difficult problem. At such times, the *function* of a composition may serve as a guideline.

It has long been noted in art history that form follows function. The limits of a work of art, be it a cathedral, the carving around a doorway, or a portrait, are often set in advance. True, there are countless ways of working within those limits, but when the destination is known, the route may be charted with greater assurance.

Function and Form in Religious Music

In music, the form of the chorale arose out of its role in the Lutheran service. Until a fairly recent period, it was the custom in many Protestant churches for the leader to "line out" a hymn, singing it for the congregation one phrase at a time and stopping at the end of each phrase. The congregation would then repeat what the leader had sung. The frequent fermatas and cadences that mark the pauses became a characteristic of the chorale form.*

At an earlier period of religious music, the recitation of the Psalms gave rise to the free-flowing, non-metrical synagogue and early church chants. The Mass lent its verbal and liturgical structure to the musical designs that embellished its performance. Again, form followed function.†

Function and Form in Dance Music

Dance music serves other purposes, produces other patterns. As we have seen, the physical movements of dancing demand a strong, insistent, often repetitive beat. Among all the world's peoples, the dance has led to the emergence of rhythm as a basic structural element of music. In western Europe especially, evenly balanced movements have given rise to symmetrical musical patterns—the repeated phrase, the period, the two-part form.‡

Widely used in European folk and popular dance music, these forms were developed by serious composers into idealized dance compositions where the basic patterns remained clearly discernible. The rhythm, phrasing, and design of the Renaissance pavane, the Baroque gavotte, the Classical minuet, and the Romantic waltz still reflect their original function as dance accompaniment. Even when, as in Stravinsky, Copland, and Villa-Lobos, specific dance rhythms emerge in asymmetrical form, they often appear within a context of over-all symmetry.§

Repetition and symmetry permit music to be readily grasped and carried in the memory—hence the universal appearance of the repeated phrase, the period, and the two- and three-part forms in folk music, popular and theater songs, marches, and the like, and in themes of Classical and Romantic compositions. On a larger scale, dance patterns often suggest forms for ballet music, the suite, and free orchestral compositions.

* See Exs. 3–5, pages 191–194.
† See page 442, Volume I.
‡ See pages 280–284, Volume I, and pages 26 and 146 of this volume.
§ As in Stravinsky's *Dance of the Coachmen*, from *Petrushka*, and Copland's *Hoe-Down*, from *Rodeo*.

Contemplation and Asymmetrical Form

Turning to another area, we come to an entirely different function of music—a function associated not with social activity but with the private world of the individual artist. Various musical forms and styles are especially suited to the expression of inner experience. From medieval times to the present, composers have projected their vision of the other-worldly, the romantic, and the dream-like in irregular patterns, long-line melodies, and free-flowing rhythms. Compositions expressing mystical or contemplative states often have a slow tempo, asymmetrical structure, and elusive harmonic patterns. Such musical characteristics contrast with the clearly etched forms and actions of the external world.

A contemplative quality appears in works as different as the Gregorian *Kyrie Alme Pater* and the *Ave verum* of Josquin des Prés,* many of the chorales, preludes, and fugues of Bach,† and the slow movements of Beethoven.‡ Various works of Ives, Bartók, Shostakovich, and Berg§ project a contemplative quality through subtly interwoven, elusive shapes. A free-flowing melody from Prokofiev's Sixth Symphony has a deeply introspective character.

Ex. 43   Prokofiev: Symphony No. 6, Op. 111, third movement

© *Copyright 1946, 1948 by Music Corporation of America, 322 West 48th Street, New York, N.Y. All rights reserved. Used by permission.*

* See pages 442 and 444, Volume I.
† See pages 192 and 201–202 of this volume.
‡ See pages 50–51 and 73 of this volume.
§ See page 15 of Volume I and pages 412–420 of this volume.

Function and form are most closely related in short pieces—chants, chorales, dance melodies, and folk and popular songs. When the scope of composition broadens, a single work often encompasses many functions. Thus a fugue may provide an intellectual concept, a religious experience, the pleasure of weaving lines, or all three at once. In operas and other large dramatic works, function and form become closely intertwined on a grand scale. In more abstract instrumental compositions of large dimension, form may grow so complex that its connection with a specific function becomes remote or non-existent.

Nonetheless, and within appropriate limits, function can serve as a guide to the understanding and use of musical form.

Summary

1. The function of music can influence its form.

2. The needs and practices of the Church have given rise to religious forms such as the chorale, chant, and Mass.

3. The patterns of dance movement have evolved into musical forms such as the repeated phrase, the period, and the two-part form.
   a. European dances have produced such forms as the gavotte, minuet, and waltz.
   b. When developed into idealized versions, their basic patterns still persist.

4. Contemplative, introspective, and mystical states of the individual composer have found expression in asymmetrical, irregular forms and free-flowing melodies.

5. Function and form are most closely related in shorter compositions. With works of larger scope, the relationship grows far more complex.

XII

Twentieth-Century Harmony

Every artistic style has its life span: its birth, age of flowering, and time of decay. So it was with major-minor harmony. Arising with the Renaissance and flourishing in the continuity of Baroque–Classical–Romantic creation, it came at last to a decline in the period from 1890 to 1910. Through the harmonic complications of late Romantic music, the differences between active and rest tones, between strong and weak progressions, became obscured. Constant chromatic alteration and modulation eventually destroyed the sense of a strong tonal center; continuous movement without a clear point of reference became no movement. Finally, the contrast of tension and relaxation that forms the core of traditional harmony all but disappeared.

A sharp break came with Debussy in the 1890s. The French composer had discovered in Moussorgsky a wellspring of fresh harmonic ideas—ideas that stemmed from Russian folk and church songs and the modal scales of

Oriental music. Turning in this new direction, Debussy abandoned Romantic chromaticism, and with it the entire tradition of functional harmony. He opened the door to the twentieth century.*

Our time has produced not one but many new styles. Composers have always differed in approach and method; but in the past, those of a given period practiced many techniques in common. Mozart, Haydn, and Beethoven, for example, shared their harmonic speech and many melodic patterns with lesser-known musicians such as Boccherini, Dittersdorf, Sammartini, and Pergolesi.

No such common language exists in our century. Diversity has reached the point where many composers differ almost entirely in technique and style. Esthetic values, moreover, have changed far more rapidly than ever before. Impressionism, folklorism, primitivism, dadaism, nationalism, quarter-tone music, neo-Baroquism, expressionism, atonality, dodecaphonism (twelve-tone technique), neo-classicism, and avant-gardism are but some of the styles and methods that have appeared (and often disappeared) in the space of a few short decades. More recently, the rate of technological obsolescence of musical styles has increased almost as quickly as those of automobile models or women's fashions. No single technique of harmony or melody has achieved universality in our time, as it did in the past.

Nor is this stylistic diversity necessarily bad. Although it may cause dismay to those who prefer a neatly ordered esthetic scene, the dissolution of traditional harmony has given rise to the widest range of artistic possibilities and to a wealth of musical masterpieces. We can benefit by examining various twentieth-century techniques of harmony and melody, even within the limits of a brief survey. In this chapter, the section on harmony covers new ways of using traditional chords, expanded tonality, and modal harmony. The discussion continues in Chapter XIII with new harmonic structures, new uses of dissonant chords, polytonality, and atonality. As in earlier times, modern harmonic devices, too, often derive from melodic impulses. The second parts of these chapters examine the nature of twentieth-century melody. The Postlude explores the union of tonality and atonality.

New Ways of Using Traditional Chords

Modern harmony began not with the invention of new chords but with the development of new uses for traditional chords. In the twentieth century, chords are used:

---

* Romantic chromaticism persisted, however, in the work of Strauss, Mahler, early Schönberg, Scriabin, and others.

1. As pure sonority.
2. Without preparation or resolution of dissonances.
3. To form a shifting tonality, by leaping from key to key.
4. In parallel motion.
5. In linear, not functional, progression.
6. In expanded tonality.

Chords as Pure Sonority

     Contemporary harmony often strives for sonority, color, or atmosphere rather than a chain of root movements marching toward a goal. Anticipating twentieth-century practice by several decades, Moussorgsky evoked a mood of wild jubilation in the Coronation Scene from his opera *Boris Godunov*.

Ex. 1   Moussorgsky: Coronation Scene, from *Boris Godunov* (1868)

In Ex. 1, two dominant seventh chords on D and A flat (keys at opposite ends of the tonal spectrum) alternate for 38 bars, moving nowhere, and forming a massive envelope of tone. Since the chords, a tritone apart, are of equal importance in the phrase, neither one establishes a tonic. The tonality remains vague and suspended for 38 bars—one of the first examples of its kind in nineteenth-century music. The object here is not harmonic progression but simply the creation of a *sonorous atmosphere*. We can appreciate the composer's indifference to traditional root movements in this passage when we understand his purpose—to suggest the clangor of cathedral bells.

Moussorgsky's concept of harmony as pure sonority stems from his absorption in Russian and Near Eastern music. Debussy adopted and expanded this concept (Ex. 2), and Ravel, Ives, and Stravinsky (Ex. 3) carried it still further.

Ex. 2   Debussy: *La cathédrale engloutie*, from Preludes, Book I

Permission for reprint granted by Durand et Cie., Paris, copyright owner, and Elkan-Vogel Co., Inc., Philadelphia, agents.

Ex. 3   Stravinsky: *Les noces*

Reprinted by permission of J. & W. Chester Ltd., London, and G. Schirmer, Inc., New York.

Among others who made use of chords as pure sonority were Bartók, Varèse, Cowell, and—more recently—Boulez and Cage.

The Free Use of Dissonance

In twentieth-century music, dissonances often appear without preparation and progress without being resolved. An early instance occurs in *Boris*. Example 4 presents a chord that might be analyzed as a French sixth (*a*), alternating with an augmented triad (*b*). Without resolving the dissonant tones, the phrase calmly ends on a I⁶ of C major. Intended as the depiction of a nightmare, the passage is remarkable for its time in the free treatment of dissonance.

Ex. 4   Moussorgsky: *Boris Godunov*, Act I

Once again, Debussy followed Moussorgsky's lead in his handling of dissonances; his methods, however, were more elegant. In Ex. 5, the seventh chords are neither prepared nor resolved, yet the progression is completely smooth, typically Debussyan in its floating sonority.

Ex. 5   Debussy: *La fille aux cheveux de lin*, from Preludes, Book I

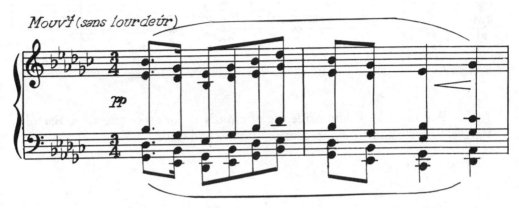

Permission for reprint granted by Durand et Cie., Paris, copyright owner, and Elkan-Vogel Co., Inc., Philadelphia, agents.

It is interesting to see how the attitude of modern composers toward dissonance has passed into the popular musical theater, where the free attack of seventh and ninth chords has long been standard practice. Note, in Ex. 6, the unprepared I^7 at (a) and the IV^9 at (b).

Ex. 6   Loesser: Joey, Joey, Joey, from *The Most Happy Fella*

Shifting Tonality by Leaping between Keys

Returning once more to *Boris Godunov*, we note another charac-teristically modern technique: *shifting tonality*.

Ex. 7   Moussorgsky: Coronation Scene, from *Boris Godunov*

In Ex. 7, the V⁷ of D flat (*a*) does not merely fail to resolve; it leaps abruptly to a chord of another key, E major (*b*). Abrupt leaps occur in traditional music; but there they usually link two well-defined keys. Ex. 7 shows successive leaps from the V of D flat (*a*) to E major (*b*), back again to D flat (*c*), to C major (*d*), and back once more to the V of D flat. Such leaping progressions establish no single key; they form, rather, a kaleidoscopic, shifting tonality, a characteristic Debussyan technique (Ex. 8).

Ex. 8   Debussy: *Les sons et les parfums tournent dans l'air du soir*, from Preludes, Book I

Parallel Chords

Still another twentieth-century practice is foreshadowed in *Boris*: parallel chord motion. Moussorgsky's opera brought to an end the five-hundred-year prohibition of such progressions. A passage suggesting medieval organum shows four voices moving boldly in parallel fifths and octaves.

Ex. 9   Moussorgsky: *Boris Godunov*, Act I

Debussy startled his professors at the Paris *Conservatoire* by improvising similar progressions, later developing parallel movement into a personal style. Example 10, a passage from *The Sunken Cathedral* (also reflecting the influence of organum), shows parallel fifths and octaves over a pedal bass.* Example 11 contains parallel dominant seventh chords,† and Ex. 12, parallel dominant ninths.‡

Ex. 10   Debussy: *La cathédrale engloutie*, from Preludes, Book I

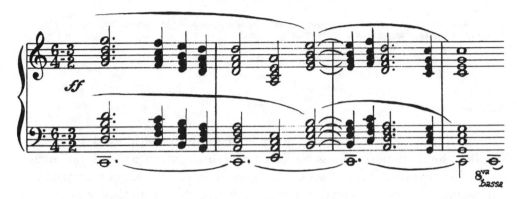

Permission for reprint granted by Durand et Cie., Paris, copyright owner, and Elkan-Vogel Co., Inc., Philadelphia, agents.

Ex. 11   Debussy: *La cathédrale engloutie*

Permission for reprint granted by Durand et Cie., Paris, copyright owner, and Elkan-Vogel Co., Inc., Philadelphia, agents.

* See also Exs. 5 and 13.
† The same work also contains parallel fourths, seconds, and non-dominant sevenths.
‡ Parallel V⁷ chords were already used by Chopin in his Mazurka, Op. 30 (see Workbook, Vol. II, Chapter X, Ex. 20c), and parallel ninths by Liszt in *Les jeux d'eaux à la villa d'Este* (1887).

Ex. 12   Debussy: *Pelléas et Mélisande*, Act I

Permission for reprint granted by Durand et Cie., Paris, copyright owner, and Elkan-Vogel Co., Inc., Philadelphia, agents.

Harmony as Linear Progression

The use of chords as pure sonority led to a radical change in harmonic thinking: the disappearance of functional progression and the emergence in its place of *linear, gliding motion*. Such motion is similar to that of Renaissance modal style, in which the bass served as another line rather than as the bearer of dynamic chord roots. A comparison of Ex. 13 with examples of Renaissance music* shows a similar gliding bass devoid of functional motion. Debussy's chords often form a band of sonority paralleling the melody—a broad harmonic movement in which chord roots carry little weight. Linear chord progression, established by Debussy, was to have an enormous influence on the further development of twentieth-century harmony. The abandonment of functional movement led to the dissolution of the hierarchy of chords within a key. Except for the tonic, chords no longer rank in order of importance. Example 13—an illustration of linear movement—shows little distinction between one scale degree and another.

---

* See page 296 of Volume I, especially the comparison between the gliding movement of Renaissance music and that of Ravel; see also Ex. 2, page 190 of this volume.

Ex. 13   Debussy: *Canope*, from Preludes, Book II

Permission for reprint granted by Durand et Cie., Paris, copyright owner, and Elkan-Vogel Co., Inc., Philadelphia, agents.

Expanded Tonality

At (*a*) in Ex. 13, the harmony seems to leave the key of D, leaping to a flat key. The suggestion of a new key is only momentary, however, for the music returns immediately to D. Chords that leap out of and back into a key are called *escaped chords*.* Progressions containing escaped chords do not modulate; they enrich a key by absorbing into it foreign sonorities to form an *expanded tonality*. Once a key has been firmly established, the momentary appearance of borrowed tones or chords need not weaken its identity. They can, on the contrary, enlarge its boundaries—either by temporary diversion (Ex. 13), or by the simultaneous appearance of diatonic and borrowed harmonies (Ex. 14).

* They are, in a sense, a more radical form of borrowed chords or diversions.

Ex. 14   Debussy: *Les sons et les parfums tournent dans l'air du soir*, from Preludes, Book I

Les sons et les parfums shows the key of A major enriched by the inclusion within its borders of the V^7 of E flat (*a*), the V^9 of E (*b*), a complex chord that resists translation into chord symbols (*c*), the V^9 of D minor (*d*), and an augmented triad on A (*e*). But rather than identify these formations by chord symbols that imply harmonic functions, we can more validly view them as freely roaming sonorities in an expanded tonality centering on A.

Seen in perspective, the expanded tonality of twentieth-century music differs from the widened tonality of the nineteenth century in degree, not in kind. Leaps from the center to the outer regions of the key now occur constantly and more abruptly, but they represent no different principle. As compared with Beethoven's Quartet (Ex. 24, page 266), harmonic diver-

sions in Hindemith's Third Sonata (Ex. 15) are more radical and occupy a
larger proportion of the music; they arise, moreover, from linear rather than
functional motion. But both are examples of expanded tonality; Hindemith
simply carries the process further than Beethoven.

Ex. 15   Hindemith: Third Sonata for Piano

The first two bars of Ex. 15 establish B flat major. At (*a*) the music
moves abruptly into the region of lowered III (D flat); at (*b*) it enters the
region of raised IV (E minor), breaking up the octave at the distance of the
tritone.* At (*c*) and (*d*), three borrowed chords lead back to re-establish the
home key B flat (*e*).

* Compare this use of harmonies on the tritone with examples from Berlioz, page 262,
and Moussorgsky, page 341.

Expanded tonality, therefore, represents a further development of the widening of tonality initiated by secondary dominants and borrowed chords. But whereas these chords introduce elements derived mainly from closely related keys, expanded tonality involves the absorption into a key of all possible tones and chords. Sometimes, as we shall see, remote borrowings either are made from several keys simultaneously or appear together with chords of the home key, resulting in the most complex and varied combinations, and vastly extending the possibilities of the tonal concept. In the works of Debussy, Ives, Stravinsky, Bartók, Hindemith, Prokofiev, and many others, expanded tonality forms one of the basic lines of development of twentieth-century music.

Modal Harmony

Earlier, in discussing modal melody (Volume I), we noted the ancient and universal prevalence of the modes. We also noted that the major-minor system—important as it was for the music of western Europe—reigned for a relatively brief period in the long perspective of history. And even during this period, the modes were not completely abandoned, persisting in European folk song and the melodic music of non-European peoples.

When the nineteenth-century nationalist movement led to a rediscovery of folk music, and when, at the same time, the Gothic Revival awakened interest in medieval chant and organum, Romantic composers began to employ modal material in compositions reflecting a national or medieval concept. Starting with Lesueur (Berlioz' teacher), and gathering momentum with Chopin, Berlioz, Liszt, Glinka, Moussorgsky, Fauré, Brahms, and Dvorak, composers began to write modal melodies and chords—generally within a broad context of major-minor harmony. During the 1880s and '90s, interest in the modes grew, reaching its peak in the early twentieth century. Modern composers, unlike those of the Romantic period, have usually avoided compromises with major-minor harmony, striving instead for a purely modal language.

Modal harmony tends to produce linear rather than functional progression.* In modal music, except for the tonic, there is little difference between the roles of one chord and another, and less distinction between strong and gentle root movements. Harmonic motion, therefore, is less dynamic than in major-minor music.

As composers turned away from the extreme tensions of nineteenth-century chromaticism, they found a refreshing alternative in modal harmony. Basically diatonic and less susceptible of elaborate harmonic embellishment, the various modes allowed for the growth of rhythmic, melodic, and

* See page 190.

orchestral complexities. The return to a clear harmonic atmosphere also permitted the rise of new types of diatonic chord structure, which many composers adopted in place of chromatic harmony.

The harmonic structure of the modes depends on the order of whole and half steps in each. Certain modes, especially Dorian, Aeolian, and Mixolydian, allow for a greater variety of chord progressions than do others. Among the most important determinants of harmonic color are the forms of the primary triads I, IV, and V found in each mode. Thus the Dorian mode has minor I and V chords but a major IV, which adds a touch of brightness to the rather dark harmonic atmosphere.

Ex. 16   Triads in Dorian

Aeolian is the darkest of the three modes: its primary triads are all minor.

Ex. 17   Triads in Aeolian

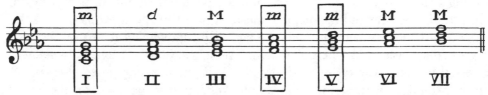

The Mixolydian mode, with major I and IV triads, is closest to the brightness of major: its minor V, however, lends a gentle quality to the cadence.

Ex. 18   Triads in Mixolydian

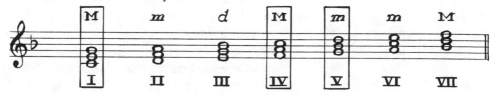

Dorian Harmony

An especially pure example of Dorian harmony occurs in the music of Moussorgsky, a master of modal style. Note, in Ex. 19, the luminous quality of major IV at (*a*) and major VII at (*b*), followed by minor V at (*c*).

Ex. 19   Moussorgsky: *Boris Godunov*, Act I

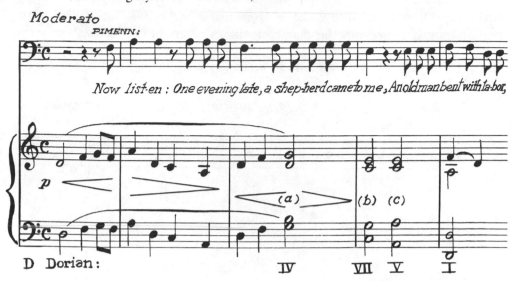

Bartók's harmonization of a Roumanian folk dance (Ex. 20) shows another aspect of Dorian harmony. The gay sound of major IV and the freshness of the progression M IV—M III[6]—M IV resemble nothing in traditional harmony.

Ex. 20   Bartók: Roumanian Folk Dances, No. 2

The character of a mode develops most clearly when its distinctive scale steps (those that distinguish it from major and minor) are called into play. Example 21 presents the characteristic scale steps of each mode.

Ex. 21   Distinctive scale steps in various modes

Aeolian Harmony

To distinguish Aeolian from the melodic minor mode, Ravel stressed the lowered 6 and 7 in a *rising* line (Ex. 22).

Ex. 22   Ravel: *Sonatine*

Permission for reprint granted by Durand et Cie., Paris, copyright owner, and Elkan-Vogel Co., Inc., Philadelphia, agents.

We have already noted Ravel's use of the Aeolian mode to express nostalgia for the far away and long ago. This archaic quality appears in a progression of seventh chords (Ex. 23). Starting with IV⁷ (*a*), the cadence on minor... traditionally through VII⁷—III⁷—VI⁷—II⁷ to a half (unusual in a modal work... Despite the strength of the root movements their drive, revealing once more the relationships of the Aeolian mode soften ...uality of modal harmony.

Ex. 23   Ravel: *Pavanne pour une Infante défunte*

Borrowed chords occur frequently in the modes, as in major and minor. Prokofiev substitutes a minor VI (Ex. 24, *a*) for the major VI usually found in Aeolian, adding further darkness to the dark character of the mode.

Ex. 24   Prokofiev: Field of the Dead, from *Alexander Nevsky*, Op. 78

Mixolydian Harmony

The distinctive character of the Mixolydian mode results from combining the brightness of the major I and IV with the gentle cadence created by the minor V. This pattern of harmonies appears to advantage in Satie's *Gymnopédie* No. 2. Note that the Mixolydian V⁷ is a non-dynamic *minor* seventh chord.

Ex. 25   Satie: *Gymnopédie* No. 2

By courtesy of the publisher, Editions Salabert, Paris.

An entirely different mood arises from a Mixolydian passage in Stravinsky's *Rite of Spring* (Ex. 26). A constantly repeated V—I pattern serves as background to a primitive-style Russian melody. The neutral quality of the harmonic movement allows the hypnotic rhythm to work its effect.

Ex. 26   Stravinsky: Dance of the Adolescents, from *The Rite of Spring*

Jazz reveals still other possibilities of the Mixolydian mode, whose lowered 7 is identical to that of the blues mode.* For the final chord of *Rhapsody in Blue*, Gershwin introduces a Mixolydian I⁷—a favorite jazz ending of the 1920s.†

Ex. 27   Gershwin: *Rhapsody in Blue*

Lydian Harmony

As we have seen, raised 4 is the sole difference between the Lydian mode and major; but it is sufficient to lend a distinctive quality to the mode. Because of this raised step, IV becomes a diminished triad, and II—a *major* triad—assumes the important role normally played by the IV.

Ex. 28   Triads in the Lydian mode

* See page 127, Volume I.

† The Mixolydian I⁷ is identical in structure to the conventional V⁷.

Two progressions appear frequently in Lydian music: (1) a reiterated tonic chord, with raised 4 appearing as a passing tone or appoggiatura in the melody (Ex. 29), and (2) a tonic chord alternating with the major II (Ex. 30).* (The raised 4 appears as a grace note at *a*.)

Ex. 29   Milhaud: *Protée* Suite

Permission for reprint granted by Durand et Cie., Paris, copyright owner, and Elkan-Vogel Co., Inc., Philadelphia, agents.

Ex. 30   Bartók: *Poargă Românească*, from Roumanian Folk Dances, No. 5

* For another example of this pattern, see the excerpt from *Boris Godunov*, page 125, Volume I.

Phrygian Harmony

The Phrygian mode is characterized by the lowered 2, with a strong tendency downward to the tonic. It has a further peculiarity: V, a diminished triad, cannot function as a dominant. The active role usually played by V is divided in the Phrygian mode between II, a major triad, and VII, a minor one.

Ex. 31   Triads in the Phrygian mode

In Ex. 32 the dominant appears as an augmented sixth chord (*a*) with its lowest tone on 2. The downward cadential pull of the lowered 2 is balanced by the upward drive of the raised 7.

Ex. 32   Debussy: String Quartet

The reiterated tonic—a frequent characteristic of Phrygian as of Lydian—appears in Ex. 33.

Ex. 33   Bartók: In Phrygian Mode, from *Mikrokosmos*

Whole-Tone Harmony

The modes most prominent in twentieth-century music are, by and large, the same as those of medieval, Renaissance, and folk tradition—a forgotten spring, come to the surface once more. To establish a new mode is a far more difficult problem, as shown by the history of the *whole-tone scale.* Known to and used occasionally by nineteenth-century composers,* it (or something very like it) was brought to Paris in 1889 by Javanese *gamelan* players. There the scale caught the imagination of Debussy, in whose music it reached its highest development.

Constructed entirely of whole steps, the whole-tone scale (Ex. 34, *a*) gives rise to harmonies of a special kind: a series of augmented triads (Ex. 34, *b*). It is the only scale with the same type of chord on every degree.

* Glinka employed the whole-tone scale in the Overture to *Russlan and Ludmila* (1842).

Ex. 34   Whole-tone scale and its triads

Because all its steps are equal, the whole-tone scale tends to lack a tonic; even when a tonal center is present, it has little gravitational pull. To prevent the harmony from merely drifting about, the sense of tonality must be emphasized by insistent repetition of the root tone. Example 35 illustrates one of the rare compositions of Debussy built almost entirely on the whole-tone scale. Note the reiterated pedal tone (B flat) in the bass; also the parallel augmented triads in the left hand. The effect is one of floating movement.

Ex. 35   Debussy: *Voiles*, from Preludes, Book I

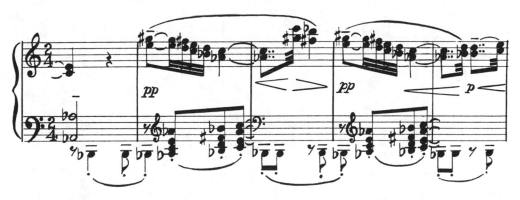

Permission for reprint granted by Durand et Cie., Paris, copyright owner, and Elkan-Vogel Co., Inc., Philadelphia, agents.

Since all triads of the whole-tone scale are of the same structure, harmony in this scale lacks variety. It also lacks a central point from which chords can depart and to which they are drawn back. As a result, whole-tone harmony has no contrast of tension and release and little forward drive; it frequently results in a tiresome repetitiveness. Debussy, Ravel, and other impressionist composers were careful to employ whole-tone harmony only in brief passages, generally interwoven with longer sections in major, minor, or other modes. More recently, composers have moved on to harmonic patterns that offer greater possibilities of contrast and activity.

Mixed Modes

Modern modal music, as compared with that of the sixteenth century, contains much greater harmonic freedom and variety. In Renaissance style, one mode was generally retained over a long expanse, often throughout an entire composition. Twentieth-century practice tends toward a free interchange of modal scales and chords; after 1900, the modes appeared more often as mixtures than in a pure state.*

Thus, the key signature of Ex. 13, page 350, indicates the Aeolian mode on D. At its very first appearance, however, the sixth tone of the scale occurs as a B *natural*—which alters the mode to Dorian. The succeeding B flat immediately changes it back again to Aeolian.

Another example (Ex. 36) begins with an interplay of two modes: the first four bars are Lydian, the next three (*a*) Mixolydian, and the last (*b*) Lydian mode once more.

Ex. 36   Milhaud: *Le pauvre matelot*

Reprinted by permission of Theodore Presser Company.

The simultaneous use of two modes offers still further harmonic possibilities. The Lydian melody of Ex. 37 appears together with a Mixolydian accompaniment—a combination favored by Debussy, Stravinsky, and Bartók.

* On this point, see John Vincent: *The Diatonic Modes in Modern Music* (New York, 1951), pages 267–284.

Ex. 37   Stravinsky: *Petrushka*

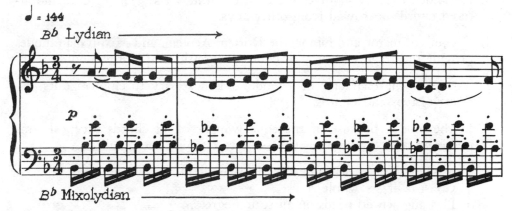

Because of the absence of a leading-tone progression, tonality* is less firmly established in the modes than in major and minor. It becomes all the more important, therefore, to emphasize the authority of the tonic by frequent repetition. Note the reiterated B flat in the bass in Ex. 37, and the insistent D in Ex. 29.

Summary

1. Twentieth-century harmony, breaking with traditional practice, has developed many new styles and techniques.

2. One basic modern approach involves the use of traditional chords:
   a. As pure sonority—chords used for color or atmosphere, rather than in functional roles.
   b. Without preparing or resolving dissonances.
   c. In shifting tonalities.
      i. With chords leaping into and out of various keys.
      ii. Around a given key center, with roaming harmonies called escaped chords.
   d. In parallel motion—including triads, seventh chords, and ninth chords.
   e. In linear, gliding motion.

* Bear in mind the broad definition of tonality given on page 33, Volume I, as the gravitational relationship of a group of tones to a central tone. In this sense, tonality exists in modal compositions as well as in those using major-minor harmony.

3. Expanded tonality involves the absorption into a key of diatonic and altered chords borrowed from other keys.

4. Except for major and minor, the Dorian, Aeolian, and Mixolydian modes provide the greatest variety of chord progressions of all the modes.

5. To define the character of a mode, it is necessary to emphasize its distinctive steps and chords.

6. In the modes, because of the equal weight of all chords except I, emphasis on tonic harmony is necessary to establish the tonality.

7. The whole-tone scale, used in early twentieth-century music:
   a. Consists of six whole steps.
   b. Has augmented triads on all scale degrees.
   c. Has a certain sameness of harmony due to its uniform chord structure.

8. In twentieth-century music, mixed modes appear more often than pure ones.

Twentieth-Century Melody

"You hear a medley of sounds, a variety of parts, a rumble of harmonies that are intolerable to the ear. . . . with all the best will in the world, how can the mind see light in this chaos?"* A criticism of twentieth-century music? No, of the *nuove musiche* (new music) of 1600, written by the theorist Artusi, in complaint against the strange styles then being introduced by those modernists Monteverdi and Gesualdo da Venosa.

We hear the same complaint today by otherwise sensitive people who believe melody went out when the twentieth century came in. Partly the charge is justified: there were as many writers of poor melody in 1960 as in 1860, 1760 or any other '60. Consider the melodic clichés of some contemporaries of Beethoven: the banal tunes of Spohr; the triteness of Zelter, the triviality of Hummel—noted composers in their time.

Our century is as rich in melody as many that preceded it, having produced the distinguished melodies of Bartók, Ives, Prokofiev, Gershwin, Revueltas, Villa-Lobos, Shostakovich, and many others. But new melody rarely attracts the same critical attention as new types of harmony, orchestra-

* Quoted in Marion Bauer: *Twentieth Century Music* (New York, 1933), page 19.

367

tion, and theatrical and symphonic structure. Melody, the most intimate avenue of musical expression, receives considerably less discussion in scholarly journals and the press than new esthetic theories, novel forms of making music by machine, mathematical analyses of sound, and the like.

One difficulty in evaluating twentieth-century melody stems from the vast diversity of its styles. No longer limited to the major-minor system, the melodic imagination of composers has expanded in many directions. Countless new influences—from jazz, Brazilian folk music, and Javanese modes to rediscovered medieval and Baroque styles—have colored contemporary melody. The experimental spirit of the age has contributed new scale patterns, quarter tones, and electronic sound; and the exploration of rhythm has added still further possibilities. It is still too soon to find order in this melodic wilderness.

Nonetheless, certain traits emerge that are common to many different modern styles:

1. Extreme range.
2. Unusual intervals and difficult leaps.
3. Varied scale patterns.
4. Free tonal movement.
5. Intricate rhythmic structure.

Basic differences between various modern melodic tendencies include the contrasts of: (1) extreme complexity and simplicity, (2) tonal and atonal structure, and (3) fragmented and long-line melody.

Wide Range

Wide-range melodies serve two purposes in traditional music, as noted in Volume I: they display certain instrumental possibilities, and they convey an extreme or dramatic emotion. In twentieth-century music, wide range tends to be the norm rather than the exception. This holds true neither for every composer nor every composition, but nonetheless it occurs so frequently that the appearance of a wide-range melody no longer suggests any special purpose or emphasis. The themes of Richard Strauss, for instance, continuing the theatrical style of Wagner, often sweep wildly from one end of the melodic spectrum to the other. Thus, Ex. 38 mounts through four octaves.

Ex. 38   Strauss: *Ein Heldenleben*, Op. 40

While the wide-range melodies of Strauss won wide acclaim within a few years after being written, those of his American contemporary Ives remained unknown for almost half a century. Even now, relatively few listeners are acquainted with this lovely theme from the *Concord* Sonata, written fifty years ago.

This melody also illustrates the practice of *octave displacement:* the last five bars are the same as the first five, except that certain tones are shifted to a different octave.

Ex. 39   Ives: *Emerson,* from The *Concord* Sonata

In a completely diatonic style, without even the few chromatic notes of Ex. 39, Copland writes a wide-range melody (Ex. 40).

Ex. 40   Copland: *Appalachian Spring*

Unusual Intervals, Difficult Leaps

The rise of new melodic pathways led to the free exploitation of uncommon intervals and difficult leaps. Reflecting the extremes of German expressionism around the early 1900s, Arnold Schönberg went further than any other composer of his time in using extensive jumps and rare intervals. Example 41 shows an augmented octave (*a*), a diminished triple octave (*c*), and a diminished twelfth (*b*).*

Ex. 41   Schönberg: String Quartet No. 3, Op. 30, last movement

* Ex. 41 also illustrates both atonal and twelve-tone melody, discussed further in Chapter XIII.

Complex intervals often arise when a melody follows the outline of altered chords. Taken in itself, the melodic line of Ex. 42a seems indefinite in its tonality. Joined to the underlying chords (42b), it is revealed as a twentieth-century descendant of nineteenth-century chromaticism. (Note the chromatic falling bass line.)

Ex. 42a   Berg: Lullaby, from *Wozzeck*, melody alone

Copyright 1926, Universal Editions, A. G., Vienna. Used by permission.

Ex. 42b   Berg: Lullaby, with harmony

Copyright 1926, Universal Editions, A. G., Vienna. Used by permission.

Followers of Schönberg often write the same for voice as for instruments—with extremely wide range and unusual intervals (Exs. 43 and 44).

Ex. 43   Berg: *Wozzeck*

Copyright 1926, Universal Editions, A. G., Vienna. Used by permission.

Ex. 44   Dallapiccola: *An Mathilde*

Reprinted by permission of Edizioni Suvini Zerboni, Milan.

Complex harmonies sometimes produce a sense of diffuseness or obscurity in a melody. To develop a tighter structure, modern composers, like those of the past, frequently use a single interval as a germ, repeating it over and over in a phrase. Debussy employed the third, Bartók the perfect fourth, Bernstein the augmented fourth, and Prokofiev the minor ninth.*

* For the Debussy example, see page 344; for the Bartók, page 392; and for the Bernstein, page 45, Volume I.

Ex. 45   Prokofiev: Symphony No. 5, Op. 100, second movement

Variety of Scale Patterns

Another characteristic of twentieth-century melody is the great variety of its scales. In addition to the traditional modes and the whole-tone scale, contemporary composers have used many non-European modes, besides inventing scale patterns of their own.

One intriguing aspect of non-European modes is their variability. In Spanish flamenco songs (influenced by Arabic music) tones lowered in one octave are often raised in another. Example 46 shows a flamenco mode with lowered 2 and 3 in the upper octave (*a*) and raised 3 in the bottom one.

Ex. 46   de Falla: Ritual Fire Dance, from *El Amor Brujo*

Other scales influenced by Oriental music possess an even more irregular structure. Example 47 shows a mode whose second, third, and fourth tones are sometimes lowered, sometimes raised.

Ex. 47   Bartók: Bulgarian Rhythm, from *Mikrokosmos*, Book IV

Certain composers, notably Bartók, employ many complex scale patterns. Familiar with a wide variety of scales, he made frequent use of one he may possibly have discovered for himself—a scale containing a raised 4 and lowered 7.*

* See also Ex. 37, page 365.

Ex. 48   Bartók: Music for Strings, Percussion, and Celeste, fourth movement

Copyright 1937 by Universal Editions; renewed 1964. Copyright and renewal assigned to Boosey and Hawkes, Inc. for the U.S.A. Reprinted by permission. All other rights by courtesy of the original publishers, Universal Editions, A. G. of Vienna.

Free Tonal Movement

Another aspect of twentieth-century music concerns the dissociation of melody from the influence of harmony. Melody, as we have seen, existed free of harmonic considerations until the early Renaissance, but in the following centuries gradually came to depend on chord structure and function. The intense chromaticism of late Romantic music weakened the influence of chord patterns over melodic movement; and after 1905 a number of composers, notably Ives and Schönberg, evolved individual styles in which melodic tones were free to move virtually anywhere, unhampered by harmonic requirements.

At the same time there developed in the work of certain composers an increasing equality of all twelve notes of the chromatic scale and, as a corollary, their increasing independence of each other. Between 1907 and 1912, Schönberg's melodies gradually became *atonal:* no single tone acted any longer as a center of gravity around which the other eleven revolved.*

Ex. 49   Schönberg: Serenade, Op. 24

* For Schönberg's later technique of organizing atonal music, the twelve-tone method, see pages 406–407.

Reprinted by permission of Gertrud Schönberg and G. Schirmer, Inc.

Atonality, however, is by no means the only method of achieving free tonal movement. Expanded tonality makes possible free melodic movement through all the diatonic and chromatic steps while still retaining one of them as a gravitational center. The second theme of Prokofiev's Violin Concerto No. 2 (Ex. 50) remains perfectly tonal while encompassing all twelve notes. In nine bars, it shifts from the key of B flat (*a*) to the regions of B major (*b*) and E flat (*c*), and then back to B flat again (*d*), the changes being effected mainly by side-slipping. Basically diatonic, the theme achieves a distinct freshness through free tonal movement.*

Ex. 50   Prokofiev: Violin Concerto No. 2, Op. 63

Reprinted by permission of Boosey and Hawkes, Inc.

Complex Rhythmic Structure

Many rhythmic techniques found in twentieth-century melody have also appeared at one time or another in the music of the past. What distinguishes contemporary melody is the concentrated use of these techniques—especially those producing irregularity, asymmetry, or a clash of accents. Example 51, for instance, contains several rhythmic irregularities within a single phrase: syncopation (*a*); changing meter (*b*); polyrhythm (the clash of an uneven rhythmic series in the right hand with a steady 2/4 beat in the left); and asymmetrical phrase lengths (the last three bars contain more beats than the first three).†

* For other melodies in expanded tonality, see Exs. 21, page 263; 24, pages 266–267; 39, page 369; and *Workbook,* Volume II, Chapter XIII, Exercise 10b.

† See also Ex. 52, page 417.

Ex. 51   Stravinsky: Soldier's March, from *The Story of a Soldier*

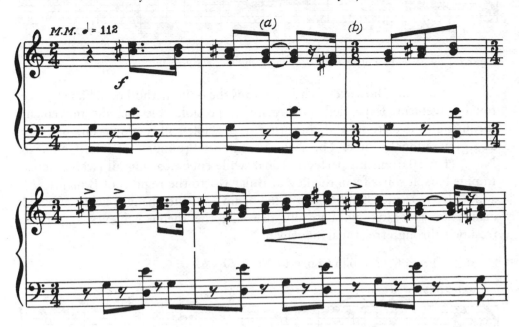

Copyright 1924 by J. & W. Chester, Ltd. Reprinted by permission.

Free-flowing and non-metric rhythms in contemporary melody have already been illustrated.*

One purely modern technique involves asymmetrical subdivision of beats within a regular metric pattern—a technique that contemporary composers borrowed from East European, African, and American Negro folk music and jazz. Thus Ex. 52 shows the subdivision of a measure into three, three, and two eighths, a pattern that occurs also in Negro spirituals† and such dances as the Charleston and the rumba.

Ex. 52   Bartók: Six Dances in Bulgarian Rhythm, from *Mikrokosmos*, Book VI

Copyright 1940 by Hawkes & Son (London) Ltd. Reprinted by permission.

* Pages 161, 166–167, Volume I.
† See "Didn't My Lord Deliver Daniel," page 168, Volume I.

The measure divides into three, two, two, and three eighths in Ex. 53.

Ex. 53   Bartók: String Quartet, No. 5

Finally, Ex. 54 shows the division of a 7/8 measure first into four plus three eighths (*a*) and then into three plus four eighths, producing variable polyrhythmic patterns.

Ex. 54   Siegmeister: Symphony No. 3

Complexity and Simplicity

In discussions of contemporary music, the term "advanced" often appears in connection with intricate techniques, implying that musical progress is synonymous with growing complexity. But art rarely follows so obvious a formula. Although a complex style frequently follows a simpler one, the opposite also occurs. Musical change tends to zigzag rather than to move in a straight line. Haydn is not a lesser composer than Rameau because his melodies, on the whole, are simpler; nor is Reger's style more advanced than Verdi's because it is more laden with harmonic complications.

In a few short decades, twentieth-century music has gone through several reversals of direction. At times, complexities have proliferated to such a point that composers, for sheer survival, have been moved to sweep them aside and start once more from the basic elements.

An early pioneer in such a return to simplicity was Erik Satie. Oppressed, like Debussy, by the chromatic excesses of his time, he rejected them all and wrote a deliberately naïve *musique d'ameublement* (furniture or "wallpaper" music).*

Ex. 55   Satie: Gymnopédie No. 3 (1888)

By *courtesy of the publisher, Editions Salabert, Paris.*

The young Stravinsky, also reacting against extreme chromaticism, turned to themes of an even more primitive simplicity. Many of his early melodies consist of a short group of notes no more than a fourth or a fifth in range. The fascination of these melodies lies in their insistent repetition, each time with a different rhythmic pattern and different accents. †

* To point up the simplicity of this melody, compare it with a flamboyant Strauss theme of the same period (pages 368–369).
† See also pages 358–359 and 390–391.

Ex. 56   Stravinsky: *Petrushka*

Copyright by Edition Russe de Musique; assigned 1947 to Boosey and Hawkes, Inc. Revised version copyright 1947, 1948 by Boosey and Hawkes, Inc. Reprinted by permission.

The folk-like simplicity of Stravinsky's early melodies formed a counterpoise to the harmonic and rhythmic complexity of such masterpieces as *The Rite of Spring* and *Les noces*. When, at a later date, Stravinsky relinquished simple for more complex intervals in his melodies, he still retained the characteristic turning, repetitive quality.* In his latest period, Stravinsky has abandoned previous techniques in favor of the twelve-tone method, moving still further in the direction of melodic complexity.

Still another composer who returned to a diatonic style after exploring intricate melodic techniques is Darius Milhaud. Having utilized a host of sophisticated methods in the vast choral panoramas *Agamemnon* and *Les Choëphores,* Milhaud startled Paris of the '20s with compositions in an almost elementary vein, reflecting Brazilian and Provençal folk songs, music-hall tunes, and early jazz. "The most difficult thing in music," Milhaud wrote in later years, "is still to write a melody of several bars which can be self-sufficient. Without this fundamental element, all the technique in the world can only be a dead letter."†

* See pages 67 of Volume I and 411–412 of this volume.

† In David Ewen: *The Book of Modern Composers* (New York, 1942), page 184.

Ex. 57   Milhaud: *Corcovado*, from *Saudades do Brazil*

The contrasts of complex and simple melody appear in the art of many twentieth-century composers. There are the differences in Kurt Weill, between the complexities of his early work and the deliberate banalities of *The Three-Penny Opera;* in Bartók, between the intricate lines of the Third String Quartet and the lyrical melodies of the Concerto for Orchestra; in Ives, between the tangled harmonies of the *Concord* Sonata and its naïve quicksteps and ragtime tunes. The music of the Mexican Revueltas likewise ranges from the involved patterns of *Sensamaya* to the delightfully simple *mariachi* tunes of the *Homenaje a Federico García Lorca.*

Ex. 58   Revueltas: *Homenaje a Federico García Lorca*

One of the distinguished melodic creators of the twentieth century, Sergei Prokofiev, passed through a period of intense complication when writing his opera *The Flaming Angel*. That he could write in a simple, lyrical manner, however, is evident in such works as the two violin concertos, the *Lieutenant Kije* Suite, and the Fifth Symphony. Neoclassic in style before the term became popular in the 1920s,* Prokofiev's melodies exhibit typically modern traits while remaining basically lyrical and diatonic. One of his characteristic scherzo-like themes is marked by wide leaps, sudden flashing runs, and sharp reversals of direction.

Ex. 59   Prokofiev: Symphony No. 5, Op. 100, last movement

Problems of Twentieth-Century Melody

Despite the great expansion of possibilities offered by the new techniques, melody has encountered serious problems in the twentieth century. Although gifted melodists have not been lacking, new harmonic

---

* Witness the Gavotte for piano (1914) and the *Classical* Symphony (1916–1917). For a melody from the latter, see Ex. 23, page 96.

devices, rhythmic combinations, and concepts of tonality, as well as new means of producing sound (by mechanical and other special agencies), have usurped the center of interest formerly held by melody. In consequence, some of the most widely known composers have been noted more for their harmonic, rhythmic, and structural innovations than for melodic substance.

The very concept of melodic line, moreover, has been questioned in certain quarters. The Viennese school (except for Berg), influenced by the fragmentary style of late Debussy, abandoned the thematic concept of melody, in which a linear motive, once stated, forms the basis of a continuous melodic expansion. Webern's *pointillism*—melody fragmented into patterns of single notes separated by wide, often dissonant leaps—broke with the age-old tradition of the flowing, singable line. It has had widespread influence in the 1960s, on Boulez, Stockhausen, Stravinsky, and many other composers. The question of whether extreme fragmentation is evolving into a new concept of melody, or whether it is a temporary phenomenon, will be settled only by the passage of time.

Ex. 60   Webern: Piano Variations, Op. 27

Reprinted by permission of Theodore Presser Company.

Regardless of the future possibilities of the fragmented style, the tradition of the long, flowing line still persists in our time—as we shall see in Chapter XIII.

Summary

1. Twentieth-century melody appears in a vast diversity of styles and techniques.

2. It often makes use of:
   a. Extremely wide range.
   b. Unusual intervals and difficult leaps.
   c. A wide variety of scales.
   d. Free tonal movement, of two basic types:
      i. Atonal melody, without a key center.
      ii. Melody in extended tonality, using all twelve diatonic and chromatic tones.
   e. Complex rhythmic structure.

3. Contemporary melodies range from:
   a. Extreme complexity to simplicity.
   b. Fragmented structure to long, flowing lines.

XIII

More about Twentieth-Century Harmony

New uses of traditional chords form one aspect of twentieth-century harmony; another concerns the emergence of new harmonic structures: eleventh and thirteenth chords, triads with added tones, polychords, major-minor triads, and chords built in fourths and fifths, in clusters of tones, and in two keys simultaneously.

Eleventh and Thirteenth Chords

Before giving way to other harmonies, the chord built in thirds appeared in two final forms: the *eleventh* chord, comprising five superposed thirds, and the *thirteenth* chord, with six.

Ex. 1   Genesis of the eleventh and thirteenth chords

As early as 1874, Wagner had used eleventh and thirteenth chords in *Götterdämmerung*.

Ex. 2   Wagner: *Götterdämmerung*

Over a softly sustained V^9, the melody leaps up to the eleventh (*a*), then down again without resolving. An inner voice, echoing the upper one, sounds the eleventh again (*b*), then resolves to the tone below. At (*c*) a thirteenth appears, adding intensity to the phrase; it leaps away (*d*) without resolving.

Decades later, Ravel used the same chords in a setting that emphasizes their dissonant quality. Example 3 shows II^{11} and V^{13} in a C major progression.

Ex. 3   Ravel: *Rigaudon*, from *Le tombeau de Couperin*

Permission for reprint granted by Durand et Cie., Paris, copyright owner, and Elkan-Vogel Co., Inc., Philadelphia, agents.

Berg, whose *Wozzeck* is noted for its complex harmonies, ended the opera on IA^{11} of G major. By contrast with the extreme intricacy pervading the entire work, the eleventh chord seems simple and almost consonant (Ex. 4). In a more complex passage, depicting the hero's incipient madness (Ex. 5), a IV^{13} appears.

Ex. 4 Berg: *Wozzeck*, Act III (four hands)

Ex. 5 Berg: *Wozzeck*, Act I

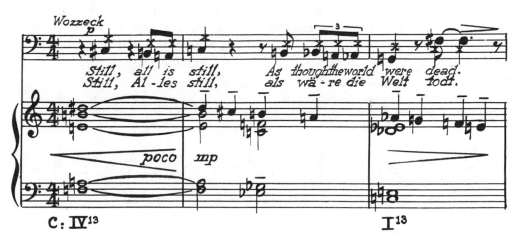

Added Tones

Another contemporary practice involves the *added tone*—a neighboring tone joined to a chord, altering its sonority but not its harmonic function. Thus in Ex. 6 the sixth degree of C major is joined (*a*) to the tonic triad. In conventional theory, the resultant chord would be considered VI$_5^6$. In the newer view, function determines identity: we call the chord a tonic triad with *added sixth* (I^{+6}).

Ex. 6   Moussorgsky: Coronation Scene, from *Boris Godunov*

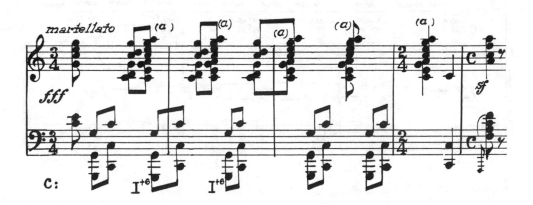

Example 7 shows the added sixth joined to triads on various degrees. In Ex. 8 (*a*), it appears in Puccini's *La Bohème* (1895); in Ex. 9, as employed by Debussy; and in Ex. 10 (*a*), in a ragtime piece of the 1890s, anticipating what later became standard practice in popular music.*

Ex. 7   Added sixth chords

* See also Ex. 6 (*b*), page 344.

Ex. 8   Puccini: *La Bohème*, Act I

Ex. 9   Debussy: *Menestrels*, from Preludes, Book II

Ex. 10   Scott Joplin: Original Rags

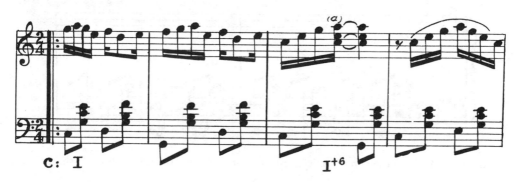

Like added sixths, other tones—seconds, ninths, sometimes also fourths and sevenths—can be joined to chords or to melody tones. Such added tones enrich the sonority without changing the basic functions of a chord or melodic line. Examples 11 and 12 illustrate added seconds, and Ex. 13, added ninths.* Example 14 contains a mixture of various added tones.

Ex. 11   Ravel: *Jeux d'eaux*

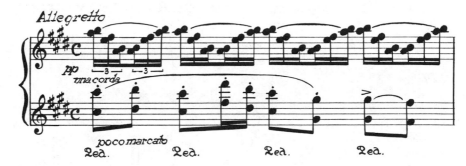

Ex. 12   Stravinsky: *Petrushka*, first tableau

Ex. 13   Stravinsky: *The Rite of Spring*, Part II

* In Ex. 13, E flat is the enharmonic equivalent of D sharp—the ninth above C sharp.

Copyright 1921 by Edition Russe de Musique; assigned 1947 to Boosey and Hawkes, Inc. Reprinted by permission.

Ex. 14   Stravinsky: *The Rite of Spring*, Part II

Copyright 1921 by Edition Russe de Musique; assigned 1947 to Boosey and Hawkes, Inc. Reprinted by permission.

Example 14 starts with one bar of I⁶ in B flat. At (*a*) an added sixth joins the throbbing chord, and at (*b*) an added fourth (plus a conventional fifth). At (*c*) the melody enters, leading to a repeated chord at (*d*). The chord now contains a root, third, fourth, fifth, sixth, and seventh—every tone of the scale but one. Distinctive in sonority, the passage suggests the mysterious quality of the scene, "Ritual Action of the Ancestors."

Chords in Fourths and Fifths

For at least five centuries (1400–1900), the third was the sole foundation of chord structure. With the appearance of chords built in fourths, the reign of tertial harmony came to an end. Chords in fourths, lacking the stability of triads, often produce a tonal vagueness. Among the first to use them were Satie, Scriabin, and Debussy.* Example 15 shows an early Schönberg example.

* See page 399.

Ex. 15   Schönberg: *Kammersymphonie*, Op. 9

Reprinted by permission of Gertrud Schönberg and Theodore Presser Company.

When poised on a strong tonal foundation, however, chords in fourths can also establish a key quite emphatically.

Ex. 16   Bartók: Concerto for Orchestra

Copyright 1946 by Hawkes & Son (London) Ltd. Reprinted by permission.

Another type of chord contains superposed fifths (Exs. 17 and 18).

Ex. 17   Bartók: Piano Concerto No. 2

Copyright 1933 by Universal Editions; renewed 1960. Copyright and renewal assigned to Boosey and Hawkes, Inc. for the U.S.A. Reprinted by permission. All other rights by permission of Theodore Presser Company.

Ex. 18   Milhaud: *Laranjeiras*, from *Saudades do Brazil*

Major-Minor Chords

Still another harmonic structure is the *major-minor chord*—a triad or dominant seventh containing both the major and minor thirds above the root, usually separated by a diminished octave. Forming a cross-relation, this chord is often used for its tangy dissonance. In American music, it characterizes the blues: Example 19 shows the chord in an early folk blues; Exs. 20 and 21, as employed by Gershwin and Copland in blues-influenced pieces; and Ex. 22, in a famous jazz-inspired work of 1923 by Milhaud. (In these examples, all major-minor chords are marked *a*.)

Ex. 19   Folk blues: House of the Rising Sun

Ex. 20   Gershwin: Concerto in F for Piano and Orchestra

Ex. 21   Copland: Concerto for Piano

Ex. 22   Milhaud: *La création du monde*

Polychords

When one diatonic chord is superimposed on another, a *polychord* results.

Ex. 23   Polychords

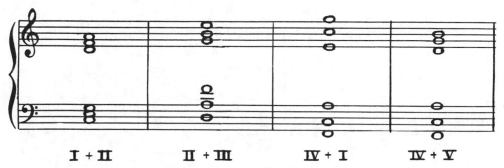

I + II   II + III   IV + I   IV + V

Characteristic of twentieth-century music, the polychord was fore-shadowed in Beethoven. A famous example, occurring in the *Eroica*, was corrected as a "mistake" by blundering nineteenth-century editors. Under a shimmering V^7 in the development section, just before the return of the main theme, the horn enters on the *tonic* triad (Ex. 24, *a*). The clashing entrance is immediately set to rights by the thunderous arrival of the orchestra with the standard progression (*b*).*

Ex. 24   Beethoven: Symphony No. 3 (*Eroica*), Op. 55

*For another striking Beethoven polychord, see the dramatic opening of the last movement of the Ninth Symphony (page 300), in which a VII^{d7} is sounded together with a tonic triad.

A similar superposition of V and I chords occurs in Richard Strauss' *Tod und Verklärung*.

Ex. 25   Strauss: *Tod und Verklärung*

Reprint permission given by the copyright owners, C. F. Peters Corporation, 373 Park Avenue South, New York, New York 10016.

It was Stravinsky in his neoclassic period, however, who first made widespread use of polychords. The *Sérénade en la* (Ex. 26) contains a variety of these chords, as does Copland's *Billy the Kid* (Ex. 27).

Ex. 26   Stravinsky: *Sérénade en la*

Copyright 1926 by Edition Russe de Musique; assigned 1947 to Boosey and Hawkes, Inc. Reprinted by permission.

Ex. 27   Copland: *Billy the Kid*

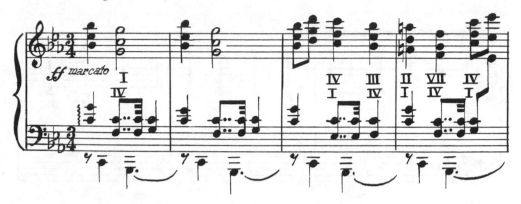

Copyright 1941 by Aaron Copland. Reprinted by permission of Aaron Copland, copyright owner, and Boosey and Hawkes, Inc., sole licensees.

The Tone Cluster

A distinctly modern invention is the *tone cluster*—a chord of major or minor seconds tightly packed together. Although suggestions of such a formation can be found in Debussy, its first extensive use occurs in a movement of Ives' *Concord* Sonata, written in 1909–1910.

Ex. 28   Ives· The *Concord* Sonata

Copyright 1947 by Arrow Music Press, Inc. Used by permission of Associated Music Publishers, Inc., New York.

The name of Henry Cowell is widely associated with tone clusters, which appear frequently in his works. In Ex. 29, we find clusters spanning two octaves—indicated by the special notation at (*a*). They are played with the forearm.

Ex. 29   Cowell: Amiable Conversation

Wallingford Riegger showed that tone clusters are as effective scored *pianissimo* as they are *forte*.

Ex. 30   Riegger: Variation 4, from Variations for Piano and Orchestra

Our time has been a period of striking advances in harmony: more new chords have been invented during the twentieth century than in the previous thousand years. The extraordinary proliferation of new harmonies prompted Paul Hindemith to write, in 1949, "Harmony has become thoroughly known; no undiscovered chord can be found."* Whether true or not, Hindemith's judgment does not mean nothing new can be found in *harmony*, for harmony is a matter of relationships rather than merely of chord structures; and no one can foretell what new harmonic relationships lie ahead.

New Chords in Parallel Motion

Modern chords, like old ones, can progress in parallel fashion. Satie was a pioneer in this technique, writing parallel chords in fourths as early as 1890 (Ex. 31); Debussy soon followed suit (Ex. 32).

Ex. 31   Satie: *Le fils des étoiles*

By courtesy of the publisher, Editions Salabert, Paris.

Ex. 32   Debussy: Sarabande, from *Pour le Piano*

Permission for reprint granted by Durand et Cie., Paris, copyright owner, and Elkan-Vogel Co., Inc., Philadelphia, agents.

Stravinsky exercised still greater freedom in his use of parallel dissonant chords. A justly famous passage of *Petrushka* contains parallel ninths (Ex. 33), and *The Rite of Spring* has parallel major sevenths over a bass moving in chromatic major ninths (Ex. 34).

* Paul Hindemith: *A Composer's World* (New York, 1952), page 138.

Ex. 33   Stravinsky: *Petrushka*

Ex. 34   Stravinsky: *The Rite of Spring*

An interesting example of parallel eleventh chords occurs in the Russian master's Octet for Wind Instruments (Ex. 35, *a*).

Ex. 35   Stravinsky: Octet for Wind Instruments

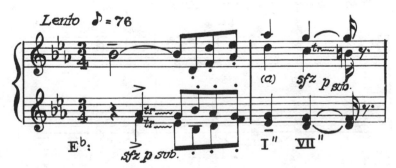

Another twentieth-century technique can be called *contrapuntal parallelism;* it consists of two or more groups of parallel chords moving independently of each other, in the manner of single contrapuntal voices (Ex. 36).*

* See also Ex. 56, page 379.

Ex. 36   William Schumann: Symphony for Strings

Like traditional harmonies, modern ones frequently arise as products of contrapuntal motion, resultants as well as sources of melodic line. New harmonic concepts arise as part of new concepts of music as a whole.

Polytonality

Polychords, escaped chords, and contrapuntal parallelism all lead to a further development of considerable importance for the evolution of modern harmonic style: *polytonality*. When two melodies or chord groups are sounded simultaneously, each in a different key, polytonality results. Suggested in certain passages of medieval music,* this technique was invented anew and richly developed in the early twentieth century. A passage from Strauss' *Ein Heldenleben* (1898) contains a G flat major chord over which a melody moves through other keys.

Ex. 37   Strauss: *Ein Heldenleben*

* Jacques Chailley, in his *Traité Historique d'Analyse Musicale* (Paris, 1947), cites a Rondeau of the thirteenth-century composer Adam de la Halle in which the upper voice (*a*) cadences in G while the middle voice (*b*) emphasizes the key of D.

Adam de la Halle: Rondeau

For another, even more daring example of early polytonality, see *Der Juden Tanz* by Hans Neusiedler, in Davison and Apel: *Historical Anthology of Music* (Cambridge, Massachusetts, 1959), page 108 of Volume I.

In 1908, Bartók, exploiting the polytonal principle more consistently, wrote a work with two simultaneous key signatures (Ex. 38). The right-hand signature is C sharp minor; the left-hand, F minor. Prokofiev used a similar technique in *Sarcasmes* (1912).

Ex. 38   Bartók: *Bagatelles*

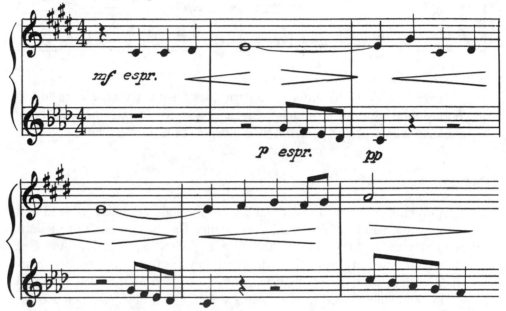

Ex. 39   Prokofiev: *Sarcasmes*, Op. 17, No. 3

Stravinsky used polytonality to depict the frustration of the puppet Petrushka. Example 40 shows the poignant effect of harmonic friction created by two voices, one in C major, the other in F sharp.

Ex. 40   Stravinsky: *Petrushka*

A distinctive harmony results from the superposition of D sharp minor and D minor triads in a poetic phrase from *The Rite of Spring*. (Note that A sharp is written enharmonically as B flat.*)

Ex. 41   Stravinsky: *The Rite of Spring*

* Composers often use enharmonic equivalents of chord tones, regardless of the "correct" spellings. Since they do not feel obliged to conform to theoretical principles, analysis of their work sometimes requires interpretation.

Ives' *Housatonic at Stockbridge* contains polytonal harmonies (C and C sharp major) that evoke a dream-like mood.

Ex. 42   Ives: *The Housatonic at Stockbridge*

Reprinted by permission of Theodore Presser Company.

Note that, like Stravinsky, Ives writes enharmonically: at (*a*) F is really the enharmonic equivalent of E sharp. (If written E sharp it would have indicated more clearly the presence of a C sharp major triad in the left hand.)

Another function of polytonality is to create the vigorous or brutal effects favored by many twentieth-century composers. An extremely dissonant combination occurs at the opening of the Dance of the Adolescents, in Stravinsky's *The Rite of Spring.** A powerful though less violent quality emerges from the joining of A and E flat minor in a work by Darius Milhaud —one of the most consistent advocates of polytonality.

Ex. 43   Milhaud: Concerto for Percussion and Small Orchestra

* See page 75, Volume I.

Reprinted by permission of Theodore Presser Company.

Contrasting with the vigor of Ex. 43, the polytonal harmonies of Ex. 44 create a delicate, sparkling sound.

Ex. 44   Milhaud: Violin Sonata No. 2

Permission for reprint granted by Durand et Cie., Paris, copyright owner, and Elkan-Vogel Co., Inc., Philadelphia, agents.

Polytonality appears in the work of quite a few twentieth-century composers, among them Debussy, Ravel, Poulenc, Milhaud, Bartók, Shosta-kovich, Ives, Copland, Gould, Blitzstein, and Revueltas. * It has been variously used: in massive chord blocks and thin contrapuntal lines, in harshly dissonant combinations and delicate textures, and in the blending of distant or closely related keys. Besides combining two keys, composers have sometimes superimposed three or more—although this practice has generally proved less satisfactory. Polytonality, moreover, is not limited to the use of major and minor modes; any two modes can be mingled, in diverse combinations. Various types of chords are likewise combined in different keys. Polytonality represents a wide range of harmonic relationships whose ultimate possibilities are still to be fully explored.

* For a Revueltas example, see pages 380–381.

Atonality

As already mentioned, the intense chromaticism of the late nineteenth century developed to a point where tonality frequently became vague and indefinite. The extreme emotionalism of many Strauss and Mahler works found expression in ambiguous harmonic textures sliding so continuously from key to key, or in between various keys, that the feeling of key itself was often lost.

Around the turn of the century, European composers were generally divided into two camps: those who, following Moussorgsky and Debussy, made a sharp break with Romantic chromaticism; and those who, like Strauss, Mahler, Scriabin and early Schönberg, developed the tonal ambiguities of chromaticism still further.

From persistent tonal ambiguity it was but a step to the total abandonment of tonality. In his Opus 11, Schönberg wove lines together in such a way that no single tone stands out as a tonic. The result (despite Schönberg's objection) became widely known as *atonality*. It represented yet another kind of break with traditional harmony as it had evolved through the centuries.

Ex. 45   Schönberg: *Drei Klavierstücke*, Op. 11, No. 1

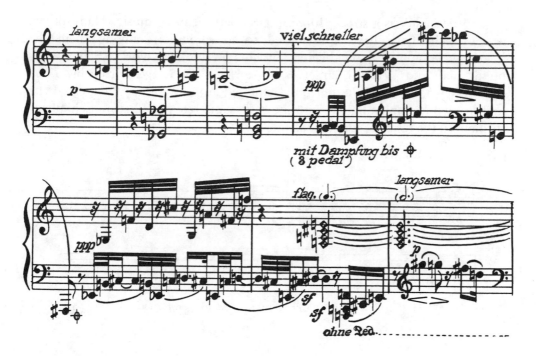

Reprinted by permission of Gertrud Schönberg and Theodore Presser Company.

Several analyses of *Drei Klavierstücke* have attempted to show that it does have a central tonality after all. Whether such analyses are or are not correct, it would be difficult in any case to find *harmonic progression* in this work. Unique in style and brilliantly organized in a structural sense, it represents the last contact between post-Romantic chromaticism and harmony. From this point on, Schönberg renounced harmony altogether as a structural force and as a means of musical motion.

With this renunciation, atonal music moved outside the realm of harmonic thought (except perhaps in a negative sense); most atonal composers are careful to *avoid* tone combinations that crèate a sense of key or harmonic progression. The absence of the organizing power of tonal and harmonic structure remained a problem for Schönberg until he developed a new structural principle, the *twelve-tone row,* which he utilized in his later compositions.* Schönberg's method, however, falls in the domains of modern counterpoint and form rather than harmony, and lies, therefore, outside the scope of this study. From the purely *harmonic* standpoint, twelve-tone style can be considered an aspect of atonality.†

* For Schönberg's own discussion of his method, see "Composition with Twelve Tones," in Arnold Schönberg: *Style and Idea* (New York, 1950).

† Certain twelve-tone compositions are tonal (at least in part), and quite a few atonal compositions do not use twelve-tone methods. By and large, however, the two techniques have been closely identified with each other.

Atonality is a strong force in twentieth-century music. Many others besides Schönberg have contributed to its evolution—among them the Viennese composer Josef Hauer, Scriabin in his last works, Schönberg's pupils Berg and Webern, and Ives. As early as 1915, Ives wrote his *Tone Roads No. 3*, in which he not only explored atonal writing but created the first known example of a twelve-tone row, some ten years before Schönberg formalized the practice into a doctrine.

Ex. 46   Ives: *Tone Roads No. 3*

Summary

1. Twentieth-century chord formations include:
   a. Eleventh chords, containing five superposed thirds, and thirteenth chords, containing six.
   b. Chords with added tones—neighboring tones joined to triads:
      i. Triads with added sixth (+6).
      ii. Triads with added second, fourth, seventh, or ninth:
   c. Chords of superposed fourths and fifths.
   d. Major-minor chords—triads or seventh chords containing both major and minor thirds above the root, usually separated by a diminished octave.
   e. Polychords—two superposed diatonic chords.
   f. Tone clusters—tightly packed groups of major or minor seconds.

2. Twentieth-century harmonic practices include:
   a. New chords used in parallel motion.
   b. Contrapuntal parallelism—two groups of parallel chords moving independently of each other.
   c. Polytonality—two series of tones or chords moving simultaneously in different keys.
   d. Atonality—music without a key center, in which no chord or tone acts as a tonic.
      i. In one type of atonal music, lines and chords move freely, independently of traditional pathways.
      ii. In another type, they derive from the twelve-tone row—a pattern governing the order of the twelve chromatic tones.

More about
Twentieth-Century
Melody

"The tradition of the long line still persists," we said at the end of Chapter XII. Can this statement be substantiated? Let us examine seven twentieth-century examples representing various types of long-line melody.*

Ravel

Why Ravel rather than Debussy? Because Debussy, for all his genius and the revolutionary nature of his vision, was concerned more with mood, color, and harmonic exploration than with linear melody. Ravel, on the other hand, never ceased to work for a long-spun, continuous line. Always precise and elegant, Ravel's melodic style passed through several phases, from the modal quality of the early *Sonatine* (page 356) to the jazzy brashness of the later piano concertos. Among his most lyrical themes is the flute solo from *Daphnis and Chloë*.

---

* For background material on the composers and their melodic styles, see Gilbert Chase: *America's Music* (New York, 1955); Arthur Cohn: *The Collector's Twentieth-Century Music in the Western Hemisphere* (New York, 1961) and *Twentieth-Century Music in Western Europe* (New York, 1965); Arthur C. Edwards: *The Art of Melody* (New York, 1956), pages 222–248, and *Practical Lessons in Melody-Writing* (Dubuque, 1963), pages 114–185; Peter S. Hansen: *Introduction to Twentieth Century Music* (Boston, 1961); Joseph Machlis: *Introduction to Contemporary Music* (New York, 1961); Wilfred Mellers: *Music in a New Found Land* (New York, 1965) and Israel Nestyev: *Prokofiev* (Stanford, 1960), pages 475–478.

Ex. 47   Ravel: *Daphnis and Chloë*, Suite No. 2

Permission for reprint granted by Durand et Cie., Paris, copyright owner, and Elkan-Vogel Co., Inc., Philadelphia, agents.

Example 47 presents a long, flowing melody, finely drawn and well able to stand alone without any harmonic background, in the old French tradition of plain chant and Troubadour song. (The harmony, not shown here, is of the simplest—a pedal point with slowly changing chordal inflections.) The delicate, sensuous line moves with such fluency that we overlook its essential classicism. Yet it is a three-part form with proportions of 8, 10, and 4 bars—as classical a pattern as one could wish. Ravel did not hesitate to use motives (*a*, *b*, and *c*) in developing the line, or to employ traditional methods of interlocking contrasted sections (the descending arabesque figure *b*, appears within both phrases 1 and 2). The rhythm is constantly varied without calling attention to itself; and the melodic curve—a bowl—descends gracefully over nearly two octaves, rising again toward the end (*d*).

In this melody, Ravel reveals his musical ancestry. *Daphnis* is colored by modality and a fluid impressionism. We also find traces of the composer's debt to Rimsky-Korsakoff, both in the *Scheherazade*-like arabesques and in the exquisite writing for the flute. Despite the shifts of fashion that have transformed Ravel from a daring avant-gardist to an old grandfather of modern music, the melody from *Daphnis* still retains its poetry and distinction today.

Stravinsky

Stravinsky's melodic gift has remained the most puzzling aspect of his talent. The melodies of his early years were either taken from Russian folk music or composed in folk style, in the tradition of older Russian masters. After Stravinsky entered his neoclassical period (with *Pulcinella*, 1918), he frankly borrowed themes from other composers and wrote melodies in a variety of styles from different historical periods—a practice that has continued into his latest, neo-Webern phase. The Octet for Wind Instruments (1923) provides a representative melody of Stravinsky's middle period.

Ex. 48   Stravinsky: Octet for Wind Instruments, second movement

Example 48 is typical of Stravinsky's "objective" neoclassical style. Although it has none of the flavor of his earlier Russian melodies, this theme nevertheless remains Stravinskian in its concentration, its narrow range, its changing meters, and above all its tendency to rotate around a single note or pair of notes. C sharp and A (neither of them the tonic) form a melodic axis, recurring again and again in the first phrase (*a*). Typical also of Stravinsky are the rhythmically irregular repetitions of these notes. This uneven yet insistent reiteration produces an hypnotic quality.

The most telling of all the repetitions occurs in the second phrase (*b*). Here the melody has slipped out of the opening key of D and seems to be heading in a new direction (*c*). Suddenly, it swoops down a major seventh (the widest of all its leaps) back to the axial tones C sharp and A, the last phrase ending similarly to the first. This "pull to the center" is a striking characteristic of Stravinsky's melodic technique.

Berg

Like the work of his teacher Schönberg, the music of Alban Berg lies at the opposite pole from that of pre-1950 Stravinsky. Whereas the Russian master proclaimed objectivity and non-expressiveness as the highest goals of the composer, Berg's music was the reflection of an intense subjectivity. As we have seen in examples from *Wozzeck*, Berg's harmonies burn at white heat, and his melodies reveal an enormous tension in their wide leaps, jagged rhythms, and chromatic wandering. A characteristic melodic utterance is the relatively restrained theme from his Violin Concerto.

Ex. 49   Berg: Violin Concerto

Reprinted by permission of Theodore Presser Company.

The opening phrase of Ex. 49 is built on a twelve-tone row: all the notes of the chromatic scale appear between the opening low G and the high F three bars later. Subsequent phrases are also based on the row. But the Berg melody differs from many other twelve-tone phrases in three respects: its character as a *theme;* its structure based on triads; and its suggestion of tonality.

Schönberg himself, and many of his followers, made clear their longing for an "athematic" music: a music in flux, unbroken by the repetition of any recognizable melodic pattern. Berg did not follow this principle in his Violin Concerto, for its first four bars, rising in thirds through nearly three octaves and ending with a leap in the opposite direction, form a clearly memorable theme. This theme, which appears many times in the course of the work, has magnificent sweep and a most tender quality.

After three bars of rest (*a*) the melody reappears (*b*), but this time inverted, dropping from high G (one tone above the climax of the first phrase) to low A, and then turning back in the opposite direction, as before. The third phrase (*c*) starts with an inverted fragment of the second (the last three notes), continues with the fragment in its original shape (*d*), presents the fragment again in retrograde inversion and augmentation (*e*), and then mounts expressively to the high G (*f*). One bar later (*g*) the original theme appears in inversion again, starting on high F sharp and ending on G (at *h*). These techniques of motive variation are identical with those found in older musical styles; to this extent, twelve-tone methods are rooted in tradition.

The second distinctive element of the Berg melody is its triadic structure. The first nine notes are built in piled-up thirds—the traditional formula for building triads. The theme might be analyzed as embodying the I, V, and II of G minor, plus a secondary dominant triad, V of II (although there is no evidence that the composer had this in mind).

Ex. 50   Chordal analysis of Berg theme

The selection of thirds as a germ and their use in forming triads lends an air of serenity to the theme and leads to the last distinguishing mark of this twelve-tone melody: its suggestion of tonality. While all twelve chromatic tones are introduced, theoretically destroying the possibility of any tonal center, Berg has arranged them in successive phrases to suggest clearly such a center, on G. Not only is G the first note of the theme; it also begins phrase (*b*), at the summit of the line. After the long descent, the melody rises once more to the same G (at *f*). Finally, the third complete statement of the theme ends on G in a lower octave (*h*). That the plan is not accidental is borne out by the ending of the entire Concerto (not shown in Ex. 49), which mounts again with the same theme and comes to rest on the same high G. In this work, as in others, Berg united the extreme chromaticism of the twelve-tone method with elements of tonality.

Hindemith

Paul Hindemith's music, which unites Baroque motivic, contrapuntal, and structural techniques with modern harmonic and rhythmic methods, is highly distinctive in style. Melodically, the composer preferred to write in a stepwise, often diatonic manner, with frequent changes of mode and key.

Influenced by Schönberg's atonal technique, Hindemith tempered free linear motion with a strong sense of tonality. Thus many of his melodies, resembling the contrapuntal lines of the Baroque, move logically from one nodal harmony to another, evolving in a tight, structural plan.*

Ex. 51   Hindemith: *Matthis der Maler*

* Review the analysis of the theme of Hindemith's Third Sonata, Ex. 16, pages 352–353.

Example 51, a fine illustration of Hindemith's linear writing, resembles an eighteenth-century contrapuntal "subject" rather than a nineteenth-century expressive theme. Its three-part form is traditional: Parts I and III present the melody as a whole; Part II forms a short development section, with a fragment of the original phrase appearing in rising sequences.

Part I introduces two motives, (*a*) and (*a²*). At (*b*) (*a²*) is repeated, with slight interval change, and extended; at (*c*) it appears freely inverted and extended again. Part II starts with (*a*) in a new key, shortened and given a new ending (*d*). Four sequences of the motive follow, at first shortened to two and a half bars, then growing shorter and leading to the emphatic recapitulation of the opening phrase (Part III) at (*e*). From the formal standpoint, Hindemith's sole concession to modern thought is the return of the original theme in a different key and its ending in still another key.

Although several changes of accidentals show this to be a twentieth-century melody, it remains basically diatonic; Hindemith reveals his anti-Romanticism by largely avoiding chromatic motion. The contemporary quality of the work derives more from its unconventional harmonization than from the melody as such; the effect cannot be guessed from one melody alone, for Hindemith's music relies on contrapuntal interweaving rather than on the character of a single line.

Bartók

One of the great melodists of our time, Bartók first became known for his violent harmonies, striking rhythms, and fresh orchestral colors. The modal, Hungarian sound of his music led some to classify him as a "folklorist" composer—thus relegating him supposedly to second rank.* But a fuller

---

* During his lifetime, Bartók's fame was relatively modest; wide recognition came only after his death.

knowledge of Bartók's work shows that one need not belong to the German, French, or Italian traditions to be a "mainstream" composer.

Having absorbed all the harmonic, rhythmic, and formal innovations of the time, Bartók utilized them to develop a rich vein of ideas. His melodies encompassed a wide range of communication, from the bleakest despair to the most light-hearted buffoonery, and restored to music a personal warmth and emotional power that had been largely blacked out by the anti-human environment of the strife-torn twentieth century.

Ex. 52   Bartók: Divertimento

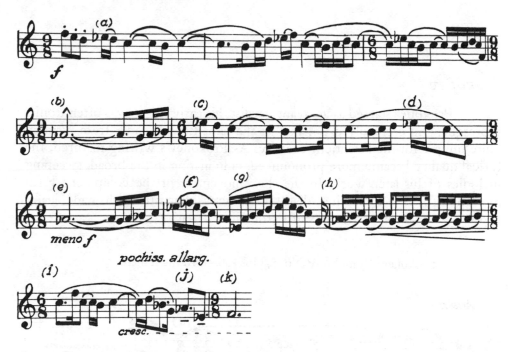

Copyright 1940 by Hawkes & Son (London) Ltd. Reprinted by permission.

Example 52 shows the long, flowing line and distinctive tonal inflections that are Bartók's hallmark. Deriving from Hungarian and other folk modes, this melody is far more sophisticated than any of them with respect to both pitch and rhythm. The mode of the opening—major, with a lowered 7 (*a*) and raised 4—is soon varied, at (*b*), by a lowered 3; and, at (*f*), by a lowered tonic (F flat). Rhythmically, it is freshly minted: although the tune runs continuously for twelve bars, *no two measures* have the same rhythm. The little three-note figure (*a*) recurs several times, but always at a different point in the bar.

Like Stravinsky, whom he resembles only superficially, Bartók bases his melody on several focal points, around which the figuration turns. These points keep changing, however. First the melody fixes on high F and C; then, at (*b*), on A flat, for an intense, long-sustained note; then, at (*c*) and (*d*), on E flat. At (*e*) the long note, A flat, returns, followed from (*f*) to (*i*) by an outpouring of sixteenth notes, the line expanding upward and downward at (*g*), and breaking, at (*h*), into an impetuous polyrhythm. At (*i*) the original focal point, C, returns strongly; and at (*j*) the line dips to the low point, E flat (in still another polyrhythm). The phrase now leads to the low tonic, F (at *k*), which had been carefully reserved for this moment. Technically brilliant, the tune is full of verve and imagination—one of the distinguished melodies by a twentieth-century master.

Prokofiev

Prokofiev started as an avant-gardist; his early music was often ironic, grotesque, and decidedly dissonant. At the same time, it had a fresh lyricism quite unique for the twentieth century. As Prokofiev's writing matured, the lyrical quality became more pronounced, culminating in the broad, sweeping melodies of his later work. In the slow movement of the composer's Fifth Symphony (1944), flowing diatonic patterns alternate with wide leaps, expressive tonal contrasts, and shifts from light to dark.*

Ex. 53   Prokofiev: Symphony No. 5, Op. 100, third movement

* See also the opening theme of Prokofiev's Sixth Symphony, pages 336–337.

The first two bars show a typically Prokofiev diatonic line, daring in its simplicity. At (*a*) the phrase rises in small leaps, dropping back again in falling sixths and sevenths. After the restraint of the pure F major, the minor ninth at (*b*) and the chromaticism of the following bars form a striking contrast. A second rise, to C flat (at *c*), adds a dark color, and the relaxation of the falling minor ninth (*d*) makes a lovely balance to the earlier upward motion. At the end, the phrase reaches repose with a cadence on the dominant of F.

For an artist to achieve such melodic simplicity requires great maturity of spirit. Prokofiev's range was wide, including the Classical Symphony, the lyrical First Violin Concerto, and the comic masterpiece, *Lieutenant Kije*. Having experienced the complexities of life (*The Flaming Angel*) and known its absurdities (*The Love of Three Oranges*), he arrived at a balance and serenity rare in the twentieth century.

Ives

Numerous references have been made in these volumes to the pioneer contribution of Charles Ives. The scope and diversity of his achievements—as yet only partly known—include anticipation of many techniques still considered avant-garde. In discussing his work, our main focus so far has been on its harmonic and rhythmic innovations.

Another facet of Ives deserves attention: his rich melodic gift. The collection *114 Songs* reveals the composer's unique insight into life and his wide sympathies, not to mention a host of striking technical devices, astounding when one considers their early origins ("Walking," which contains polytonality, ragtime, polyrhythms, and other contemporary techniques, dates from 1902). Ives' interests included transcendentalism, in the song "Serenity"; robust social satire, "Nov. 20, 1920"; a Charlie Chaplinesque vision of life in the back alleys, "General William Booth Enters Heaven"; New England landscape, "Thoreau"; and a classic purity of mood, "Evening."*

* See also the melody from the *Concord* Sonata, page 369.

Ex. 54   Ives: Evening

© 1939 by Associated Music Publishers, Inc., New York.

Ives remains the despair of analysts; his melodies, like his harmonies and rhythms, are the prisoners of no system. In his own words, "If [a song] feels like walking along the left hand side of the street—passing the door of physiology or sitting on the curb, why not let it? If it feels like kicking over an ashcan, a poet's castle, or the prosodic law, will you stop it?"

Faced with this warning, it seems irrelevant to search for a key to Ives' style, to point out an irregular interval here, a strange scale there, or the contrast between the wayward opening and the almost motionless ending of "Evening." But Ives was nothing if not an interpreter of words and the silent thoughts behind them. When his melody chooses to settle down on two notes (a) for the delicate warblings of the nightingale, and to end in a pure E major after starting out in a scrambled B flat, this was Ives' response to Milton's thought "Silence is pleased."

Summary

1. Long-line melodies as well as fragmented ones are characteristic of twentieth-century music.

2. Ravel's melodic style, traditional in structure, reflects his interest in modality and impressionism.

3. Stravinsky's neoclassical melodies tend to circle around one or two notes.

4. Berg's melodic style, built on twelve-tone methods, often has, nonetheless, thematic character and a suggestion of tonality.

5. Hindemith's melodies are generally in neo-Baroque style. Diatonic and motivic, they are often suited to contrapuntal development.

6. Bartók's melodies are often in freely fluctuating modal style, marked by constant rhythmic variation.

7. Prokofiev's melodies often combine flowing lyricism, sudden tonal shifts, and dramatic wide leaps, in a highly individual manner.

8. Ives' melodies often represent a distinctly original mingling of modern techniques with a spirit of serene introspection.

Postlude

Three types of musical motion—harmonic, melodic, and rhythmic—have formed the substance of our investigation. Seen in perspective, their relations with each other—and with the motion produced by counterpoint, form, and tone color—have varied constantly in the music of different epochs and in different lands. Now one and now another element has come to the fore: in Africa, rhythm; in Indonesia, sonority; in medieval Europe, counterpoint; and in the post-Renaissance Western world, harmony, melody, form, and orchestral color.

During the twentieth century, the relationships of the various musical elements have changed with bewildering speed. In Debussy's music, harmony and color made striking advances, overshadowing melody and rhythm. With the early Stravinsky, harmony developed still more boldly and rhythm emerged as a commanding element, while melody and form were placed in the background. Schönberg's twelve-tone style elevated abstract structural and contrapuntal techniques to a central position, casting melody in a secondary role and all but dissolving harmony. Berg restored lyrical melody to an important place, and gave twelve-tone methods a highly dramatic significance. Hindemith joined Baroque counterpoint to a free yet solid tonality. Ives, Bartók, and Prokofiev, each in his own way, blended modern melodic, harmonic, and rhythmic techniques in a highly personal fashion. Needless to say, these composers were not alone in creating syntheses of contemporary elements. Countless others have contributed to esthetic and musical values; a catalogue of the achievements of twentieth-century composers would fill many volumes.

Among the voices of our time, there have been those that since the 1920s have announced the end of tonality as a musical force. Others have proclaimed flowing melody a relic of the past. Yet the demise of tonality and flowing melody, like the report of Mark Twain's death, has proved greatly exaggerated. In the decades since such predictions were made, an impressive number of tonal masterpieces based on linear melody have appeared. Besides experimenting with recently developed techniques—atonality, twelve-tone methods, *musique concrète*, pointillism, music of chance, electronic sound, and others—musicians have continued to draw sustenance from flowing lines and the tensions and relaxations of tonal structure.

Some composers—notably Hindemith, Berg, Bartók, Ives, and Riegger—have shown that tonality and atonality can, in fact, be fruitfully reconciled. A work such as Riegger's Variations for Piano and Orchestra has each variation beginning and ending on B flat. For most of its course, the music follows atonal, twelve-tone patterns. But the repeated return to B flat causes this note to be heard as a tonic, and its alternate relinquishment and restatement as a departure from and return to tonality.* Tonal and atonal elements are also interwoven in Ives' *Concord* Sonata (1909–1910), Berg's *Wozzeck* (1914–1921), and numerous works of Riegger, Varèse, Blomdahl, and many other contemporary composers.

Such an interplay of tonal and atonal elements is, by extension, nothing but a modern version of the contrast between clear and ambiguous tonality often found in Beethoven. In that master's work, the opposition of tonally definite and indefinite passages played a dramatic role.† Later, with the music of Chopin and still more with Wagner's operas, the areas of tonal ambiguity became proportionately larger; and in the work of Berg and Riegger, predominant. Yet the difference remains one of degree; the basic contrast between stable and fluctuating areas still persists. From such a contrast, a new concept of harmony has emerged, in which both tonal and atonal elements play important structural roles.‡

* See page 219, Volume I, and Ex. 26, c, Chapter XIII, *Workbook*, Volume II.

† See pages 170–171 and 284. The musicologist Edward Lowinsky (in *Tonality and Atonality in Sixteenth-Century Music*, Berkeley, 1962) views the roots of atonality stretching as far back as 1550. "Chromaticism in the sixteenth century represents a full-fledged movement . . . that marked a total break with the tonal thinking of the past . . . and planted the seeds of atonality."

‡ For further discussion and examples of the mixture of tonal and atonal elements, see Rudolf Réti: *Tonality, Atonality, Pantonality* (New York, 1958), pages 112–119 and 136–139.

During its long and varied history, tonality has passed through many stages of development, from the modal tonality of the middle ages and the Renaissance, through the major-minor tonality of the Baroque–Classical–Romantic periods, to the expanded tonality of the twentieth century—which includes all types of modes, chord combinations, and whole-tone and polytonal structures. Seen from this viewpoint, atonal passages can form one element of yet another kind of expanded tonality embracing many different types of harmonic structures.

Various ways of joining together compositional techniques formerly considered incompatible appear in a number of twentieth-century masterpieces. Bartók's *Improvisations on Hungarian Peasant Songs* combined diatonic melody and polytonal harmony. Berg included triad formations in his atonal Violin Concerto. In *Three Places in New England*, Ives superimposed diatonic Civil War and ragtime tunes over polytonal and atonal harmonies. Irregular as such combinations may appear to the theorist, in the hands of a master they lead to new syntheses. It would be folly at this stage to attempt a systematization of modern techniques, which would force them into a Procrustean bed. Musical unities spring not from theoretical formulas but from the personal, unpredictable imagination of composers.

Like tonality, the long melodic line can be found, surprisingly enough, still very much alive. Although faced by a host of aggressive new musical forces, melody retains a central role in the work of those composers who find their individual way among devious paths. In America, a living spring of tune and rhythm continues to surge up from below, from the music of dance bands, theater musicians, and jazz improvisers. Jazz persists on its lusty way (although its death knell, too, has been rung more than once), leaving the taverns and jam sessions every so often to poke its way into the rhythms and themes of the serious American composer. Just as German musicians from Walther von der Vogelweide to Hindemith drew sustenance from the patterns of German folk music, just as French masters from Perotin to Milhaud were refreshed by the influence of French peasant songs, so too does the American composer often derive a vital essence from the common music of his own time and place. "Everything," wrote Charles Ives, "from a mule to an oak, to which nature has given life, has a right to that life, and a right to throw into that life all the values it can."

Indexes

Index of
Composers and
Compositions

Note: An (m) indicates a musical example in the text. Except for anonymous works, musical compositions are listed under their composers. **Boldface** type indicates pages on which the major discussion of a subject appears.

Ah, vous dirai-je, maman, 175(m)
All Through the Night, 6(m)
America, 147(m), 149
Arbeau, Thoinot:
  Pavane, 81(m)
Arlen, Harold:
  Blues in the Night, 91–92(m)
Au clair de la lune, 132–133(m)
Aura Lee, 23–24(m)

Bach, 16*n*, 23, 26, 58, 59*n*, 67, 68, 79, 105, 132, 140, 191, **194–196**, 202, 203, 204*n*, 221*n*, 235, 242, 243, 244*n*, 247, 248, 289, 296, 297, 299
  Ach wie flüchtig, ach wie nichtig, 87(m)
  B minor Mass:
    Crucifixus, 3, 204*n*, 214
    Kyrie, 165(m)
  Chaconne in D minor, 204*n*, 214
  Chromatic Fantasy, 306*n*
  Ein'feste Burg ist unser Gott, 131(m), 132(m)
  English Suite No. 4, Sarabande, 67(m)
  English Suite No. 6, Sarabande, 23(m), 241
  Fantasy in G minor, 306*n*
  French Suite No. 2, Minuet, 63(m)
  French Suite No. 3, Minuet, 31–32(m)
  French Suite No. 5, Gavotte, 114(m),

Bach (continued)
    154–155(m), 247, 248
  Gott sei gelobet und gebenedeiet, 196–197(m)
  Gottlob, es geht nunmehr zu Ende, 44(m)
  Helft mir Gott's Güte preisen, 86(m)
  Ich dank dir schon durch deinen Sohn, 201–202(m)
  Invention No. 4, 111–112(m)
  Invention No. 8, 104–105(m)
  Invention No. 14, 101(m), 109(m), 237
  Little Fugues and Preludes, Fugue No. 2, 68(m)
  Meine Seele erhebet den Herren, 197(m)
  O Ewigkeit, du Donnerwort, 192–194(m)
  Partita No. 2, Sinfonia, 230–231(m)
  Passacaglia in C minor, 204*n*
  Saint Matthew Passion, 297–298(m)
  Sinfonia No. 13, 83(m)
  Six Preludes, Prelude No. 5, 69(m)
  Toccata and Fugue No. 3, for Clavier, 167(m)
  Vater unser im Himmelreich, 128, 191(m)
  Was mein Gott will, das g'scheh'allzeit, 58(m), 59(m)
  Well-Tempered Clavier, Book I:
    Fugue No. 1, 40(m)
    Fugue No. 2, 119(m), 120(m)
    Fugue No. 16, 139(m)
    Prelude No. 5, 105–106(m), 242–

Index
of Subjects

433